The Saints of Santa Ana

The Saints of Santa Ana

Faith and Ethnicity in a Mexican Majority City

JONATHAN E. CALVILLO

OXFORD
UNIVERSITY PRESS

Oxford University Press is a department of the University of Oxford. It furthers the University's objective of excellence in research, scholarship, and education by publishing worldwide. Oxford is a registered trade mark of Oxford University Press in the UK and certain other countries.

Published in the United States of America by Oxford University Press
198 Madison Avenue, New York, NY 10016, United States of America.

Library of Congress Cataloging-in-Publication Data
Names: Calvillo, Jonathan E., author.
Title: The saints of Santa Ana : faith and ethnicity in a Mexican majority city /
Calvillo, Jonathan E.
Description: New York : Oxford University Press, [2020] |
Revision of the author's thesis (Ph.D.)—University of California, Irvine, 2016. |
Includes bibliographical references and index.
Identifiers: LCCN 2020022195 (print) | LCCN 2020022196 (ebook) |
ISBN 9780190097790 (hardback) | ISBN 9780190097806 (paperback) |
ISBN 9780190097820 (epub) | ISBN 9780190097837 (online) |
ISBN 9780190097813 (updf)
Subjects: LCSH: Mexican American Catholics—California—Santa Ana—
Ethnic identity. | Mexican American Protestants—California—Santa Ana—
Ethnic identity. | Communities—Religious aspects—Catholic Church. |
Communities—Religious aspects—Protestant churches. |
Ethnicity—Religious aspects—Catholic Church. | Ethnicity—
Religious aspects—Protestant churches. | Santa Ana (Calif.)—
Religious life and customs.
Classification: LCC E184.M5 C35 2020 (print) |
LCC E184.M5 (ebook) | DDC 305.8009794/96—dc23
LC record available at https://lccn.loc.gov/2020022195
LC ebook record available at https://lccn.loc.gov/2020022196

To my parents, Lydia and Alvaro Calvillo, who taught me to walk with el pueblo, with a strength and spirit beyond my own. To my brother, David Calvillo, for his wisdom and love. To Puanani, my partner in adventure, the love of my life, may we continue to create culture and imagine worlds together. To our Kalea, Mahalia, and Jonathan, may you continue to ask questions that keep us rooted, and may you always remember where we came from. Para mi gente de "Santana," sigamos cruzando fronteras juntos.

Contents

Acknowledgement

I am grateful to the many people that helped move this project forward. Boston University School of Theology was exceedingly supportive of my research and writing. I especially appreciate the feedback and encouragement provided by Mary Elizabeth Moore, Nancy Ammerman, Rady Roldan Figueroa, Cristian De La Rosa, Daryl Ireland, Courtney Goto, Christopher Schlauch, Nicolette Manglos-Weber, Shively Smith, Rebecca Copeland, Luis Menéndez-Antuña, Filipe Maia, Yara González-Justiniano, Theodore Hickman-Maynard, Christopher Evans, and Judith Olsen.

I appreciate the conversation partners I have met on the journey, some who have persisted across the span of the project. The project would not have been realized without the guidance of Stan Bailey during my time at the University of California, Irvine, and beyond. The feedback I received from Jennifer Lee, Glenda Flores, Jacob Avery, Yader Lanuza, and Mark Villegas proved to be invaluable. The LPC project provided critical insights toward this project, and I am grateful for the ongoing dialogue it facilitated; the mentorship I have received from Gerardo Martí and Mark Mulder has been a gift. Various scholars have left a mark on the project through our interactions within academic guilds, including Daniel Ramirez, Jennifer Scheper Hughes, Russell Jeung, Robert Chao Romero, Aida Ramos, Jerry Park, Richard Flory, Lloyd Barba, Erica Ramirez, Kristy Nabhan-Warren, Tony Lin, Jason Sexton, Grace Yukich, Rodolfo Estrada, Victoria Perez Rivera, Nancy Yuen, Brad Christensen, Gaston Espinosa, Erualdo Gonzalez, Jess Mason, and Gabe Veas. Edwin Johnson provided needed insights and motivation at key junctures.

It has been a pleasure to work with the team at Oxford University Press. I appreciate that Theo Calderara saw the potential in this project early on and facilitated a supportive experience throughout. Theo's review process and the feedback provided by the anonymous reviewers were crucial. The Forum for Theological Exploration was a source of support unlike any other, compelling me to do rooted scholarship. I am especially grateful for the ongoing support of Patrick Reyes at FTE. The Louisville Institute not only provided critical funding but also provided access to key thinkers in my field from a variety of backgrounds and traditions. I am thankful to Edwin Aponte and Don Richter for their personal and institutional generosity.

I am indebted to the people of Santa Ana, Santaneras and Santaneros, who were willing to share their stories with me and to make their lives accessible to me. The hospitality I received and the friendships that were built along the way have forever shaped my soul. I am honored that Julie Leopo provided the image for the book cover. I appreciate the insider knowledge provided by Erika Sanchez, Jose Aleman, and Marcos Lopez.

Finally, I could not have done this work without my familia, who held me up when I could not go forward, and spoke clarity into my life when the future was unclear. Thank you.

Introduction

The Spirit of the Barrio

I bid Mario Pineda[1] farewell, not knowing it would be the last time I would see him in person. A happy-go-lucky young man whose family hailed from Michoacán, Mexico, he and I parted ways in a manner typical of young men in the neighborhood: Our right hands quickly clasped against each other then slid off into a fist bump. The sun was setting, and the lit-up windows of the sixteen apartment units in Mario's complex exuded the warmth of working adults and extended families convening for dinner. In the distance, the thick, wavy baseline of funk music pulsated through the California evening sky.

As Mario cracked open the door to his family's apartment, I caught a glimpse of the altar to La Virgen de Guadalupe in the living room. The altar was composed of a small shelf holding a central, colorful foot-tall statue of *La Morenita*, accompanied by candles and paper flowers. Green, white, and red streamers, the colors of the Mexican flag, were braided together and emanated from the altar toward the ceiling. Mario and his family did not have to prove their faith in Jesus Christ or La Virgen de Guadalupe—their practices embodied their faith. They, along with many of their central Santa Ana neighbors in their majority Mexican neighborhood, often expressed their Catholic faith publicly through neighborhood celebrations and parish-based festivals. Indeed, their faith was more than personal, it was communal. As reflected in their home altar, their faith and their Mexican identity were closely intertwined.

Still, a type of faith struggle was afoot in the Pineda household. Mario's parents had lost faith in the prospects available to them in the

[1] I use pseudonyms for all informants, and for the names of some of the congregations sampled from.

The Saints of Santa Ana. Jonathan E. Calvillo, Oxford University Press (2020). © Oxford University Press. DOI: 10.1093/oso/9780190097790.001.0001.

United States, Mario explained to me. In the aftermath of the 2008 economic recession, families like Mario's were devastated by what Omi and Winant called "the largest regressive racial redistribution of resources to have occurred in U.S. history" (2014:227). The working-class, immigrant neighborhoods of Santa Ana, California, were exorbitantly pummeled by this financial crisis. Rising deportations under the Obama administration served an additional blow. Mario's father, Mario Sr., wanted to move the family back to his ancestral lands in Mexico, a place that Mario hardly knew, having come to the United States as a child.

I noted the photos of deceased grandparents displayed in the Pinedas' living room; it was to the land of these loved ones that Mario Sr. hoped to return. The same photos would seasonally function as altar centerpieces during *el Dia de Los Muertos*, reminding the Pinedas of their lineage. I imagined that family members would discuss their next steps at the dinner table or in the living room as these saints and ancestors looked on.

Mario entered the apartment and shut the door behind him. The lock clicked. The family's fate would soon be sealed. In the days to follow they concretized their plans to return to the land of their ancestors. Taking a leap of faith, the Pinedas abruptly moved back to Mexico. Through social media, I later learned that Mario had settled into his new home and that the family altars too had accompanied the family. Through the crossing of borders, the Pinedas had kept their faith.

Faith permeated most facets of life for the Pinedas as faith was a matter of survival for them; such was the case with many other immigrants I would encounter when studying faith and ethnic identity. Numerous scholars make similar observations (Hirschman 2004; Portes and Rumbaut 2014). For the Pinedas and many of their neighbors, faith was a critical ingredient toward establishing a sense of belonging in a trying context; it informed how these residents envisioned and enacted forms of collectivism. Faith was ever present in the negotiations made while crossing borders and boundaries, providing a sense of stability in the midst of drastic change. Faith provided tools for moving about within foreign and familiar spaces, shaping the very understandings of people's positionalities within these contexts.

Understanding the Moment

Beginning my doctoral studies on the tail end of the 2008–2009 recession,[2] I had set out to investigate how religion influenced the ethnic identities of Mexican immigrants. Specifically, I planned to compare the ethnic identity formation of Catholic and evangelical Mexican immigrants, paying special attention to how these distinct Christian traditions influenced notions of Mexican ethnicity individually and collectively. Scholarship on immigrants had so often emphasized ethnicity as a central organizing principle of immigrant solidarity (Portes and Rumbaut 2014). The pervasiveness of religion in the lives of immigrants from Mexico seemed especially apt for reinforcing this solidarity. Ethnicity and religion, it seemed, worked in concert with each other.

Yet, even as the share of Latinxs[3] in the Catholic church was expanding (Ospino 2014), so too was the share of evangelicals in the Latinx population increasing (Cooperman et al. 2014). Moreover, the Catholic church in the United States was becoming more Latinx, and Latinxs as an aggregate were becoming less Catholic. The opportunity to understand how these trends in religion were affecting the ethnic cohesion of the Mexican-origin population seemed timely. Communities like Mario's working-class neighborhood in central Santa Ana formed the backbone of this Mexican majority "Latino City" (Gonzalez 2017) and offered rich opportunities, I surmised. It was also a time of political and economic upheaval, and the residents of my selected field sites were being confronted with significant life decisions. The cohesion of the community was being tested, and I could hardly ignore what was happening in that moment.

Santa Ana's religious communities had been unduly affected by the recession. Rev. Lee De Leon, a pastor from Templo Calvario, one of the largest churches in the city, reported that 15% of his church's congregants were in the process of returning back to their countries

[2] I started my doctoral studies in the Fall of 2009 when the effects of the 2008 recession were still being felt.

[3] I employ the term Latinx, a gender-neutral, gender-inclusive term, to refer to people of Latin American descent in the U.S. I use gendered cognates of this term, such as Latina or Latino, when particular informants or cited sources apply this terminology.

of origin (Carcamo 2011). While non-citizens underwent both forced deportations and self-deportations, in some cases US citizens, often children, also left the United States with family members. Mario's family, parishioners of Inmaculado Corazon Catholic church, self-deported. Their parish too was experiencing the shakeup.

Many parishioners in these Latinx-dominant parishes perfectly and tragically fit the profile of households most vulnerable to predatory lending in the early 2000s (Tienda and Fuentes 2014). Older barrios, like those in Santa Ana, bore the brunt of foreclosures (Tienda and Fuentes 2014), with numerous popular news outlets reporting on the trend in the city (Gittelsohn 2008; Hagerty 2009; Christie 2011). One *Wall Street Journal* article characterized Santa Ana's foreclosure housing market as "blazing hot" (Hagerty 2009). Some homebuyers and investors readily benefited from the life crises of some Santa Ana residents. Even renters like Mario's parents and his neighbors were directly affected. The construction industry and the service sectors that employed many in the neighborhood imploded. As an outgrowth of this financial upheaval, churches themselves were struggling to sustain operations. Pastor De Leon's church laid off a number of staff members, and temporarily discontinued certain programs vital to the community (Carcamo 2011).

Yet, many of Santa Ana's Latinx immigrant residents, authorized and unauthorized, continued to live their lives in the city, hinting at another story that was emerging: Many Mexican immigrants in Santa Ana were weathering the storm through a sense of hope rooted in faith practices. Faith sustained the individuals and households that faced some of the most trying situations. Faith infused these residents with a sense of fight that kept them pushing on, in the face of immediate financial needs, deportation, and sustained inequality. The faith of local congregants was a faith largely built into the rhythms of everyday life; it was communal and quotidian. Congregations had a visible role in this, but so too did the lived religion enacted in the neighborhood spaces of central Santa Ana.

Santa Ana residents engaged in a high degree of organizing and planning in their homes and neighborhoods around activities centered on and infused by faith. Congregations helped shape the strategies with which residents engaged in their social interactions. Yet, it was through lived religion, the faith expressions embodied by nonexperts in everyday ways (Ammerman 2007), that Santa Ana residents enacted a type of public resilience in their neighborhoods. I began to recognize that it was through an examination of lived religion that immigrants could be given a fuller and more nuanced representation as subjects of their own future, exercising agency, and not just as objects, as Martinez (2013) cautions against. I committed myself to walking alongside of Mexican immigrants in Santa Ana, paying particular attention to the lives they led in their residential communities.

Along with my ethnographic research among Santa Ana residents, a review of Santa Ana's Latinx religious history helped me to situate the current moment within broader streams of social and political developments reaching back into the nineteenth century. On the one hand, the precarious status of many Mexican Santa Ana residents was the present-day effect of a series of policies and social mechanisms wielded upon working-class Latinxs at local, national, and international levels, drawing from their life labor while constraining their spheres of life. The much-needed labor for Orange County had historically been provided by the residents of barrios throughout the county, with Santa Ana home to the greatest number of these barrios; residents of these barrios faced a variety of exclusionary policies even as their labor was solicited. On the other hand, for Santa Ana's Mexican residents, faith consistently functioned as a resource in the struggle for dignity and collective legitimacy. Latinxs played an important role in the founding of religious institutions, for example, and religious communities often provided spaces wherein Latinxs could exercise agency. Furthermore, Latinxs have had a variety of religious options for over a century in Santa Ana.

While researchers today trumpet a recent "shift" in Latinx religiosity away from Catholicism, I came to find that Santa Ana's barrios were home to distinct religious traditions for over a century. To understand Mexican ethnic identity in the region, I recognized that I needed to understand the ongoing history of spatial and social exclusion along with the religious choices faced by the residents of Santa Ana's barrios.[4]

[4] The results of this historical analysis are primarily contained in Chapter 2 of this volume.

The narratives of faith, inequality, and ethnic identity I encountered in historical documents of a century past were at times eerily similar to accounts I took in through contemporary face-to-face interactions.

Building Ties in Santa Ana

My own experiences of faith and ethnic identity formation would play a significant role in how I moved about in the field of inquiry. My choice of Santa Ana as a research site came from very personal interactions with the city. In my childhood imagination, Santa Ana, California, was a city of churches. Santa Ana was warmth emanating from human bodies crowded together in worship gatherings. It was music reverberating through old speakers. It was the staccato cadence of a preacher's voice filling a church sanctuary. It was the aroma of beans, rice, and fresh tortillas floating through church kitchens. It was a feeling of breathlessness after chasing other children alongside of church parking lots. These are among my earliest memories of Santa Ana. When my Pentecostal family and I visited the city, it was usually to attend any of a wide array of church activities: special services, outreach events, concerts, too many to remember. We periodically visited several churches in the city, a few among the many. As my mother once said, "En Santa Ana, hay una iglesia en cada esquina" (In Santa Ana, there's a church on every corner).

In these Santa Ana churches, people looked like me, spoke like me, ate the foods I was familiar with, and sang the songs that I knew. This was not the case just anywhere in Orange County, California. Still, born and raised in a Latinx Pentecostal church where my parents were busy lay leaders, this network of churches was part of my social world. The embodied interactions at these churches during this formative life stage significantly shaped who I was. The experiences oriented my sense of who "my people" were and etched a particular social map upon my psyche. Deep down in my bones, when we visited Santa Ana, I felt that I belonged. My family of Pentecostal, Mexican-immigrant parents and second-generation children was normal in Santa Ana, that much I knew. In this city, our faith and ethnicity came together seamlessly.

It was not until my late teens that I got to experience the pulse of the city in more extensive fashion, by living in one of the central city barrios. In the Summer of 1997, I took an internship with a local non-profit organization that allowed me to work among primarily Mexican-immigrant families residing in central Santa Ana. I had completed my freshman year in college and was strongly motivated to become more engaged with community work. What I thought would be a summer long experience turned out to be the start of a close bond with a city that I would eventually call home.

That summer, I noticed the way that religion was integral to the public identities of local residents. Faith was a powerful force in my up-bringing, but what I observed in Santa Ana was a neighborhood-based, communally expressed religion that I had rarely experienced firsthand. Many of the gatherings that I initially saw simply as neighborhood parties, I soon understood as being celebrations of the sacraments. That is, after particular sacraments were partaken of at church, celebrations would follow in the neighborhood. The sacrament of Baptism enacted at church often carried over into neighborhood celebrations of the infants who had been welcomed into the family of God. The welcoming of these infants into the journey of faith included a neighborhood-based welcome. The sacrament of the Eucharist as expressed in the first communion was also often celebrated in the neighborhood after children partook of it at church. Christ's bodily sacrifice and his continued presence with his people were often remembered in the neighborhood whenever this Eucharistic tradition was celebrated. The sacrament of Confirmation was sometimes celebrated in the neighborhood as well, but not as frequently as baptism and first communion. Weddings were less frequently celebrated in the neighborhood, as off-site rented halls were used more frequently, but sometimes wedding-like quinceañeras were celebrated in the neighborhood. While quinceañera ceremonies are not themselves a sacrament, they did constitute an important point of connection to the church, with special masses being held for young ladies coming of age. Quinceañera ceremonies provided reminders to participants of the importance of the sacraments. All in all, the centrality of the Catholic sacraments was amplified by the celebratory rhythms of neighborhood life.

In order to put together these community affairs, families in the neighborhood would come together to plan. The ties of *compadrazgo* and *comadrazgo* among those designated as godparents undergirded the social capital embedded in the community. Women in the neighborhood were especially at the forefront of maintaining community ties (Treviño 2006), of organizing events, and of ensuring that proper steps were taken in observing the sacraments. Open air courtyards in densely populated apartment complexes would double as banquet halls, with balloons and streamers and all. Sound systems from apartment units would pump up the music to treat party attendees. Local DJs exercised entrepreneurship, creating their own industry and revolutionizing neighborhood parties. All the while, faith was tied into these celebrations, both through personal devotional practices and through ecclesial ties. As I established relationships with people in the community, I received invitations to these events, both to mass and to neighborhood celebrations.

The personal, Catholic faith of local residents became vivid to me as I lived and worked in the community. I would observe the dedication of one woman, for example, who led catechism classes from an apartment unit. The living room of that apartment would be filled to the brim with children from the neighborhood. I met a volunteer at our nonprofit who would write to young men and women in prison, encouraging them in their Catholic faith. They often sought her out when their incarceration term was completed. Quite lively were the organizing efforts of local residents when feast days would come about, particularly the day of La Virgen de Guadalupe. Through my work, I gained the opportunity to experience firsthand the celebrations in honor of *La Guadalupana* at a community level. Hundreds of residents from particular neighborhoods would take to the streets to express their love and devotion to the patron saint of Mexico.

A minority of people were of Protestant background like myself, and they too came to my attention. I got to know the Oneness Pentecostal family where the women in the household distinguished themselves in the neighborhood by always wearing long skirts in public and rejecting the use of makeup. I interacted with the Baptist pastor that held church in an apartment unit down the street from where he lived. I watched how the Salvation Army ran a neighborhood program for children from a huge mobile home every week. Occasionally I encountered a group from Victory Outreach conducting outreach events targeting gang affiliated young men and young women on the streets where we ran our programs. The Protestant presence among locals in the neighborhood was clearly in the minority, but it was felt, and it was diverse in its institutional expressions. Awareness of this minority was expanding among the Catholic majority and evangelicals were growing increasingly visible, and increasingly vocal. Change was afoot in the city's religious landscape.

About a dozen years after my first stay in Santa Ana, I would find myself a resident in the city, about to embark on my doctoral studies. By then the city was home. I had never really left since my first summer working in the city, staying connected through a variety of formal and informal ties, eventually living in the city for over a decade. I was set on studying immigrant sociocultural incorporation, ethnic identity formation, and religious belonging. Santa Ana seemed to me the ideal context to embark on this course of study. I would build on my ties to the nonprofit world and to faith-based grassroots institutions to capture a cross-section of stories from the residents of central Santa Ana. With two religious groupings having considerable following in the city, Catholics and evangelicals, I would focus my research on understanding how religious affiliation within these two groups influenced ethnic identity formation, and how the growth of evangelicalism among Mexican immigrants was influencing local notions of collective ethnic identity.

Defining the Field of Study

Early on, I decided that my study would focus on the working-class communities of central Santa Ana. I recognized that these were the communities most vulnerable to being marginalized by the social and economic policies of the time. These communities were home to high concentrations of Latinx residents, and also reflected high rates of poverty. Historical patterns of segregation experienced by

Latinxs had contributed to ongoing experiences of social distance from the white middle class, and many Latinxs had responded by forging strong co-ethnic communities. Local residents were invested in the wellness of their neighborhoods, and often this was expressed through acts of collectivism centered on faith. These strong ethnic investments in the city had given rise to a vibrant religious ecology[5] that had served Latinx residents for over a century. I expected that in light of the vulnerability of local immigrant communities, religion would serve as an ever-important resource for sustaining a collective ethnic support system.

At this stage in the life of Orange County, Santa Ana's county home, there were many other Latinx dominant neighborhoods that were home to great numbers of working-class residents. Yet, there was something special about living in Santa Ana. Many residents of the city, past and present, expressed exuberant pride in their ties to the city and an awareness that this city represented a history—an ethnic history. The label used by many locals to tie themselves to the city of Santa Ana—*Santanero/a*—contained various shades of meaning. Not all Santa Ana residents identified with the term Santanero, but it seemed particularly prevalent among people connected to the working-class, Latinx-majority neighborhoods of central Santa Ana. Implicitly, especially for many central Santa Ana residents, to be a Santanero signaled ties to local neighborhoods and commitment to collective action therein. Some Santaneros struggled as immigrants, both in their process of migration and their process of settling in the United States; many US-born Santaneros struggled through processes of being racialized often linked closely to racialized perceptions of the city itself espoused by outsiders (Lacayo 2016). Identifying as a Santanero might signal familiarity with these types of struggles. Many self-identified Santaneros also embodied a sense of hope about the future of the city, expressed through activism and entrepreneurship. Moreover, Santaneros were often invested in the well-being of the city and in building a sustainable future for the city

[5] Eiesland (2000:11) provides a helpful definition of religious ecology: "The patterns of relations, status, and interaction among organizations as they are embedded within a specific environment."

that included the working-class, Latinx core of the city. Santa Ana was a place of memory for Latinxs, a place to recall victories and losses, but it was also a place where ethnic community was made real, where an ethnic past was brought into the present and onward into the future.

Some residents of the city had been referring to themselves as Santaneros for years now and it struck me that the term aptly fit my informants. The term Santanero reflected the way that many locals pronounce the name Santa Ana—pushing both words together to form a single word—*Santana*; most, if not all of the people I spoke with for this project used this pronunciation of the city name. Particularly among local Spanish speakers, *Santana* was the "correct," colloquial way to say the name of the city. The term *Santanero* became popular among a segment of Santa Ana residents of a younger generation. A magazine, named *Santanero Zine*, for example, published by Santa Ana local Eric Cocoletzi, was one platform that brought the term to a broader audience (Arellano 2013), though the term itself had already been in use among local residents. Santanero is a term which, to me, characterizes the soul of the city, particularly the soul of the Latinx, working-class community of *Santana*.

Questions of ethnic identity and of ethnic collectivism took on a level of urgency for Santaneros that understood what it was to struggle. Ethnic solidarity and collectivism for Santaneros were largely rooted in localized networks of co-ethnic support. However, differences in key identifiers of ethnic belonging, could call into suspicion one's commitment to the broader community. Ethnic commitment mattered to Santaneros, particularly to working-class immigrants, for whom community—or *comunidad*—was more than an abstract idea. Religion often functioned as a primary platform of ethnic collectivism. It could provide the ethos that enabled exchange and care within the ethnic community in a broad, public sense. Religious difference could make for tenuous ethnic ties. Thus, as I would find out, religion was internally policed in part because it pointed to one's commitment to the broader ethnic community, a community that for many could be signaled and delineated along concrete, material, geographic terms.

Centering the Study

Initially I designed this study as a mostly interview-based investigation on how Mexican immigrants articulate their notions of ethnicity across religious lines.[6] I expected to find noticeable differences in the preferred ethnic labels of evangelicals and Catholics, for example. My expectations were only partially confirmed. While I observed some nuanced differences of ethnic identification correlating with religious differences, there were also significant similarities across affiliations. Salient differences began to emerge in other arenas related to ethnic identity, however. Subjects' responses suggested that the way that ethnic community was lived out in the neighborhoods of Santa Ana, for example, significantly differed across religious lines. Instances of direct interaction across religious lines, and how people talked about the religious "other" also emerged as important loci of ethnic identity formation.

To supplement my interview data, it became clear that I needed to spend more time in the field, within the social worlds and social spaces of spiritual sustenance that were most meaningful to the Mexican immigrants I was walking alongside; this included churches, neighborhood-based gatherings, and home gatherings. An important difference across religious lines that did emerge from analysis of interview data centered on the theme of identity continuity. That is, through religion, in the midst of experiences of social dislocation and through migratory journeys, subjects grappled with notions of a sustained and authentic self, integrated with their pasts.

In the end, I conducted in-depth interviews with fifty Santa Ana residents, all Mexican immigrants, twenty-five of them Catholics, and twenty-five of them evangelicals. The majority of interviewees were of working-class socioeconomic status. Most worked in the service sector, in construction, or in light industry. A handful of interviewees approximated middle-class status and worked mostly in the fields of education and/or human services, but they too lived in majority-working-class neighborhoods. Interviewees ranged in age from

[6] I discuss research methods in Appendix A.

nineteen years of age to sixty-five years of age, and had been in the United States in the range of ten years to sixty years.

My sample is not representative of Santa Ana in its entirety, nor even of the city's Mexican-origin population in its entirety. Notably, later-generation ethnic Mexicans were not part of this sample and neither were upper-middle-class Santa Ana residents interviewed. There are neighborhoods in the city of predominantly middle-class and upper-middle-class households, especially on the edges of the city. As noted by Agius Vallejo (2012), there is a "growing middle class Mexican-American presence" in the city, yet this group is not the focus of this book. Informants in this book are overwhelmingly residents of central Santa Ana's working-class, immigrant dominant, Mexican majority neighborhoods.

Nearly all interviewees resided on the western side of central Santa Ana, west of the famous Bristol Street, with a majority clustered within a roughly one-mile radius of Immaculate Heart of Mary Catholic Parish. The Immaculate Heart of Mary parish provides a helpful frame of reference for situating the social ecology of the study as the majority of my informants were familiar with the parish, regardless of whether or not they were parishioners there. About a fifth of informants lived farther out, on the edges of the city core, but maintained connections to central Santa Ana through familial ties, church involvement, and/or work; most of these outlying residents had previously lived in the city core. All interviewees were members of Latinx-majority churches in Santa Ana. In addition to my fifty in-depth interviews, I conducted dozens of informal, ethnographic interviews with Santaneros who participated in the religious communities familiar to my original fifty interviewees. These additional interviewees provided important insights into lived religion, ethnic networks, and the creation and sacralization of ethnic space.

The completion of in-depth interviews required a multi-pronged approach. As I learned through the process of data collection, making myself available was of utmost importance because many of my informants had limited availability. Many informants worked multiple jobs and cared for multigenerational households. The time that they made available to me was of utmost value. As such, I became efficient at conducting short interviews when necessary, but made sure to conduct follow-up interviews if the initial interview had been truncated. On average, I spent at least an hour interviewing each informant, but in some cases interviews were broken up into multiple conversations. I had contact with and spoke with most of my interviewees on multiple occasions, given the extensive time I spent in neighborhoods and religious communities. In some cases, I had follow-up conversations with informants that explored topics we had covered in our formal interviews. In other cases, I merely interacted with them informally and on their terms, typically in a public setting involving their religious communities. This approach allowed me to access multiple channels of data from individual informants.

At this juncture it is also important to clarify that this project was not designed as a parish study. My focus was on Santaneros' understandings of ethnic identity as expressed in their broader social spheres of the city and neighborhoods. Certainly, churches helped to socialize the congregants I interviewed, and as such I reference church experiences whenever informants brought them to the fore. Congregants' perceptions of the religious other, however, were uniquely enacted in their face-to-face interactions outside of church, I observed. Thus, for this volume I privilege how Santaneros engaged in church and religious activities outside of traditional church gatherings held inside of church buildings. I spent extensive time inside of church buildings during my research. Nevertheless, I recognized a new possibility in exploring how churches were influencing congregants' notions of ethnic identity and ethnic community in more diffuse ways. This was made possible through my engagement of religious collectivities, typically tied to churches, but whose activities were enacted "*en la comunidad*" or in the community.

In holding steadfast to my general question about religion and ethnic identity among Mexican immigrants, a broader question came to dominate this study. How does religious affiliation influence the production of ethnic space among Santaneros, especially in the face of religious difference and religious change? More than ethnic identity as a notion that individuals carry within them, the theme of ethnic space allowed me to investigate how physical space was imbued with ethnic meaning through personal and public practices of faith. Histories of exclusion, preferences in self-identification, views about the past, beliefs about the spirit world, and opinions about the ethnic neighborhood, all contributed to notions of ethnic space. These religious practices contributed to understandings of Santa Ana as a space that held value for the ethnic Mexican community. And as I conclude in this volume, notions of ethnic space would serve as a proxy for ethnic identity itself, signaling that relationships to Santa Ana as an ethnic space could be deployed in the construction of ethnicity.

Santa Ana Demographics

The unique place of Santa Ana within its broader region is reflected in its demographic realities. The city of Santa Ana rests at the heart of a famed region, Southern California, and an infamous county, Orange County. As the county seat, Santa Ana provides space for the headquarters of county governance. Santa Ana also contains several federal service centers such as the Ronald Reagan Federal Building, and is home to a Mexican consulate office. Santa Ana was established as a US township in 1870, under the guidance of founder William H. Spurgeon. Once Spurgeon connected Santa Ana to a regional stagecoach line, Santa Ana came to be the urban hub of a generally agricultural area (Harwood and Myers 2002). World War II brought about significant developments as industry expanded in the region, catapulting the growth of Santa Ana. In the years from 1960 through 1990 Santa Ana saw astounding growth as its population nearly tripled from 100,350 to 300,000 (Harwood and Myers 2002).

A city at the heart of Orange County California's thriving economy, Santa Ana's working-class Latinx residents constitute a substantial segment of the Orange County labor force. Composed of thirty-four cities, Orange County is home to eleven out of the one hundred wealthiest cities in the nation; three Orange County cities are in the top ten.[7] This contrasts with the experience of Santa Ana's majority-working-class population. Reflecting the experience of this substantial

[7] See Miller (2016).

population, a 2004 report from the Rockefeller Institute declared Santa Ana the toughest place to live in the nation:

> [Santa Ana] displays many of the same characteristics associated with hardship in the older "rust belt" cities listed [in another section]: a central city that represents a low, possibly shrinking share of population in the metropolitan area; stuck within inflexible city boundaries; with limited new housing stock; and tough social challenges, such as having nearly six out of every ten adults over 25 years of age having less than a high-school education. (Montiel et al. 2004)

Much of Santa Ana's working-class population moves across spaces of abundance and struggle. They act as the hands of the service sector, as house cleaners, landscapers, construction workers, warehouse employees, and restaurant staff.

Data on Santa Ana as my study first got underway signaled the city's ongoing status as a gateway city. Nearly 50% of Santa Ana was composed of foreign-born residents (U.S. Census Bureau 2010). Latinxs constituted 78.2% of the city's population whereas whites composed 9.2% (U.S. Census Bureau 2010). While 43.2% of California's population spoke a language at home other than English, 82.9% of Santa Ana residents above the age of five spoke a language other than English at home (U.S. Census Bureau 2010).

In regard to education, Santa Ana had a significantly lower percentage of high school graduates when compared to state level figures. Among Santa Ana residents above age twenty-five, only 51.9% were high school graduates, while in the general Californian population 80.8% of the residents had graduated from high school (U.S. Census Bureau 2010). Even more pronounced was the difference in completion of bachelor's degrees. With 11.7% of residents above age twenty-five earning a B.A., Santa Ana barely surpassed a third of the percentage of state residents that had earned the same (U.S. Census Bureau 2010).

The issue of overcrowding continued to draw attention as Santa Ana households on average were composed of 4.35 members, while the state average was 2.91 members. This effect was further compounded by the fact that over 40% of Santa Ana residents lived in multi-unit structures, more than 10% higher than the state figure (U.S. Census Bureau 2010). Median household income in Santa Ana was $54,399 while the state figure was $61,632. Finally, poverty in Santa Ana was reported by 19.5% of its residents whereas only 14.4% of the overall state population reported this status (U.S. Census Bureau 2010).

As the study drew to a close, Santa Ana continued to count on a significant proportion of Latinx residents. With roughly 1.03 million Latinx residents in the entire county, Santa Ana is home to slightly more than a fourth of the county's Latinx population, with 257,000 Latinx residents (U.S. Census 2017).[8] Santa Ana also continues to be one of the most densely populated cities in the nation. The concentration of Latinx residents in Santa Ana uniquely positions the city as a mega-enclave of sorts (Gonzalez 2017). To put Santa Ana's population in perspective, it is a city comparable in population size to Cleveland, OH, Honolulu, HI, or St. Louis, MO, though at a national level the city might be less known than these other cities. Thirty miles south of Los Angeles, Santa Ana is overshadowed by its significantly larger neighbor. Yet Orange County and Santa Ana are spaces with identities all their own, and Latinxs wanting to connect with an ethnic enclave need not brave Los Angeles traffic to find co-ethnic community. Santa Ana is especially important to the region's Mexican-origin population. Ongoing cultural celebrations, and expansive ethnic economies publicly embody Santa Ana's place as an ethnic hub.

Even as Santa Ana is a center of activity for Latinxs in the region, particularly Mexicans, Latinx Santa Ana residents have continued to struggle with exclusionary boundaries in order to legitimize their local presence. Recent generations of local Latinx activists hearken back to legacies of justice work. Issues that capture the efforts of city-based activists today include advocacy for immigrant rights, combating gentrification, ensuring the rights of LGBTQ individuals, decrying educational inequality, and spearheading health and housing initiatives. That Santa Ana is home to many residents endangered by their legal status makes the issues above all the more pressing given the heightened vulnerability of some residents. An estimated 10,000

[8] The total population of the city is roughly 330,000.

people marched through Santa Ana as part of the national marches for immigrants' rights that took place on May 1, 2006. The city council, the first among US big cities to be composed entirely of Latinxs, eventually validated the sustained, arduous efforts of activists by declaring the city a "Sanctuary City."[9] With undocumented immigrants estimated as being 27% of central Santa Ana's population (Marcelli et al. 2015), spaces that allow locals to sustain homeland ties are highly valued. In many a central Santa Ana household, residents contend with the realities of having family members, friends, and neighbors struggling through issues of legal status, if they do not struggle with these issues themselves. Social boundaries of class, race, immigration status, and political influence continue to shape the experiences of Santaneros, particularly their sense of ethnic identity. Navigating religious identity was inextricable from these realities.

Navigating the Religious Ecology through this Volume

Liset glanced at me from her downcast countenance, contradicting the jovial manner that I typically knew her to exemplify. She must have had a day off from her usual job of cleaning offices on Saturdays, I imagined. Finally turning her face in my direction, revealing a facial expression that was half smile, half frown, she waved her hand at me briskly. The last time I had spoken to Liset I had crossed paths with her at one of various evangelical churches in the city that I had visited in the last year. Now I was seeing her at a rosary prayer meeting in her neighborhood of Townsend Street. It turned out that she no longer attended the evangelical church. I wondered if her uncharacteristically timid demeanor revealed a sense of shame that I might mention something about her evangelical visit to the people around her, or worse yet, to the deacon in charge of the event. I had no interest in doing any of that. I sent over the biggest smile I could muster and when I spoke to

[9] See Cindy Carcamo, "Santa Ana Declares Itself a Sanctuary City in Defiance of Trump," *Los Angeles Times*, December 7, 2016. The Santa Ana city council voted on sanctuary status on December 6, 2016.

her made no mention of the last place I had seen her. Because I had lived in Liset's neighborhood of Townsend St. for two years, I had met Liset several years prior.

A woman in her early fifties, sporting short, tousled brown hair atop her diminutive stature, Liset had come to the United States from her native state of Guerrero and had found support in various faith communities around town. "Que bueno que nos acompañas aquí en la Townsend" (That's good that you accompany us here at Townsend), Liset told me. When I had last seen Liset, she was contemplating membership at an evangelical church, but ultimately opted not to join that church. As Liset and I chatted after the event, she indicated that she was no longer visiting any evangelical churches. She did, however, find solace in the neighborhood prayer gatherings sponsored by *Inmaculado Corazón*, as the local Catholic parish was known by many residents.

As a single mother, without an extensive family network in the surrounding area, Liset's neighborhood support system was of utmost importance. The group that she prayed with was composed mostly of women who lived close to her. A next-door neighbor, a friend from across the street, a husband and wife that lived down the block, these were among the people that Liset had gathered with to pray the rosary on Townsend St. in Santa Ana. The group moved through several of the many apartment courtyards lined up across the span of a quarter mile block. Prayer stations had been set up mostly in spaces between apartment buildings. One of the stations where I had spotted Liset joining the thirty or so participants was out on the sidewalk. For Liset, the boundaries of religious belonging had been blurred for a season, but it appeared that she was reconfiguring her place within the religious ecology and strengthening her ties within her ethnic community.

Many Santaneros like Liset negotiated the boundaries of ethnic identity through religious practices. In Chapter 1, I discuss how religion provides particular boundary markers related to ethnic identity and ethnic community. I provide a snapshot of two of Santa Ana's religious communities, one Catholic and one evangelical, to demonstrate the ritualized approaches of ethnic identity construction tied to each respective religious tradition. Critical differences between these two communities emerge in relation to understandings of the past, a dimension closely linked to ethnic identity construction. Distinct understandings of history, I argue, lead to diverging patterns in how peoplehood is experienced across these groupings. In this chapter I also lay out a theoretical framework for how I approach ethnic identity formation. Specifically, I introduce the social boundary approach I employ to explain how ethnic identity is maintained and negotiated, both within groups and across groups.

Like Liset, many Santaneros faced a religious ecology offering diverse religious options. In Chapter 2, I describe how Santa Ana's distinct Latinx majority religious ecology, with its many religious options, came to be. I propose that the religious ecology navigated today by Santaneros like Liset is tied to the histories of local religious institutions and to patterns of racialized, ethnic exclusion. I chronicle how the ethnic identities that residents like Liset have had to contend with today emerge from a history of negotiations and struggles that Mexican-identified individuals have long contended with. Religion, I note, has often been used by whites in the construction of exclusionary boundary markers against Latinxs. Nevertheless, I argue that the emergence of Latinx-majority religious communities have also provided Santaneros like Liset with opportunities to exercise agency and leadership.

In Chapter 3, I examine how Santaneros like Liset articulate notions of who they are ethnically. I conceptualize group differences in ethnic self-identification as an extension of the boundary work being done among Catholics and evangelicals. Generally, most respondents, both Catholic and evangelical, identify as Mexican. A subset of respondents identify using a pan-ethnic label such as Latina/o or Hispanic. Whereas both religious groups show similar patterns in the labels of ethnic self-identification that they select, Catholics and evangelicals employ diverging discursive strategies to qualify their responses. Catholics exhibit more confidence in their responses to questions of ethnic self-identification. Evangelicals engage in extended discursive labor to legitimate their ethnic labels. I argue that these diverging discourses uncover contestations within the broader ethnic community about what legitimate ethnic identity should look like.

Just as Liset faced the prospect of religious change, in Chapter 4 I discuss Latinx religious identities through the lens of change and continuity. Discussions of Latinx religions often focus on religious change, and this chapter seeks to uncover the tension between change and continuity. For evangelicals, the experience of religious conversion becomes a marker of evangelical identity. Some Catholics, too, have experiences of religious renewal which closely approximate religious conversion. For evangelicals, conversion experiences are closely linked to rupturing with the past. For Catholics, religious renewal is a way to solidify ties to the past, both religious and ethnic. Essentially, Catholics have a stronger sense of continuity with the past and evangelicals tend to emphasize discontinuity with the past. Ultimately, I address the dilemma of how experiences of religious renewal and religious change relate to ethnic identity maintenance. Understandings of the past matter for ethnic identity because they structure the collective memories that people have at their disposal to bolster a sense of shared history. Religious traditions inform adherents as to what elements of the past matter, and how they matter.

In Chapter 5, I describe how the patterns of religious commitment for Santaneros like Liset are often articulated through a sense of engagement with divine and spiritual entities. This particular pattern signals commonality between Catholics and evangelicals in that members of both groups place an emphasis on receiving spiritual guidance from spiritual entities as they make choices about their choices of religious commitments. Though Catholics and evangelicals differ in some of the specific practices they engage in in order to communicate with spiritual entities, the expectations of spiritual guidance are similar. I argue that these notions of spiritual dialogue are especially meaningful in relation to the diverse religious ecology that Santaneros navigate. Religious commitments and religious identities are made all the more concrete as they are affirmed through expectations of divine guidance. In navigating the ethnic space of Santa Ana, divine dialogue shapes the relationship between ethnic space and spirituality.

As with Liset, for many Santaneros religious affiliation largely influenced opinions about the *barrio*, or ethnic enclave. In Chapter 6, I examine how Catholic and evangelical affiliation influences understandings of the barrio. Relationships to the ethnic enclave matter, I argue, because the ethnic enclave is a concentration of ethnic resources that distinctly shape ethnic identities. Catholics understand the barrio as a "community," denoting both physical neighborhood and tight-knit support networks. The barrio functions as a space for communally performed rituals of collective memory for Catholics. On the other hand, evangelicals tend to view the barrio as a place that is in need of redemption. To evangelicals, the barrio is the target of evangelistic efforts. Evangelicals generally conceive of their place in the barrio as a catalytic role, aimed at bringing about transformation therein. Both Catholics and evangelicals are highly invested in the ethnic enclave, but their differing views provide them with different channels of access to localized ethnic resources.

In the Conclusion, I bring together the various forms of boundary negotiation presented in previous chapters to discuss how they contribute to the production of ethnic identity and ethnic space. Ethnic space, I argue, serves as a mechanism for the reproduction of ethnic identities. For Catholics, religion shapes the boundaries of ethnicity as a retrospective, locally anchored, communally embodied identity. For evangelicals, religion shapes the boundaries of ethnicity as a future-looking, regionally dispersed, voluntarily selected identity. I do not argue that one of these typologies is the "correct" way to be ethnic. I do, however, discuss how each tradition has a distinct role to play in the production of ethnic space. I conclude by making observations about how ultimately the maintaining of ethnic space and of ethnic identities is an intergenerational endeavor. I close by reflecting on the ethnic identities being forged by later-generation Latinxs in light of what they are inheriting from their parents.

Seeing the Sacred While on the Field

In one of my early years of working in Santa Ana, on staff at Kidworks, a neighborhood-based non-profit organization, we had the opportunity to run an afterschool program within an apartment complex. During one of our programs with elementary-aged children, a foodbank had provided us with numerous types of bread that we would be donating to families in the community. We placed the bread on a table outside of our center, and would soon be inviting the parents of children to have their pick of the bread. Some children playing outside of our homework center, without our permission, began to throw pieces of bread at each other. Soon, a food fight ensued. In a matter of seconds, bread was flying across the apartment courtyard. To our dismay, the children throwing the bread ignored our directives for them to stop.

Seconds later, an apartment resident came to our rescue. Doña Elvia forcefully stepped beyond the door frame of her apartment, a woman of portly form and of expansive voice, she visibly quivered with anger as she spoke in that moment. Standing at the center of the apartment courtyard, she bellowed out to the abruptly formed crowd of children, "¿Que están haciendo? ¿Que no saben que la comida es sagrada?" (What are you doing? Don't you know that food is sacred?). As the words escaped her mouth, the bread ceased from going airborne. Her presence and voice accomplished what several of us could not do. She caused the disobedient children to behave. Those children that needed to return home did so; others came back to us and got in line. Soon a group of children were cleaning up the mess that had accumulated, and the loaves that were left intact would be distributed to parents.

As a team of children and teens picked up what remained on the floor, one child had the audacity to throw another piece of bread through the air. Without missing a beat, a young girl of about five years of age attempted to berate the offender by repeating the words of Doña Elvia, who had since gone back to her apartment: "¿Que están haciendo? ¿Que no saben que la comida está sangrada?" Her final words, spoken in an ascendingly high pitch, were slightly off from the original quote. She ended with a phrase that translates as, "Don't you know that the food is bloody?" A few children chuckled, but most stayed quiet, perhaps fearing that Doña Elvia would once again emerge.

The incident stuck with me for two reasons. On one level, the young girl's erroneous transmission made for a comical memory. On another level, the original words of Doña Elvia stayed with me because they spoke volumes about the spirituality that was embodied by many a Santanero. Food was sacred. Certainly, food met a critical need. But more than food being sacred because of some utilitarian value, the sacred could be found in all of creation. The sacred could be found even in the crumbs of bread that were being tossed to and fro. The sacred was present throughout the world. As a devout Catholic woman, whom I got to know for several years, Doña Elvia's words, spoken with authority, reflected the Catholic imagination (Greeley 2000) and more precisely the Mexican Catholic imagination, as proposed by Socorro Castañeda-Liles (2018). I believe as Doña Elvia spoke she found approval in the gaze of La Virgen de Guadalupe who from her altar looked onto the scene but a few feet away.

I would later contemplate these ideas of the sacred being present in the most mundane of items and events. In my Protestant upbringing, I had been raised to understand that there needed to be a separation between Christians and the world. In part, this rested on an understanding of God's distinction from the world. Yet, as I moved through the spaces of Santa Ana, now as a researcher, I wondered how I might shift my vision to capture understandings of the sacred in the most basic everyday interactions, and in the simplest of items. I realized that in part, I had a basis from which I could do this work, one that I gained from the very tradition of my birth. Growing up in Pentecostal churches, I was taught that the Spirit of God moved in the present moment and operated in the day to day realities of human existence. I was taught to discern Spirit/s and to make myself available whenever the Spirit was at work. Could I, as an ethnographer, tap into that aspect of my upbringing? If Doña Elvia could teach me to see the sacred in the bread, in the midst of a food fight, why would I not be able to tap into the tradition of my upbringing as well, to pursue a sense of Spirit in the lives of my Santanero neighbors?

In this study, I aimed as an urban ethnographer, a scholar of immigration, race and ethnicity, and religion, to capture the ways that Santaneros demarcated the sacred in their processes of ethnic formation in public and semi-public neighborhood spaces. I observed how space was sacralized, and in some cases demonized, amidst ethnic expression. I traced how intra-ethnic lines were drawn, and sometimes flouted, along understandings of the sacred. I examined how the movement of the sacred within time itself could vary broadly according to distinct religious traditions. As I would discover, both Doña Elvia and the little girl were correct. In her faux pas, the child had extended Doña Elvia's assertion; in her faux pas she had transubstantiated the bread. So too, the very streets of Santa Ana are *sagradas* and *sangradas*. The hard labor of struggle, the last breaths of life, from a long lineage of Santaneros had settled into the pavement and on these streets the Spirit/s moved.

1
A City of Saints

There are saints[1] everywhere in Santa Ana; the name of the city is a reminder of their presence. In front yards, on street corners, and at restaurant counters, saints make themselves known. Saints operate within crowded public spaces, and in intimate, protected, private spaces. Some saints clamor for attention, while others quietly, diligently go about their work. Certainly, they can also be found in churches, but they are not confined to churches. Many saints have belied confinement, traversing geographic boundaries to reach their current homes. In fact, some of them have traveled quite a distance to reach Santa Ana. Still others are native to the land and have come from nearby. Santa Ana is a city of saints, a saintly place, a holy place. *Un lugar santo*. Saints make the place sacred. Indeed, they make many things sacred, including the most mundane of items. On numerous occasions I witnessed the streets, the lines delimiting neighborhood and community, the channels of everyday exchange, being made sacred. As I lived and breathed these streets, I experienced the very boundaries of belonging being marked by saints in the holiest of terms. For *Santaneros*,[2] the residents of Santa Ana, particularly for those that are Mexican immigrants, this sacralization is an everyday reality.

Honoring Saints

Melissa's voice cut through the din of hundreds of parishioners streaming out of the crowded sanctuary: "My mom is surprised that you're here. I mean, you're not supposed to be here because you're

[1] Students and alumni of Santa Ana High School, a historic school in the region, are referred to as "Saints," a detail well known in the city.
[2] The use of this term is explained in the Introduction of this volume.

The Saints of Santa Ana. Jonathan E. Calvillo, Oxford University Press (2020). © Oxford University Press.
DOI: 10.1093/oso/9780190097790.001.0001.

Christian,[3] not Catholic, right?" The inquiry, more rhetorical than interrogative, relayed a question that Melissa's mother had posed to her over the phone. At nineteen years of age, Melissa had to convince her mother that she had not prematurely left the mass honoring La Virgen de Guadalupe.[4] Having bumped into me, Melissa now had a credible witness to her participation. Melissa, in fact, had no plans to leave early; to the contrary, armed with a high-grade camera, she had taken it upon herself to photograph the evening's proceedings. For Melissa, as with multitudes of her Santa Ana, California, neighbors, this was a highly anticipated night. I had set out to study the mechanisms of religion that shaped the ethnic identities of Mexican immigrants in Santa Ana. The night was golden.

Though I momentarily wondered if my own religious difference would present a barrier to my participation, my doubts about being included quickly dissipated. A cluster of roughly thirty residents, including Melissa's family, beckoned me to join them in a procession back to "La Myrtle," their home neighborhood. My involvement with Kidworks, a local community organization, introduced me to Myrtle St. two decades prior. The energy that crisp winter evening at the local parish, Inmaculado Corazon, was palpable and readily spilled out into the surrounding city streets. La Virgen de Guadalupe, in statue form, would be carried through central Santa Ana streets and placed back at her rightful home, a carefully crafted public altar nestled amid two densely populated apartment buildings. As our group snaked through the throng of revelers, I caught glimpses of other Guadalupan images emerging from the sanctuary, en route to their respective barrios. Additional Guadalupan artifacts processed into the church sanctuary anticipating the start of the next in a series of masses.

Religious participation that evening defined a locally pervasive vision of ethnic identity. For many in Santa Ana, this night was the annual apex of a personally and collectively felt sense of peoplehood, where notions of ethnic belonging were publicly inscribed upon the cityscape through religious devotion (Vega 2015). The night's festivities marked December 12 as *El Día de La Virgen de Guadalupe*,

[3] Residents often used the term "Christian" or "*Cristiano*" to refer to Protestants.

[4] The concern demonstrated by Melissa's mother reflected the tendency to "monitor and chaperone" young women in immigrant households for the sake of upholding their honor, as discussed by Nabhan-Warren (2005:36).

a date commemorating the nearly five-centuries-old narrative of La Virgen de Guadalupe appearing to Juan Diego, a peasant of indigenous Mexican origins (Elizondo 2006) living in colonial Mexico c. 1521. Following generations of Marian veneration, recognition of this holiday by the Mexican state became official in 1895, signaled by a national coronation ceremony of La Virgen de Guadalupe's image (Matovina 2009; Traslosheros 2002). Among US Catholics, it is now the most popular of Marian feast days (Deck 2015),[5] denoting the influence of Mexicans and Latinxs on US religion.

The Guadalupan devotees that I stood alongside were participating in a classic display of ethnoreligiosity, a religious tradition where the boundaries of faith are tightly linked to the boundaries of ethnic identity (Dillon 2003; Mora 2006). The sonic resonance of that evening was particularly apt in conveying the strong implications that devotion to the Virgin de Guadalupe has for Mexican ethnic identity. The lyrics of a tune sung at that and other similar events made the linkages resoundingly clear:

Desde el cielo una hermosa mañana[6] (2x)	*From heaven on a beautiful morning*
La Guadalupana (2x)	*The Guadalupan*
La Guadalupana bajó al Tepeyac.	*The Guadalupan came down to Tepeyac*
La Guadalupana (2x)	*The Guadalupan*
La Guadalupana bajó al Tepeyac.	*The Guadalupan came down to Tepeyac*
Desde el cielo una hermosa mañana . . .	*From heaven on a beautiful morning*
Suplicante juntaba las manos (2x)	*Pleading She joined her hands*
Eran mexicanos (2x)	*They were Mexican*
Eran mexicanos su porte y su faz.	*They were Mexican, her stance and face*
Eran mexicanos (2x)	*They were Mexican*
Eran mexicanos su porte y su faz.	*They were Mexican, her stance and face*
Desde el cielo una hermosa mañana . . .	*From heaven on a beautiful morning*
Desde entonces para el mexicano (2x)	*From then on for all Mexicans*
Ser Guadalupano (2x)	*Being Guadalupan*
Ser Guadalupano es algo esencial.	*Being Guadalupan is essential*
Ser Guadalupano (2x)	*Being Guadalupan*
Ser Guadalupano es algo esencial.	*Being Guadalupan is essential.*

[5] There are a number of feast days that commemorate special events in the life of Mary the mother of Jesus. In addition, some Marian feast days commemorate what devotees consider supernatural apparitions of Mary such as the Día de la Virgen de Guadalupe.

[6] There are slight variations of these song lyrics in circulation. There are also a number of other verses that are traditionally included in the singing of this song. Some of the additional verses were also sung on the occasion described here, but I have only included those verses relevant to the adjoined commentary.

The words sung by devotees of *La Virgen*, known as *Guadalupanos*, reflect the mutual reinforcement between devotion to *La Virgen*, and ethnic identity: "For all Mexicans, being Guadalupan is essential." This assertion is predicated on the belief that La Virgen de Guadalupe represents the Mexican people in various ways: She is believed to represent the Mexican people in a spiritually mediative role, pleading for her devotees before Jesus Christ. At a more mundane level, her image is understood as embodying Mexican features (Matovina 2009). As the song lyrics remind devotees, "They were Mexican, her stance and her face."

En route to Myrtle St., the procession would cross into Townsend St., a neighborhood known by Myrtle St. residents as home to a street gang in direct conflict with the local gang on Myrtle St. Melissa pointed out to me that some of the residents on Myrtle St. had relatives that lived on Townsend St. The rows of apartment buildings, with pairs of buildings typically surrounding respective central courtyards were not much different from the housing configurations on Myrtle St.; neither were the residential demographics of notable difference. Yet, I was quite familiar with Townsend St. as I had lived there for two years, and knew all too well that the gang rivalry was a serious issue. The concrete sidewalks had absorbed blood from both sides of the rivalry. I also knew that the overwhelming majority of residents there were hardworking people committed to maintaining the well-being of their households. I asked Ricky, a teen, if he thought it would be dangerous for the procession to cross into Townsend St. "No, because we have La Virgen. They can't do anything to us," Ricky responded. Ricky believed that the image being carried was powerful, and would shield everyone from any attacks. He was right. The procession would arrive at its home destination to much fanfare, ready to situate *La Virgencita* in her rightful place, a place of honor that residents had built for her. A small house-like structure within an apartment courtyard awaited her arrival. Devotees would have a chance to exchange memories and contemplate Guadalupe's presence in their lives.

Elements hearkening to a shared ethnic past abounded that night in Santa Ana as participants commemorated La Virgen de Guadalupe. Children wore costumes representative of Juan Diego's indigenous culture and social class. Young boys donned white pants and shirts, sown of *manta*, a rugged cotton fabric worn loosely in rustic fashion. Young girls wore dresses with stitched flower patterns and hair braided into tight spirals resting on their heads. The attire drew a cultural tie between these urban residents and Mexican indigeneity. The incorporation of dance also highlighted pre-colonial cultural streams intermingled with salient colonial influences. Some events I visited in previous years incorporated Aztec dance troupes reminiscent of pre-conquest times. Other events incorporated *Matachines* and *Chinelos*, two dance traditions that embodied the fusion of European and indigenous culture, telling stories of colonial contact through movement. The aroma of traditional foods, tacos, tamales, and pozole, permeated the festive environment. Mexican flags ubiquitously reminded participants from whence these traditions hailed. For many of these participants, the most authentic way to be Mexican was to be Guadalupan.

Ethnoreligiosity Reformed

At La Gran Cosecha Sobrenatural (LGCS), "saints" were also centered in reference to ethnoreligious devotion. At this independent Pentecostal church, the term "saints" was applied quite differently from how it was used by the parishioners of Inmaculado Corazon. "*Somos santos, sanos, prósperos, bendecidos, saludables y fieles a la Visión que Dios nos ha dado*." These words echoed through the sanctuary as one hundred or so congregants recited them with gusto. The lead pastor of LGCS, Pastora Mirvella, would periodically lead her congregation through these and various other declarations at the start of the Sunday morning worship service. The phrase "somos santos" stood out to me: "We are holy," or understood differently, "we are saints." The leaders and congregants of LGCS frequently talked about this "saintliness" as something meant to characterize their life, their *testimonio*. The life of these congregants was intended to be a life of holiness characterized by ascetic practices and strong commitment to God and to church. As described by one of the leaders of the church, Obed, "We believe that God calls us to be luminaries, as his word says, with holiness of life and to be testimonies of our faith."

The "saintliness" talked about at LGCS was not an ethereal reality but rather one that was spatially expressed and embodied. The borrowed space that LGCS met at was "sanctified" space according to the people of LGCS. That is not to say that members viewed the space as intrinsically holy or sacred. Rather, sanctification of physical space required spiritual labor. It meant that people had come in for early morning prayer, day in and day out, throughout the week. It meant that on the days there were services, people prayed to "prepare the territory." It meant that on certain days, congregants and leaders fasted from any food. This commitment to sanctifying the space of the church was a value that Pastor Solis, the founding pastor of LGCS, instilled in his congregation. Solis invested in his circle of leaders to shape them as models for the rest of the congregation to follow after. Solis asked that "all of my leaders, as an obligation, come an hour early and dedicate that hour to prayer. What happens? God sanctifies the place where prayer happens."

Having sanctified their space, the community members of LGCS were engaging in forms of spiritual devotion that blended ethnic identity and religious belief and practice. September 16, Mexican Independence Day, was being observed by the church community. One of the church leaders, *hermana* Katy, took to the stage during the worship service to give announcements. *Hermana* Katy, speaking with restrained joy evidenced by her beaming smile and slowly enunciated words, explained to congregants that this particular day was set aside to celebrate Mexico's independence from Spain. "The church is commemorating this historical moment by having our team of dancers and musicians put on a special performance," she announced. She further added, "We have the opportunity to remember that this is part of our history, Amen?" A few "Amens" were uttered from among the congregation. There was a sense of newness in this moment. Pageantry was not uncommon at this church, but this particular occasion required some explaining. The one hundred or so members in attendance sat in the sanctuary, a rented space in a mainline church, in eager expectation.

Dressed in long flowing dresses adorned with green, white, and red frills, to match the colors of the Mexican flag, a team of girls twirled and danced to several songs that were being played by a live band.

The eight girls, ranging from four to eighteen years of age, clapped onto tambourines as they danced in unison. Two of them waved long undulating pastel colored flags. This was an intimate setting, where most congregants and attendees knew everyone else in the room. Still, performance was taken seriously, with members of the dance team meeting weekly to practice.

Like with the Guadalupan dancers, the dances that were performed by these young people were a mixture of elements from various cultures, albeit of a different blend. The wardrobe, in color and style, represented Mexican folkloric attire but the style of music being played approximated soft rock. The songs being sung were evangelical Christian praise tunes. The style of dance being performed was meant to portray a type of festive Jewish dance, a tribute to the tie between Christian tradition and the Hebrew scriptures, revered by Christians as the Old Testament. In this particular congregation, symbols and imagery tied to the Old Testament were commonly spotlighted during worship gatherings. Pictures of the Hebrew Tabernacle, the blowing of Jewish shofar horns in trumpet fashion, and the playing of Hebraic sounding music, drew a connection between these Latinx evangelical believers today, and the Hebrew people of ancient times. The victories and travails of ancient Israel, and their encounters with the divine, their experiences of the holy and their communal quest for holiness, were brought to the forefront.

Paralleling the Catholic celebration, this Pentecostal church took their celebration beyond the walls of their building. The leader of the dance team was invited to the stage by Pastor Mirvella, and she announced to the audience that the team of young ladies, accompanied by several young men dressed in military fatigues, would be going out onto the street to perform their dances in public. This was a strategic moment for the church. During this time of the year, the downtown area of Santa Ana was abuzz with thousands of revelers celebrating Mexican independence in a carnival environment. The dance team would be going out into public space to perform some of their dances before the crowds.

These young children and teens, under the guidance of their leader, gathered in a public square, connected a cellular phone to portable speakers, launched their first song, and began to dance in fashion similar to their church performance. A few dozen people circled around to watch them dance. Some onlookers took pictures of the performance. The reception was generally positive, some rewarding the young people with smiles and applause. The Mexican folkloric attire combined with Jewish dance was a novelty to people. As some people came by to inquire about the dance team, they were invited to the church. The team and the church took great pride in the efforts being made through these young people. Many of the church members, themselves converts from Catholicism, were committed to the work of "sharing the gospel" to those that were not of the same faith, most typically among their co-ethnics. When I spoke to the leader of the dance team, she clearly communicated the motive of their performance: This was an opportunity to evangelize.

Religion and Ethnicity among Immigrants

The comparison of Catholics and evangelicals in Santa Ana is timely in nature. The expressions of religious faith made public on the streets and neighborhoods of Santa Ana, California, signal changes that are afoot in the religious dynamics of US Latinx communities. On the one hand, the US Catholic church is becoming more Latinx, as exhibited by the dominant presence of Mexican devotional practices at Immaculate Heart of Mary. On the other hand, the Latinx population is becoming less Catholic. These changes have elicited astonishment from observers of religion in light of Latinxs' strong traditional association with Catholic affiliation. Mexicans, the largest national origin group among Latinxs, have arguably identified with the Catholic Church since the early colonial days of Nueva España, and more so by the time that Mexico gained its own nationhood (Bowen 1996; Deck 2015; Fortuny Loret de Mola 1994; Lopez 2009).[7]

[7] To assert Mexico's strong historical ties to the Catholic Church, one need not negate that the relationship between church and state has at times been tumultuous (Schmitt 1960). Mexico's constitution included anti-clerical provisions that were enforced at varying levels in the nation's history and were once the cause of a war known as the Cristeros Revolt. The rebellion's name refers to those that supported the Catholic Church, with Cristero denoting those "Of Christ" or "For Christ."

A barrage of publications, both popular (Dias 2013; Hagerty 2011; Salguero 2013) and academic (Jones, Cox, and Navarro-Rivera 2013; Kosmin and Keysar 2009; Lugo and Pond 2007; Mulder, Ramos, and Marti 2017) draw attention to the growth of Protestant, evangelical, and Pentecostal[8] adherence among Latinxs at the national level. The ethnic Mexican population too has shown shifts in religious adherence, despite being the Latin American origin group with the highest rate of Catholic adherence (Cooperman et al. 2014). As a point of comparison, of the nearly 120 million residents in Mexico (INEGI 2015), 81% identify as Catholic (Cooperman et al. 2014). On the other hand, among the population of 33.7 million Mexican origin individuals in the United States, only 61% identify as Catholic (Cooperman et al. 2014).

Still, ethnic Mexicans in the United States remain the most Catholic Latinx ethnic group (Cooperman et al. 2014). Reflecting these statistical realities, Santa Ana is home to lively Catholic parishes that are bursting at the seams, even as the cityscape is dotted by Latinx evangelical churches, with everything from storefront congregations housing a few dozen members to large dominant congregations that boast more than a thousand members. What happens to Mexican ethnic identity when it is decoupled from a historically salient marker such as adherence to Catholic religious tradition? How do individuals enact membership within a local ethnic enclave when they do not partake of the primary spaces of belonging for that group? A number of scholars have engaged these and closely related questions.

Various scholars have undertaken the task of directly comparing Latinx Catholics and Protestants in relation to how religion sustains ethnic identity formation. Most empirical studies that intentionally sample from both Latinx Catholics and Protestants, and employ some

[8] I have chosen to use the term evangelical, most generally in this volume, as that is the term that most Latinx Protestants in Santa Ana identify with. According to national level research from the Pew Research Center, "Evangelical Protestants outnumber mainline Protestants among Latinos by roughly three-to-one" (Cooperman et al. 2014:32). In Santa Ana, I observed that most Protestants, including Pentecostals, identified as evangelical. Conversely, though all evangelicals are technically Protestants, I observed that many Latinxs who self-identified as evangelicals in Santa Ana rarely used the term Protestant and some found the term strange or foreign. Latinx mainline Protestants were an exception as they were more comfortable identifying as "Protestants" than their evangelical counterparts.

level of control for demographic variables, conclude that Catholic affiliation contributes to a more salient ethnic identity than Protestant affiliation for Latinxs. Marquardt (2005), for example, posits that Latinx Catholic congregations present stronger transnational ties than do their Protestant counterparts. Several studies suggest Catholic parishes are stronger than Protestant parishes at sustaining particular national traditions (Alarcon et al. 2016; Freier 2008, 2009), especially the use of national symbols (Vila 2005; Vasquez 1999). In addition, some research suggests Catholic parishes are more committed to local ethnic enclaves, in contrast to more dispersed Protestant constituencies (Freier 2008, 2009; Hurtig 2000). Conversely, research suggests that Protestant affiliation is experienced by some as an assimilatory force, particularly as it encourages integration with whites (Alarcon et al. 2016; Lopez-Sanders 2012), promotes "hybridity" alongside of whites (Juffer 2008), and in some cases lacks an explicit discourse on faith and ethnicity (Hurtig 2000). Quantitative studies suggest that Latinx Protestantism is weaker at assisting members in maintaining Spanish language usage at home (Calvillo and Bailey 2015) and that being Protestant is linked with saying that Christian identity is central to being American (Taylor et al. 2014).

However, several comparative studies suggest Protestantism can also sustain robust Latinx identities. Flores (2014), in his study of Latinx-majority gang rehabilitation programs, notes that the Pentecostal sites he studied effectively adapted their message and programs to Chicano street culture in ways that differentiated them from Catholics. Menjívar (1999, 2003) notes the propensity of some Latinx evangelical churches to cater to specific national-origin groups by maximizing the organizational flexibility of evangelical churches. Williams and Mola (2007) note that both Catholic and evangelical churches in their study excelled at meeting the needs of their Latinx members. More work is needed to identify how the intersections of religion and ethnicity among Latinxs play out differently for Catholics and evangelicals and how the growth of evangelicalism has influenced collective processes of ethnic identity formation.

While studies of ethnic identity within immigrant faith communities have done well in highlighting the ongoing correlation between these two dimensions of identity, many questions remain as to *how* ethnicity and religion interact. The presupposition of ethnicity as a given in the field of immigration studies (Wimmer 2009) has had a major influence in understandings of how ethnicity and religion intersect. Primordialist notions of peoplehood are decried in the social sciences, yet such views still functionally creep in (Wimmer 2013). This orientation can be seen in the manner with which categories of ethnic belonging are presupposed to supersede other categories (Brubaker 2004). As Schiller et al. note (2008), ethnicity for immigrants is conceptualized as the primary pathway of societal incorporation. Ironically, even as assimilation theory essentially tracks the attenuation of ethnic difference, it takes the "ethnic group" as a perennial category. Ethnicity, especially when it is punctuated by racialized markers, is assumed to be the most salient mode of self-identification. In terms of research design, as Wimmer posits, ethnicity is assumed to be an "explanans" rather than an "explanandum" (Wimmer 2009:244). Certainly, there are cases where ethnicity serves as a master status, the most salient identity that a group of social actors adheres to. Yet, this is something that should be scrutinized rather than assumed. Better understandings of how religion sustains, and/or alters, ethnic identity can be gained from comparative approaches that allow for the contingent nature of ethnicity.

Religion and Ethnicity Forming Communities of Memory

As suggested in the two vignettes drawn from Catholic and evangelical congregations at the beginning of this chapter, Catholic and evangelical practices of devotion among Santaneros may divergently orient devotees in relation to understandings of ethnicity. Though the events in question were meant to commemorate distinct days, the types of elements related to the past that were emphasized and the manner in which such elements were embodied varied. For Catholics that night, the performance of peoplehood was closely linked to an origin story, the birth of a "*raza*," encapsulated by the patron saint of Mexico, la Virgen de Guadalupe, and embodied through participation in the rituals that commemorated her manifestation. For evangelicals that day, the performance of peoplehood was largely based on interpretations of the history of the Hebrew people presented in the Biblical texts and embodied in a communal quest for personal piety. For the Catholic parishioners, taking their celebration to the streets enacted a tradition of hospitality inviting neighbors to join in the festivities. For the evangelical congregants, taking the celebration to the streets was an opportunity to preach to neighbors, a traditional practice of evangelicals. Both Catholics and evangelicals were reproducing ethnicity, and specifically Mexican ethnicity; yet, both groups were doing it with distinct pasts in mind, and with distinct ends driving them. Such distinctions were not solely the territory of these two churches. As my interaction with members of religious communities across the city would reveal, a religious boundary consistently operated between and within Catholic and evangelical communities broadly.

In discussing the relationship between ethnic and religious identities generally, defining ethnicity provides a helpful starting point. Social scientific scholarship has traditionally conceptualized ethnicity as being undergirded by perceptions of a shared past. In an oft-cited definition, Schermerhorn denotes ethnicity as "real or putative common ancestry, memories of a shared historical past, and a cultural focus on one or more symbolic elements defined as the epitome of their peoplehood" (1978:12). Retrospective understandings of ethnicity can be found prior to Schermerhorn's exposition, with Weber notably including similar elements in his definition of ethnic groups: "Those human groups that entertain a subjective belief in their common descent because of similarities of physical type or of customs or both, or because of memories of colonization and migration; conversely, it does not matter whether or not an objective blood relationship exists" (1968:389). Schermerhorn and Weber's definitions notably both parse out two distinct manifestations of ethnicity related to the past: Ethnicity is characterized by a sense of having a "common ancestry," and is accompanied by memories of shared collective history.

To identify with an ethnicity is largely to assert membership within a community of memory. To be part of an ethnic group is to express who and where one comes from. It is to affirm that a particular collective history is also part of one's personal history and to acknowledge that a place of origin, a region of origin, occupies space in one's emotional topography. Ethnicity is to feel moved by the collective memories tied to a community, and to cultivate these memories for oneself, feeding them and allowing them to take on a life of their own. Ethnicity is to grieve the suffering of the ancestors and to be enraptured by the victories of the elders; it is to count oneself within an imagined community for whom an intellectual edifice has been constructed from the building blocks of perceived pasts together. The boundaries of ethnic membership are largely marked by these notions of a shared past and often enacted as cultural expressions understood as inherited traditions. In as much as these notions of a shared past are embraced collectively, the boundaries of ethnic membership are delineated in a much clearer and more salient fashion.

Religion functions as an apt platform for the maintenance of ethnicity, given its capacity for sacralizing ties to the past and doing so in a way that calls the faithful to wholly—both emotionally and physically—render their devotion. Religion can encapsulate aspects of ethnic history and seasonally remind devotees of their origins. Ritual and liturgy are intended to sustain ties to the past, and often ethnic meanings are projected onto these. By socializing the body into practices of devotion, religion allows the faithful to signal to each other that they are ultimately working in concert toward the same goals, as previously established by the saints of old. Religion can also bring about drastic divergence from the past, but in such instances a new interpretation of the past often replaces prior interpretations. Converts and revivalists may reinterpret their pasts, or understand themselves as being engrafted upon a different, and/or new community of memory. Both through change and continuity, religion maintains a close relationship to ethnicity in light of its connection to the past.

When devotees orient their sense of a common past and common origins around religious membership, there are often particular aspects of religion that emerge as the primary signifiers of ethnic belonging. Political, institutional, and historical processes, among other spheres, legitimate certain signifiers as the recognized markers of collective identity. In religion, not all aspects of a tradition function as ethnic identifiers. Yet, quite often particular aspects of a religion come to symbolize the epitome of peoplehood for a group.

The framework of *social boundaries* conceptualizes how particular symbols come to be perceived as the epitome of a group.[9] Social boundaries are modes of identification that lend meaning to categories of belonging, and reinforce notions of in-group commonality and out-group difference. Proponents of the social boundary approach challenge popular models of ethnicity that emphasize culture writ large as the hallmark of ethnic membership. Proponents of the boundary approach instead posit social boundaries that are delineated by markers that function as authenticating signals of group belonging. Culture as a whole can be extensive, and can be expressed in a variety of ways. Boundary markers provide a way to wade through the plethora of cultural practices, allowing group members to authenticate membership based on more particular symbols. Often, people negotiate the meaning of markers, or the very inclusion of certain markers, as a means of defining membership. That is, contests over symbols, have implications for the very boundaries of belonging themselves. As people engage boundary markers, boundaries themselves may change, and/or people that were once positioned within or without a particular boundary may traverse it (Barth 1969). Such processes may be summed up as the contestation of markers, members, and meaning.

Notions of a shared past, encapsulated in religious practice and tradition, serve as potent social boundary markers, delimiting the bounds of ethnic membership. There is a capacity for in-group legitimacy to emerge as individuals affirm a shared past and shared interpretations of the past. The performance and proclamation of shared understandings of the past can function as vivid authenticating symbols, relationally and cognitively, signaling the strength of a collectivity. That is not to say that all markers of ethnic belonging are immediately oriented toward the past. Political organizing, artistic tastes, linguistic expressions, even reliance on somatic markers, among other things, can function as ethnic boundary markers seeming to spring forth in a present

[9] I draw from the work of scholars such as Barth (1969), Brubaker (2002), Alba (2005), and Wimmer (2013) in arguing that the boundaries delineating ethnicity exist as processes rather than as static entities (Loveman 1999; Bailey 2008). These boundaries transition between thick or thin (Cornell and Hartmann 2006), bright or blurred states (Alba 2005). The location and meaning of boundaries can expand, contract, invert, and undergo redefinition (Wimmer 2013).

moment. Yet, often these items also retain notions of a shared past, of historical transmission, or of cultural continuity. One of the most entrenched modes of belonging that has implications for ethnic group formation, racial identification, is itself constructed on perceptions of biological inheritance and commonality, though the substance and meaning of what is inherited is often contested between in-group and out-group members. Moreover, modes of marking ethnicity are often predicated on perceived retrospective elements. The legitimacy of these identities is rooted in appeals to traditions transmitted across generations. How far back such transmissions must come from to be authentically ethnic expressions is not based on a hard and fast rule. The perception of transmission, the sense of continuity, is what holds weight. In as much as religion provides a channel for sustaining ties to the past, religious markers readily function as proxies for the reproduction of ethnic identity.

The Importance of Place in Ethnic Identity Formation

Alongside retrospective elements of ethnicity, spatial dimensions of ethnicity contribute potent material toward the formation of social boundaries. For communities that have been especially confined by physical and geographic boundaries of exclusion, social boundaries are often experienced in concrete, physical ways. Scholars have thus contended with notions of how marginalized communities establish a sense of legitimacy and a sense of belonging within their social contexts. Scholars have proposed alternative forms of citizenship, for example, that do not always coincide with legal-juridical designations, but which encompass participation and belonging within local life (Coutin 2013; Fishman 1968; Sassen 2002); these forms of citizenship have variously been termed substantive citizenship, cultural citizenship, and social citizenship.

The notions of "ethnic belonging" (Vega 2015) and of "urban belonging" (Castañeda 2018) further elucidate how Latinx immigrants within particular contexts of reception establish themselves. Vega describes ethnic belonging as accounting for "those daily acts that construct ethnic identity and weave an ethnic sense of belonging necessary for cultural citizenship efforts" (2015:179). Castañenda describes urban belonging as the "subjective feeling of belonging that responds to real social integration that includes economic, political, and institutional integration" (2018:6). Ethnic identity, according to these scholars, can be a form of immigrants enacting rootedness in their context, even as they sustain ethnic differences through connections to co-ethnics and to the homeland. These conceptual frameworks emphasize local contexts.

In line with the foundation laid by this body of work, I too center the role of the local, noting that ethnic identity formation is highly mediated by the social dynamics of localized spaces. The production of ethnic space is the means by which immigrant, Mexican *Santaneros* come to construct a space of their own. Ethnic space, as I conceive of it, serves as a complementary concept to notions of alternative citizenship and notions of local belonging with a greater emphasis on the production of space itself (Lefebvre 1991). Ethnic space is space imbued with ethnic meanings via the projection of ethnic history, the presence of ethnic symbols, and the performance of ethnic traditions. More than just speaking of an ethnic enclave, I propose ethnic space as a concept that encompasses the temporal nature of ethnic performance, as these can be transitory and temporary productions. Likewise, the focus on the production of space accounts for both in-group and out-group agents that contend over ethnic meanings associated with a particular geography. Often, understandings of ethnic space held by people in power contrast with those held by members of marginalized communities. Furthermore, within the community itself, understandings of ethnic space can vary significantly. In Santa Ana, as I argue, the negotiation of ethnic boundaries is closely linked to varying understandings of ethnic space.

Negotiating Religious Differences

As I interacted with Santaneros, I often observed how religious practices and symbols came into play in the negotiation of ethnic membership within ethnic spaces. Rodrigo Alonzo understood in a painstaking manner how religious difference could bring tension within a life arena closely linked to ethnic community—the family. I first struck up a conversation with Rodrigo, a forty-five-year-old immigrant from Mexico City, on a sunny afternoon as I walked by his home in a neighborhood where I had interviewed other informants. A stout man of bronze skin tone, Rodrigo easily maneuvered his lawnmower over his front yard. As Rodrigo worked, I complimented him for the meticulous care evident in his craft. He informed me that he ran a small landscaping business for a living. As we conversed, our attention turned to the statue of La Virgen de Guadalupe situated prominently on his front yard. I noticed that three small, outdoor spotlights installed on the lawn were pointed toward the stone image of the Holy Mother. I asked Rodrigo about his relationship to La Virgen de Guadalupe. "That's something I love to talk about," Rodrigo responded, his eyes gleaming underneath the shadow of his baseball cap. Rodrigo went on to explain what *La Virgencita* meant to him as a Mexican man.

"I don't really see how someone can be *really* Mexican and not be *Guadalupano*," Rodrigo asserted. "I am proud to be faithful to *La Virgencita*. This is something very special that we have as Mexicans," Rodrigo assured me. Drawing close to me, and taking on a more urgent tone, Rodrigo added "it's up to us to maintain it!" For Rodrigo, being devoted to La Virgen was a duty not only to the Catholic church at large, but also to his ethnic group. The devotion expressed by him and other *Guadalupanos*, according to Rodrigo, was making an impact beyond the diasporic Mexican nation. People of disparate ethnic backgrounds, including non-Mexicans, were being drawn to La Guadalupana, an observation that Rodrigo spoke of with great pride. He noted, "I know of [white] *Americanos* that also consider themselves *Guadalupanos*. Yes! They're noticing what she's about! They're seeing what she can do!" Rodrigo was more than happy to invest energies in reminding others of the connection between Mexican identity and La Virgen de Guadalupe. He gave the impression that he understood this as his contribution to his ethnic group, and to the world.

Just as he was passionate about discussing his devotion to La Virgen de Guadalupe, Rodrigo was also emotionally moved when narrating the emergence of conflict related to *La Virgencita* between him and his sister Hilda. Hilda had converted to evangelicalism and it was difficult for Rodrigo and his family to accept her decision. She had been raised in a devout Catholic home, but now, married and with a family of her own, had chosen to affiliate with an evangelical church, embracing a "born-again" evangelical identity. Rodrigo voiced his inner turmoil, stating, "I mean, she's my sister. I don't know why she would do that. How could you give up on something like that? That's the faith that we have always had." He continued, "We still talk and everything. She's still my sister." Rodrigo was hopeful about maintaining a relationship with his sister, even as he disagreed with her religious conversion.

Tensions became particularly heightened in the Alonzo household, per Rodrigo's account, one day when Hilda showed up at Rodrigo's home with images of La Virgen de Guadalupe and other saints. Hilda told Rodrigo, "I can't keep these anymore because I'm a Christian now." Rodrigo's voice quickened as he retold this portion of the story. For someone with a printed sign on his front door admonishing visitors that his home is a Catholic home and that they do not accept literature from other religions, this was quite a blow. As Hilda handed these religious items over to Rodrigo, "She began to cry and cry," Rodrigo described. "There were big tears coming out of her and she kept crying," he continued. He further recounted, "then she laid these items down on the kitchen table and I tried to make her see what she was doing. I told her that I could never give up those things because they are so dear to me and that I didn't know how she could do it." Rodrigo noted that Hilda choked back tears as she explained to him that she "could no longer worship those images." She said she saw things differently now and that "her faith was only in Jesus Christ." Rodrigo was frustrated at Hilda's response, in part because he too saw his faith as rooted in Jesus Christ, but he also felt a sense of urgency to "honor the images, that she was treating so badly." So Rodrigo obliged her request and received everything that she left. He secured these items in a place of honor in his home.

In the aftermath of this incident, Rodrigo recounted that he spent time reassuring his mother that Hilda would be fine since she still believed in the same God as them. Their mother was noticeably upset by this incident, according to Rodrigo, and needed assistance to come to grips with Hilda's change. As Rodrigo described, she was most concerned that Hilda had "forgotten that she has a mother." The phrase "remember that you have a mother," was used by Rodrigo multiple times during our conversation. The phrase had a double meaning in this case. The mother in question was both their biological mother and the Holy Mother. Rodrigo's response to his mother was that "[La Virgen de Guadalupe] will be there when Hilda needs her." In his accounts, Rodrigo presented himself as both a peacemaker and as someone who vigilantly watched the boundaries of ethnoreligious authenticity.

Rodrigo's assertion that devotion to Guadalupe was an ethnic identity marker had implications for his exchange with Hilda. Hilda's distancing from Catholic faith, and specifically from devotion to Guadalupe, meant that Hilda had distanced herself from her family and from her ethnic group, in Rodrigo's estimation. Yet, Hilda had maintained some semblance of respect in that she did not dispose of the images, but rather returned them to Rodrigo's home where they would be cared for. Moreover, this move was a type of boundary negotiation. She had some level of respect for the ethnoreligious icons, even if she herself made clear her religious turn. Even through moments of conflict, the maintenance of differences between Catholics and evangelicals generally did not lead to hateful acts, or to acts of violence, but rather to negotiations of stability. Evangelical and Catholic parishioners negotiated between a desire for differentiation, and a desire for sustained relational ties. Moreover, this interaction was to some extent an attempt to negotiate the symbols of belonging, and not necessarily an act of Hilda renouncing her ethnic identity.

Constructing Ethnic Identity

Cases such as those of Rodrigo and Hilda are important as they exemplify in-group or intra-group negotiations related to constructions of ethnic identity. As Jimenez et al. (2015) argue, the boundaries of ethnicity can also be shaped by intra-ethnic difference, not just by negotiations between the in-group and out-group. Even as in-group efforts of identity construction draw from "the raw materials of history, cultural practice, and pre-existing identities to fashion their own distinctive notions of who they are" (Cornell and Hartmann 2006), salient fissures around these dimensions may emerge among co-ethnics. In the context of salient intra-ethnic boundaries, fissures are enlivened by the practice of "ethnic authenticity" policing (Jimenez 2008:1558). Authenticity policing delimits legitimate membership within a group along various dimensions typically related to key markers of group belonging. In this process, members of a group test the authenticity of other individuals by examining their relationship to particular symbols, the key boundary markers noted previously. As Nagel posits, "questions of authenticity are not limited to the realm of ethnicity. We see authenticity of identity, behavior, or group membership challenged in other social realms as well: 'Who is really poor?' 'Who is really a Christian?' 'Who is really a man?' " (2000:101).

The weight of authenticity policing is aptly described by Carter, specifically within the context of African American students (2003:138):

> Racial and ethnic groups create cultural boundaries to demarcate both intergroup and intragroup differences. That is, groups create internal cultural boundaries to separate the "real" ("authentic") from the "not real" ("inauthentic") co-ethnic, and individuals construct self-conscious ways in which they use "natural" and specified characteristics to signify group affiliation (Tuan 1999). As groups socially construct what is authentic, their members use myriad in-group cultural codes and signals. Hence, authenticity work requires signifiers (Peterson 1997), and these signifiers often embody non-dominant cultural capital.

Carter's description has implications for other types of marginalized communities as well, suggesting that marginalized communities place value on cultural capital that is deemed as non-dominant vis-à-vis broader society. Symbols that are deemed as less prestigious or of peripheral status in the broader society may carry potency within the space of the marginalized community. In the working-class communities of Santa Ana, elements of culture that have traditionally been outside of the mainstream may especially come to signify group membership.

Though in the US context, Protestants have historically been a majority, in Mexican majority communities, Protestants are a minority.

Catholic religiosity, which in previous eras was marginalized in US society, may serve as a potent marker of ethnic membership. Even as Protestant affiliation might provide Mexican Protestants with certain privileges in broader society, in the local context the cultural capital they employ may situate them as outsiders within their own neighborhoods. Moreover, particularly among those whose life opportunities are stringently linked to life in the ethnic enclave due to legal status, or socioeconomic status, the privileges of a national majority religious affiliation may be more symbolic than material. As Fortuny Loret de Mola notes, "Members of Mexican immigrant [minority] religious communities in the United States constitute a population that historically has been marginalized at the social, political, and economic levels. They also have been constructed by Mexican Catholics as the inferior 'Other,' the non-Mexican, the ignorant" (2002:33).

Demarcating Boundaries

Catholic adherents in the barrio were strongly aware of their majority status among co-ethnics. Religious symbols and religious traditions abounded in the public spaces of central Santa Ana. Holiday seasons were times of community solidarity, with celebrations such as the day of *La Virgen of Guadalupe*, *las posadas*, Christmas, and Easter. Special days of praying the rosary also abounded in public spaces. In addition, family-based celebrations such as weddings and quinceañeras had strong religious overtones, which were all the more magnified given the public nature that these celebrations were carried out with. For those involved consistently in these "patterns of social interaction," in-group members were readily able to confirm who was part of the group and who was not (Barth 1969:15). This boundary marker of participation was made all the more salient as others opted out of participating (Jimenez 2010). That is, as participants became aware of non-participants, the boundaries of religious difference were highlighted.

In order to draw attention to evangelical acquaintances that no longer participated in the social spaces that Catholic respondents were embedded in, a number of Catholics employed colloquial labels in reference to evangelicals. The two terms that were most prevalent were "Hallelujahs/Aleluyas" and "Hermanos." When discussing with Beto Flores some of the different churches in his area, particularly those that worshiped in a spirited manner with a praise band and loud music, Beto commented, "We used to call those '*Aleluyas*.'" As Sanchez-Walsh (2003) recounts from her interaction with Pentecostals, this is a term that Catholics have been using to label evangelicals and Pentecostals for some time. The term emerged given the way that many Pentecostals shout out "Aleluya!" at climactic moments in their worship services. Labeling Pentecostals as "Aleluyas" was meant to identify them with the loud clamor and perceived emotional outbursts of Pentecostal worship (Navarro 1998; Ramirez 1999). This is not just a Latinx practice, as it can be found in white and black Pentecostal churches. It is, however, a particularly common label employed by an older generation of Latinx Catholics to identify Pentecostals. For Catholics, this served as a marker of difference that drew a contrast with more solemn Catholic liturgies.

The term "*hermanos*" displaced *aleluyas* as the most common way of referring to evangelicals in Santa Ana. The phrase, "he became an hermano" / "she became an hermana," was sometimes used to denote that someone had converted to evangelical Christianity. The label of hermano derived from the common use of the term among evangelicals themselves. Evangelicals call each other hermano/a, which means brother or sister. Often, evangelicals prefaced the name of co-religionists with the term hermano/a. Phrases like, "Let's call hermana Castillo to the stage," or "Dios le bendiga hermano Garcia," could be heard frequently on any given Sunday within the evangelical churches I visited in Santa Ana.

"The *hermanos* come to my neighborhood," Alicia Suarez, one of my informants, mentioned as she recounted a recent incident. Alicia, a woman in her late fifties who had migrated from the Mexican state of Guerrero, was highly involved at her parish, Inmaculado Corazon. Upon inquiring further, I discovered that the "*hermanos*" she was referring to were actually Jehovah's Witnesses. Several Catholic respondents made this designation during my interviews. In fact, four of the Catholic subjects I interviewed referred to Jehovah's Witnesses as *hermanos*, either confusing them for evangelical Christians, or conflating the groups. The boundary marker of non-Catholic religion coupled with the evangelistic efforts typical of Jehovah's Witnesses was enough to place them in a category with evangelicals in the religious taxonomy of some Catholics. This discovery suggested that for Catholics, there was a salient Catholic and non-Catholic boundary. Non-Catholics did not necessarily experience a sense of boundedness to each other, though, unless there was another unifying religious identity that drew them together. Jehovah's Witnesses and evangelicals, for example, did not view themselves as allies. Various types of evangelicals, however, were saliently aware of their non-Catholic status, and were likewise aware of a shared evangelical identity, albeit at times a loose one.

A notion of the imagined religious other would sometimes emerge in subtle ways. Jesús Ibarra, for example, talked about a church that had been started close to his home. I was aware of the church, and pointed out to him that the church used the term "Catholic" in their name. The church, which was no longer in operation at the time of our interview, was apparently a type of independent, non-Roman Catholic church. Jesús exclaimed,

> Oh! We have to be careful of these types of churches. You have to be careful of how churches try to reach our people. They may take advantage of what people don't know! Not just that one there. There are a lot of groups. There are a lot of these types of churches that pop up and people just don't know. People go looking because they don't know.

Jesús's brow furrowed and his usually warm, serene voice become firm and punctuated by elevated volume.

While Jesús here was not explicitly mentioning evangelicals, his widening of the scope in referring to "a lot of these churches that pop up" most likely included the many evangelical churches that had been started in his area. In terms of church start-ups in Jesús's community, all were evangelical congregations, except for the one we spoke about that was Catholic but not Roman Catholic. Still, Jesús was generally warm to most people in his neighborhood, and I observed him on several occasions interacting with others of different religious backgrounds in an exceedingly positive manner. For Santaneros like Jesús, religious others were mostly to be avoided when their religious beliefs were on display for the purpose of converting Catholic people, especially within ethnic space. Jesús was bothered by a general sense that non-Catholics would try to convert Catholics to a different faith. For Jesús, proselytizing efforts were an important marker of difference that signaled that non-Catholics and evangelicals were to be viewed with suspicion. Jesús expressed no ill will on religious others in general.

Challenging Boundaries of Belonging

Evangelicals were far from passive in the process of boundary work within the religious ecology. An account given by Mariela Sanchez, a member of an independent Pentecostal church, illustrates how inter-religious tensions in the community were often exacerbated by evangelical efforts to assert their particular faith practices. Mariela lived in an apartment complex where she had developed a number of friendships among neighbors. After having established some of these relationships, Mariela became an evangelical and clearly denounced her Catholic faith. Her relationships with her friends began to change because of how she expressed her faith among them. Mariela explained:

> A neighbor would invite me to parties. Recently she invited me to another neighbor's party. During the party, they did their rosary praying. I sat there with them and prayed to God while they were praying the rosary. Except, I never named La Virgen, because she doesn't exist. I only called out to God, "Yes, Lord, Hallelujah." I prayed in the way that I pray, and they turned around and stared at me! Because I was there with my hands lifted, because I am not ashamed of who I am and in whom I believe, that he is the king of kings and lord of lords. I said "Lord, bless this home, I know they know about you in their own way, they know you." When I opened my eyes, they were all looking at me. The host was looking at me. Before we ate, I also prayed, I prayed for the food, "Lord, bless this food and this home." They kept looking at me. I was not embarrassed. I noticed that many of the people present that day began to

> distance themselves from me. The person that invited me doesn't talk to me as much as she used to. But I said, "Lord, I didn't do anything."

Mariela had been an evangelical Christian for a relatively short amount of time, roughly two years, when this incident took place. Her actions generated tensions with her neighbors, and likely fortified negative views about what it meant to be an evangelical Christian among Mariela's Catholic neighbors. Mariela herself was intentionally engaging in a type of boundary work, distancing herself from Catholic forms of prayer by asserting an evangelical form of prayer. For Mariela, this likely meant that she would have less access to the spaces that her friends experienced as spaces of comfort.

Reactions to evangelicals' face-to-face evangelistic efforts provided clear forms of boundary negotiation. Miguel Luna, for example, recalled a situation where he was speaking to evangelical Christians who were walking through his neighborhood inviting people to their church. Miguel described the situation in the following manner:

> There go the hermanos! They're here in our neighborhood talking to people; inviting them to their church. Talking to them about the Bible.[10] They started to ask me if I was saved. I turned it on them and asked them "Are you saved?"[11] They told me, "Yes, we're already saved, and we're sure of it." They were trying to say that I'm not sure! So if they're so sure, since they say they are, I told them, "Well let me go bring a gun and I'll shoot you with it. After all, you're sure that you're saved!" After that they left and they stopped bothering me.

As Miguel told me this story, he raised his hands in agitation and motioned as if he were pointing a gun at someone in his front yard. Our conversation was made all the more vivid because it was taking place in his front yard, precisely where Miguel indicated that this confrontation took place. Miguel was actively involved in community-based religious activities in his neighborhood; his neighborhood was

[10] Miguel was in no way against the Bible, and actually claimed to enjoy reading it.

[11] Ridgely (2019:13) discusses how such a question of being saved "doesn't translate well into a Catholic context."

a safe space of sorts. I witnessed Miguel volunteering for community-based celebrations, helping to provide food for celebrations, organizing other volunteers, and helping to clean up after several celebrations.

Miguel embodied a sense of ownership about "*mi comunidad*" (my community), as he referred to his neighborhood. It bothered Miguel to see non-Catholics attempting to gain converts in his community, in his ethnic space. He too conflated Jehovah's Witnesses with evangelical Christians at other points in our conversation, but the particular incident described in his story involved evangelicals. Deploying a designation of religious others, Miguel remarked, "All these different kinds of religions show up here!" As he spoke those words, he nodded his head angrily, the greying hair atop his partially balding head swaying forward. My interactions with Miguel did not suggest that he held personal vendettas against religious others but rather that he viewed religious proselytizing as a threat to community solidarity.

Spatialized Identities

The contestation of ethnic space proved to be an ongoing form of boundary negotiation among Santaneros. For Catholics, ethnic space carried spiritual meaning in that it was imbued with communal energy and religious symbols tied to an ethnic past. Central Santa Ana functioned as ethnic space especially because it was a space of ethnoreligious devotion. The streets and neighborhoods were marked by the symbols of Catholic devotion. In large part, Catholics had worked to form communities of memory embedded within the context of reception. The markers of participation in Catholic communities signaled ethnic belonging. The saints inhabited the streets, blocks, and homes of Santa Ana.

For evangelicals, local ethnic space mattered too. To lay claim to the space meant that evangelicals had freedom to express their faith orientation. Conducting outreach in the neighborhood was itself an expression of ownership of the space, or at least an expression of desired ownership. Through evangelicals' style of participation, or lack thereof, within the Catholic majority community, evangelicals marked themselves as different. The direct attempts at proselytization reinforced this. In these face-to-face exchanges, boundaries were being negotiated.

Ethnic identity, in this case, was not just an ethereal reality but was also an embodied and concretized experience. Ethnic membership as articulated by a substantial number of Catholic Santaneros was predicated on questions of whether religious commitments to Catholicism would remain, or whether non-Catholics would continue to carve out their own niche in the community. As will be demonstrated in the next chapter, Latinx populations in Santa Ana, especially ethnic Mexicans, have long had to negotiate their place within Santa Ana. Religion has functioned as a resource in these negotiations, but it has also been a marker of intraethnic difference. The present experiences of Mexican Santaneros are in many ways a reflection of the past struggles that shaped the ethnic identities of previous generations.

2
A Century of Saints

Religious identities and ethnic identities have long been negotiated in relation to each other among Latinx and Mexican-identified individuals in Santa Ana and its surrounding region. Santa Ana's county home, as a famed hub of religious activity, has produced salient religious identities that are intricately intertwined with ethnic identities. For the last fifty years, Orange County has arguably been home to one of the most influential religious ecologies[1] in the nation. Both Catholic and evangelical sectors witnessed significant expansion in the region. Having broken away from the Archdiocese of Los Angeles in 1976, the Catholic Diocese of Orange, encompassing Orange County, has witnessed tremendous growth in the last several decades. One local journalist, Caitlin Yoshiki Kandil (2017), points to the Diocese of Orange as "the Catholic Church's future." The Diocese is now home to 1.3 million Catholics (Krekelberg 2016). A substantial portion of this growth is due to migration from Latin America and from Asia. Along with Latinxs, the Vietnamese community has especially made a mark on the diocese (Ninh 2014). This expansion is felt not only in the pews, but also in leadership. Among the diocese's 263 priests, twenty-four are Latinx and fifty are of Asian heritage (Kandil 2017). In 2017, half of all priests ordained in Orange County were Vietnamese.

Kandil (2017) cites Father John Moneypenny, director of vocation for the diocese, in observing that "Every church in Orange County would be considered a mega-church in other dioceses on the East

[1] I herein draw from Ammerman's (1997) work on religious ecologies which posits religious organizational fields as ecological systems wherein the vitality of individual organisms (read organizations) is subject to contextual factors, including the state of other organisms. Such a perspective acknowledges that institutional competition may exist, and that institutional innovation may result from this competition. In addition, institutions function interdependently.

The Saints of Santa Ana. Jonathan E. Calvillo, Oxford University Press (2020). © Oxford University Press.
DOI: 10.1093/oso/9780190097790.001.0001.

Coast or center part of the country." Moneypenny further explains that many parishes see upwards of ten thousand attendees on a typical Sunday. That is certainly the case in various Santa Ana parishes. Tarra McNally, assistant director of evaluation at the University of Southern California's Center for Religion and Civic Culture, explores the repercussions of these trends geographically: "If you're the Archdiocese of Los Angeles, you're the largest in the United States, and then the Diocese of Orange is the fastest growing, you're definitely going to have the Vatican listening to you more than the Archdiocese of Philadelphia" (Kandil 2017). In other words, the center of Catholicism in the United States is shifting to Southern California, and Orange County is a major part of that. The purchase of the Crystal Cathedral, and its subsequent dedication as the Christ Cathedral, the centerpiece of the Catholic Archdiocese of Orange, drew much attention, and was in part attributed to shifting ethnic and religious demographics (Do 2016; Kopetman 2012; Lovett 2018).[2]

Evangelicals also continue to make a major impact on Orange County. Orange County has produced some of the most recognizable names in evangelicalism, and some of the most visible and visited Christian churches in the region, if not the nation (Arellano 2008; Dochuk 2010). The barrios of Santa Ana find themselves within shouting distance of churches such as Calvary Chapel, Calvary Church, and Rock Harbor church, among others. The Trinity Broadcasting Network (TBN), known for its charismatic, Pentecostal, and word-of-faith-leaning Christian programming is a stone's throw away from Santa Ana. A trip on the freeway provides access to regional megachurches with international reach. Saddleback, Mariners, and Eastside, among others, are congregations that have experienced notable growth in the last two decades and whose congregations number in the thousands. Orange County also gave birth to several popular

[2] The Crystal Cathedral congregation filed for bankruptcy prior to selling its building to the local Catholic Archdiocese. With an aging white congregation, and a surrounding population that was increasingly Asian American and Latinx, the Crystal Cathedral struggled to sustain its operations. A growing Latinx congregation associated with the Crystal Cathedral cut ties to the original congregation and began meeting elsewhere. Under the Catholic Archdiocese, the parish is now more indicative of its Asian American and Latinx neighborhood demographics.

church movements. The Vineyard movement, for example, has been a major catalyst of charismatic Christianity in the United States. Likewise, Calvary Chapel is a movement known for a casual, contemporary style of worship, and a strict adherence to a verse-by-verse style of Bible teaching. Much of Orange County religion, especially its evangelical streams, has been associated with conservative politics (Blum 2012; McGirr 2015), but it is yet to be seen how the county's changing political landscape will be reflected in the local religious ecology. From within this larger local landscape, Santa Ana has emerged as a vibrant religious ecology in its own right.

A Latinx Religious Ecology

With scholarship and media attention primarily fixated on famed institutions and on visible mega-movements in Orange County, the vibrant Latinx-dominant religious ecology of Santa Ana has gained scant scholarly attention. Nonetheless, Santa Ana's Latinx religious ecology today is actually home to a high concentration of influential institutions, international movements, and grassroots networks; it is a religious ecology inhabited by high-powered leaders, and humble neighborhood-based entrepreneurs. With a unique Latinx-dominant religious ecology over a century in the making, the city is a quiet catalytic node tied into Latinx religious networks regionally and internationally.

The growth of the city's Latinx population, the salient boundaries of exclusion and inequality experienced by many of the city's immigrant, working-class residents, and the energetic religious culture of the broader region, have contributed to a vibrant Latinx religious ecology diffused throughout the entirety of the city limits, but especially concentrated in central Santa Ana. There are dozens of Latinx-majority churches in Santa Ana. While the religious census only lists a total of 125 congregations of any kind in Santa Ana (U.S. Religion Census 2010), not just Latinx, this number is likely underestimated because of uncounted Latinx congregations. It is difficult to give a precise count of the Latinx-dominant congregations in the city, but based on a review of church listings along with firsthand observation of the built environment, I estimate about eighty churches. Zoning laws in Santa Ana make it particularly difficult to convert facilities into church spaces. Likewise, Santa Ana has one of the lowest rates of green space per resident, among all big cities in the United States (Scauzillo 2014), meaning that there is little open space to be developed in the city. This same reality translates to Santa Ana being an area where few new church facilities, in the traditional sense, are being built. Churches are limited in where they can meet, and yet numerous Latinx churches have been founded in the spaces available to them.

A Sanctuary of Saints

Even as Santa Ana is embedded within Orange County's religious ecology, Mexican-identified individuals of previous generations participated in an ethnoreligious space that was often socially distinct from the white religious ecology. An examination of Santa Ana's history from a century past reveals that Mexican-identified individuals, and even predecessor populations of current-day ethnic Mexicans, negotiated categorizations tinged by class, race, and nativity in the ethnoreligious ecology of Santa Ana; religion often functioned as a marker of ethnic difference and as a means of negotiating ethnic difference, both inter-ethnically, and intra-ethnically. Catholicism, for example affirmed the social legitimacy of Mexican communities by offering critical resources to the community, even as it came to serve as a marker of difference within a broader Protestant-dominant society. Catholicism helped to sustain transnational ties, provided important space for local organizing, and offered opportunities for local Latinx leaders. On the other hand, Protestant leaders that facilitated the emergence of Protestantism among Latinxs often framed Mexican Catholicism as deficient. This proved to be a persistent theme in Protestant discourse on Catholics. The rise of Latinx Protestantism added a dimension of religious choice—and competition—within the Latinx community. The presence of Latinx Protestant leaders contributed to the growth of Protestantism among Santa Ana's Mexican communities. As patterns of Mexican and Latinx exclusion persisted in Orange County society, and the Latinx population expanded in

Santa Ana, a lively Latinx-centric religious ecology emerged in Santa Ana—one with racialized implications.

Establishing Geographic Boundaries

The history of Santa Ana's religious ecology reaches back to contributions made by the Acjachemen people, a native population still present in the region.[3] Indeed, several informants hinted at ties they had to the native people of the land. One local resident's recollection of having Acjachemen neighbors in Santa Ana, and a local Latinx Pentecostal pastor's indication that several of his congregants were Acjachemen, suggested the present-day importance of this indigenous population. Likewise, a local newspaper highlighted the Acjachemen presence in the city, retelling the story of Adelia Sandoval, the current spiritual leader of the Juaneño Band of Mission Indians, another name for the Acjachemen people (Brazil 2019). Sandoval, it turns out, grew up in Santa Ana. A fortuitous perusal of church records helped me to more clearly tie in the relationship between Santa Ana's religious ecology and the original people of modern-day Orange County.

As historians point out, a tragic and brutal incident marks a critical shakeup in the history of the Acjachemen. In the year 1812, as people worshipped in the sanctuary, the stone church at Mission San Juan Capistrano succumbed to a violent earthquake, leaving forty deceased victims in its wake. The victims were overwhelmingly women and all were members of the Acjachemen people (Vélez 2017). Some of the victims were likely alive when the Acjachemen first encountered Father Junipero Serra, founder of the Mission San Juan Capistrano. Founded in 1776, the mission was the first major European settlement in what would eventually become Orange County, California. The Stone Church was left in ruin, bearing testament to the native lives that were lost on that fateful Sunday. The Acjachemen parishioners would go on to worship within other sanctuaries at the mission, first within

[3] Records indicate that the Tongva people also lived in the region, with one of their villages, Pasbenga, located within what would eventually become Santa Ana (Koerper and Magalousis 1988).

an older chapel, and a year later within a newly built granary (Vélez 2017). Sanctuaries would not shield them from the change.

Tremors were not unknown in the region that would become Orange County. Indeed, when Father Juan Crespi set out to explore the region in 1769, the Franciscan friar wrote in his journal that he and his expedition team experienced four temblors while camping alongside a local river. Fr. Crespi named the river, "El Dulcísimo Nombre de Jesús de Los Temblores" (The sweetest name of Jesus of the earthquakes; Guinn 1911:83). Still, in the region, a quake of the magnitude that toppled the stone church had not been experienced—or at least remembered (Vélez 2017). Colonization of the region thereafter occurred at a rapid rate. After Mexico gained its independence from Spain in 1821, and gained control of Alta California by extension, it discontinued its mission system. By 1834 the missions would be secularized. Mission San Juan Capistrano would be sold by California's last Mexican governor, Pío Pico, in 1845. Life would never be the same for the Acjachemen people. Many now bore Spanish names and spoke Spanish. Across generations, many Acjachemen retained their Catholic faith. The United States soon took control of the territory.

Some Acjachemen people would head in the direction of the very river memorialized by Fr. Crespi. As Crespi noted in his journal, "To the soldiers, this river is known by the name of Santa Ana" (Guinn 1911:84). These Acjachemen people would find sanctuary near the riverbanks camped by Crespi, in the budding city of Santa Ana. Just as they had helped to build the mission, some Hispanicized native people contributed to Santa Ana's growth, and to the faith communities therein. Some would come to be identified as Mexican, even if not by choice.

Temporarily Mexican

The records of one Santa Ana resident whose family had roots in the old mission, provides a window into how Mexican identity in Santa Ana was a contested category tied to spatial politics and religion. The name Della Molina-Cruz came to my attention while perusing a commemorative book celebrating the one-hundred-year anniversary of

St. Joseph Catholic Church in Santa Ana. In this historical account sponsored by the church, Della bears the first Spanish surname among the parishioners commemorated. Born Della Molina in 1892,[4] Della resided for most of her life in Santa Ana. She was baptized and confirmed at St. Joseph's, where she would grow up to become a lifelong pillar of the parish. Renowned in St. Joseph's centennial book for her service as a "sponsor" to many parish children, presumably at baptism and/or confirmation, Della's constant participation in this role bore witness to her exemplary faith commitment. According to the centennial book, "She belonged to the Altar and Rosary Society and she and her daughters used to go to the Mother of Perpetual Help devotions every Wednesday night" (Green 1987:15). Into her elderly years, Della remained a faithful member of her parish, with a parish priest visiting her weekly. Affectionately known by parishioners as "Mama Della," she passed away in 1985.

State records reveal several important details regarding how Della and her family were positioned along ethno-racial lines. In the 1910 census (U.S. Census Bureau 1910a), Della and her family are listed as Mexican. Her family, the Molinas, were initially designated as "W," meaning "white," but that particular label is literally overwritten with the letters "ot," which stand for "other." On the margin of the census sheet, the word "Mexican" is stamped alongside the individual names of Della and all of her household members. In the 1920 census (U.S. Census Bureau 1920), now married to James V. Cruz, Della is listed as white. In a decade, Della had gone from "other/Mexican," to "white." In the 1930 census, the Molina-Cruz household, living in Santa Ana, is now listed as "Indian" (U.S. Census Bureau 1930), and the family's last name is listed as "Cruze." That same spelling follows the Molina-Cruz household into the 1940 census where they are again designated as "white." Two additional documents from that same decade, amended birth certificates, suggest that Della and Jim chose the family name "Cruze," an anglicized version of "Cruz," and chose to identify as "American Indian" (State of California 1941, 1949).

[4] County records list disparate birth years for Della Molina, including 1891 and 1893. Church records indicate 1892.

Della likely spent her younger years being classified by society as Mexican. She had Spanish surnames, her mother spoke Spanish, and a segment of her family migrated from Mexico (U.S. Census Bureau 1910a). Yet, as she grew older, larger political processes factored into her ethno-racial designations. 1930 marked the first census year that "Mexican" was included as an official racial category (Ortiz and Telles 2012). 1930 was also the first census year in which all Native Americans were granted birthright citizenship (Ngai 1999). That year, the Molina-Cruz household was identified as Indian. On the other hand, in 1940, the Census Bureau instructed enumerators to identify Mexicans as white, heeding protests from the Mexican government and LULAC to remove "Mexican" as a racial category (Ortiz and Telles 2012). The Molina-Cruz household was essentially classified with the Mexican population by being designated as white.

Della's ethno-racial designations were typically at the mercy of census enumerators, and census policy at the time, but given a choice, she identified as Native American, and went by the name Cruze. Parish records suggest that Della herself continued to identify as Native American. The Parish centennial book indicates that Della's mother "was a Mission Indian (Shoshone), born and baptized in San Juan Capistrano" (Green 1987). Della's maternal family would have been part of the Acjachemen tribe, dubbed Juaneños because of their geographic proximity to the San Juan Capistrano Mission, and often referred to in older documents as Shoshone, because of linguistic ties to the Shoshone tribe.[5]

To be identified as Indian in Della's early years of life was looked upon unfavorably by many within Orange County society. A gruesome milestone in the city's ethno-racial history illustrates this point, marking and marring Della's year of birth: The lynching of Francisco Torres, a Mexican man, was a highly publicized incident that took place in Santa Ana (Haas 1995). Torres was accused of murdering his supervisor after having a mandatory poll tax extracted from his paycheck.

[5] Shoshone is an incorrect designation for the Acjachemen people. A more accurate description of the relationships between the Acjachemen and the Shoshone would be to say that the Acjachemen and the Shoshone languages share the same linguistic root of Uto-Aztecan.

Evidence suggests that Torres, due to a language barrier between him and his supervisor, did not understand why his paycheck had been reduced (Lee 1969). In court, Torres claimed that the altercation with his supervisor was an act of self-defense (Lee 1969). The confrontation took place on the property of famed performer Madame Modjeska, who employed both men. Torres was described in one newspaper as "a low type of the Mexican race, evidently more Indian than white" (Haas 1995). Another reporter, from the *L.A. Times*, described Torres as "in no way superior to an Indian" (Lee 1969). For these white reporters, being Indian was conceptualized as a status of inferiority associated with primitivism and barbarous character. Simply wielding this designation was intended to elicit in readers a sense of threat and danger toward the subject described. Della was born into this world.

On the other hand, for individuals such as Della, being labeled as "Mexican" and having social proximity to Mexicans would have precipitated assimilation into the growing Mexican population and social distance from whites. Haas (1995) notes that former residents of San Juan Capistrano, such as Della's parents, left behind the pueblo lifestyle of the old mission town and relocated to the burgeoning county hub. At the turn of the nineteenth century, with Mexican barrios in nascent form, Mexican-identified residents increasingly experienced discrimination from whites (Haas 1995). As Mexican migrants arrived in the first decades of the twentieth century and solidified Mexican barrios, some Native Americans assimilated into the Mexican barrios. According to Santa Ana historian Mary Garcia, some Indians came to Santa Ana to find work, settled in Santa Ana's older barrios, and "by osmosis they became Mexican." Garcia herself recalls a childhood memory wherein after visiting the home of a neighborhood playmate, she came to find that her friend was Acjachemen. In her history of "Logan Barrio," one of the oldest Mexican barrios in Santa Ana, Garcia makes a remarkable observation about the racialized, spatial politics of the region:

> Mexicans from the Southwest, members from the Acjachemen Indian Tribe (Juaneños), Californianos, and newly arrived Mexicans from across the border moved into the area. Society labeled them "Mexicans from Logan." (Garcia 2007:14)

As Della moved toward adulthood, she would have witnessed the emergence of the citrus culture in the region, between 1900 and 1930, when Santa Ana's Mexican population went from twelve families to nearly four thousand residents (Gonzalez 1994:63). With the availability of jobs providing a migratory pull factor, and the Mexican revolution of 1910 providing a push factor, the ethnic Mexican population in the region expanded (Lopez 2009). As Gonzalez indicates, Mexicans lived in segregated *colonias*, where housing was substandard (Gonzalez 1994). Because a substantial number of workers were agricultural laborers, the type of efforts exerted were quite taxing on the body. Case notes in his early interactions within Mexican *colonias* that residents were often ailed by chronic medical conditions (Case 1902). From 1900 through 1930, the *colonias* turned barrios were the norm for Mexican laborers. These would eventually develop into urban neighborhoods, with some, such as Delhi, Logan Barrio, and Artesia (Walker 1928), still ethnic hubs today. As Walker notes, when rents became more reasonable, Mexicans sometimes moved closer to whites, spurring white "displacement." During this period, Mexicans composed roughly 15% of Santa Ana's population (Gonzalez 1994).

One identifier that Della would have shared with most Mexicans in Santa Ana was her Catholic identity, a dimension functioning as a salient point of distinction in Orange County society. As stated previously, Della remained faithful to her Catholic faith through her church participation. In a time of major transition, the church afforded members of the Molina-Cruz household a chance to be a part of a social institution at the center of the city, both figuratively and literally. As an active parishioner, "Mama Della" would have crossed ethnic, racial, and class lines within church spaces. Yet, for much of her early life, Catholic affiliation would have situated Della as a religious other within Orange County society. Often, European immigrants were the target audience for formative parishes in California at the turn of the previous century, as noted by Lopez (2009). Certainly, European immigrants were a major constituency to the first Catholic parishes in Orange County (Lawrence 2012; Montrose 1961). Nonetheless, Della's case indicates that some non-white individuals in Santa Ana could be integrated into local parishes.

Even as Catholicism united Della to Mexican co-residents, her choice to remain at St. Joseph's indicated that she distinguished herself from the larger Mexican community. The majority of Mexicans from nearby Logan Barrio helped to found Our Lady of Guadalupe parish in 1922, which would serve a predominantly Mexican audience (Garcia 2007). Logan Barrio was close to St. Joseph's, but Mexican residents desired a parish of their own, and thus founded Our Lady of Guadalupe on Third Street and Grand Ave. Della and her family would remain at St. Joseph's, while the majority of Mexican households in the area turned to Our Lady of Guadalupe parish. Church affiliation sustained ethno-racial differentiation for Della.

To identify Della as "Mexican" does not do justice to her family history, even if it was an element of her ascribed ethno-racial experience. The resilience of Della's identities rooted in precolonial Acjachemen histories overshadowed her ascribed label of Mexican. Certainly, political processes solidified or stifled the particular options at her disposal, but Della and her husband James appeared to have exercised some degree of agency. Della's story provides hints as to how Mexican identity in the United States was ascribed and contested not only at higher levels of government but also by individuals at the personal and household level. As ethno-racial labels carried social and political weight, individuals contested labels to avoid vulnerability and to maximize opportunities. Such processes continue today, even at the intra-ethnic level, and religion provides material with which individuals within ethnic spaces negotiate ethno-racial identities. While Della's case may seem distant from the cases of Mexican immigrants explored in this volume, her story illustrates how processes of ethno-racial negotiation have long been present in the Mexican-identified spaces of Santa Ana. And as explored subsequently, religion emerges as an important resource for negotiating identity.

Religion as a Social Boundary

Religious difference was at times a point of tension in Santa Ana that carried ethno-racial implications. Dubbed the "gospel swamp" as early as 1873, an area encompassing the marshlands in southern Santa

Ana and beyond was known for tent revivals, a high "proportion of preachers," and significant "piety and church-going" (Epting 2014). In a majority-Protestant region, Catholic affiliation was looked at as religiously distant. Certainly, this was amplified by a national climate that long saw Catholics as an outgroup. National sentiments were largely fueled by an ascriptive coupling of immigrant and Catholic identities that triggered nativist sentiments. One nativist group that became active nationally, the American Protective Association, or APA, worked to gain traction in Santa Ana. The group stoked national fears in 1893 when it published in a Detroit newspaper what it claimed was a secret papal encyclical encouraging Catholics to rise up in arms in the United States:

> We likewise declare that all subjects of every rank and condition in the United States, and every individual who has taken an oath of loyalty to the United States in any way whatever, may be absolved from said oath, as from all other duty, fidelity, or obedience on or about the fifth of September, 1893, when the Catholic Congress shall convene in Chicago, Illinois, as shall exonerate them from all engagements, and on or about the feast of Ignatius Loyola, in the year of Our Lord 1893, it will be the duty of the faithful to exterminate all heretics found within the jurisdiction of the United States of America. (Wiltz 1958)

The threat never materialized, but the group continued to instigate fear among white Protestants of a Catholic onslaught.

The history of St. Joseph, Della's parish, illustrates the ways in which Catholic identity was questioned by some segments of Orange County society. St. Joseph, originally called Our Lady of the Rosary, was built and dedicated in 1887. In its fledgling years, it was a mission church attended to by St. Boniface, the oldest parish in the county, serving the predominantly German colony in Anaheim (Montrose 1961). In 1896, four years after Della's birth, St. Joseph Church burnt down (Armor 1921). Some parishioners suspected that the APA had set the fire. Though the cause of the fire was never ascertained, the APA did make their presence known in another form related to this incident. Renowned actress Helena Modjeska would be inaugurating the Santa Ana Opera House and committed to offering the proceeds from her performance to St. Joseph Church. Madame Modjeska, as she was known, was an immigrant from Poland and a devout Catholic who brought her fame to the United States and settled in Orange County. The APA circulated word that they would organize a boycott of Modjeska's performance as the money would be donated to the Catholic church. As church members raised money for the church, they were accused by a local paper of "organizing an army of Mexican Catholics" (Bricken 2011). For these anti-Catholic voices, one way to generate fear toward Catholics among white Protestants was to associate the Catholic church with Mexicans.

Churches like St. Joseph already served a diverse array of parishioners, and it was precisely this diversity,[6] one that encompassed immigrants from various origins, that incensed nativists. The APA, prior to their threatening to boycott Madame Modjeska, had successfully mounted other campaigns in the area. The APA, for example, was committed to obstructing Catholics from reaching public office in the county. Joseph Yoch, a key member of St. Joseph (Bricken 2011), became a target of the APA's efforts when he campaigned for re-election as County Supervisor in 1894 (Guinn 1902). According to local church historian Bricken (2011:18), "Yoch's Catholic faith became a major subject in the election with his opponent claiming that only true Protestants were worthy of civic office since Catholics held a loyalty to a foreign government, the papacy." Yoch ultimately lost the election, though he continued to be active in the county as a banker and business owner. Other actions propelled by the APA included the "purging" of the Santa Ana library from books that were deemed Catholic or Jewish. The librarian was fired because of her "Catholic leanings" (Bricken 2011:18). Not all non-Catholics hoped for the demise of St. Joseph. As Montrose, a local church historian notes, "Hard as was the blow, the congregation encouraged by Bishop Montgomery and assisted by the help from non-Catholics, set to work to build the present neat church. The church was dedicated in 1896 by Bishop Montgomery under the invocation of St. Joseph." Some non-Catholics,

[6] St. Joseph, in its early years, seemed to function as a precursor to what Hoover (2014) calls a "shared parish."

then, acted in direct opposition to the APA by helping to rebuild the church and by attending the fundraiser put on by Madame Modjeska.

As the emergence of citrus culture made salient the social boundaries between Mexican laborers and whites, religion served as an additional marker of difference. McWilliams notes that throughout the citrus belt, "the workers are Spanish-speaking, Catholic and dark-skinned, the owners are white, Protestant, and English-speaking. . . . the whole system of employment, in fact, is perfectly designed to insulate workers from employers in every walk of life, from the cradle to the grave, from the church to the saloon" (1946:219).[7] Though McWilliams ignores the presence of white Catholics, and Mexican Protestants, his observation conveys the general perception of religion emboldening ethno-racial boundaries.

In some cases, the establishment of religious institutions serving the Mexican population brought about a form of ethnic distinction that was favored by members of the Mexican community. According to Lint Sagarena (2009) and Lopez (2009), the Catholic church did not always excel at serving ethnic Mexicans, choosing instead to prioritize Europeans migrating into the area. An element of this experience was felt by Mexicans in Santa Ana.[8] A critical mass of Mexican residents from Santa Ana's early barrios raised funds to build their own Catholic parish, Our Lady of Guadalupe Church on 3rd and Grand, established in 1922. As Garcia (2007:50) notes, "the Logan residents, together with other Mexicans from other parts of the city, organized a street fair fiesta to raise funds for their own Hispanic parish." Through these efforts, Our Lady of Guadalupe was born. Garcia (2007:50) describes parish life in the following manner. "Now parishioners had a place not just for Sunday mass but for all their other religious activities including their 'jamaicas' (fiestas). During the month of May the very young girls would go to take flowers to the Virgin Mary at church." Eventually, more parishes serving Mexican barrios in Santa Ana would be established, starting with Our Lady of Guadalupe in the Delhi

[7] McWilliams's account depicts citrus culture in his current day of the 1940s, and in the decades leading up to his day.

[8] Some parishes engaged in efforts of "Americanization" (Hoover 2014; Odem 2004). It is possible that Mexican residents hoped to shield themselves from such efforts as these would have alienated Mexicans from their cultural traditions.

neighborhood in 1927, tied to the original parish of the same name.[9] Having these churches provided an important form of sanctuary, of ethnic space, to Mexican residents of Santa Ana. These places meant that members of Santa Ana's barrios had an institution that focused on serving them, and allowed for cultural celebrations to take place. In Santa Ana, it was also important that many Spanish speaking priests, especially from Mexico and Spain, were available to serve Mexican residents (Iribarren 1974), countering some of the trends highlighted by Lint Sagarena (2009) and Lopez (2009).

Early twentieth-century parishes were also known to strengthen ethnic identities by strengthening ties between ethnic Mexicans who had long resided in the United States and more recent arrivals from Mexico. Such was the case when a group of Catholic sisters fled the Cristero Revolt of Mexico in 1926 and eventually landed in Santa Ana. The sisters were R. Mother Belen Rico, M. Loreto Arredondo, M. Emerenciana Pastor, M. Maria del Buen, Consejo Andrade, and M. Magdalene Hernandez. These sisters were instrumental in founding the St. Francis Retirement home in the Artesia St. Barrio, which historian Mary Garcia points out has continued to be a resource for elderly Latinxs in the area. Upon arriving in Santa Ana, the sisters crossed paths with a priest, Fr. Origel, that fled Mexico under like circumstances (Walker 1928). Some local residents, too, arrived from Mexico during this volatile period (Gurza 2000). Together, these Catholic religious and lay residents replenished cultural traditions in a Mexican community that by one account was losing its Mexican identity (Walker 1928). As Walker recounts, "some of the Holy Week ceremonies of the Catholics of Mexico were this year revived by Father Origel, at Delhi" (1928:75). The church literally provided refuge for religious refugees (Young 2015), and their faith in turn impacted the local Mexican population. This was an early case of transnational faith in action.

Though Catholicism functioned as a boundary marker within broader society, ethnicity functioned as an intra-religious boundary

[9] Our Lady of the Pillar (1965), in the Artesia-Pilar neighborhood would follow.

among Catholics.[10] The relationship between Our Lady of Guadalupe, on 3rd and Grand, and St. Joseph is particularly illustrative of this pattern. Many of the Mexican residents that helped found the Our Lady of Guadalupe parish lived in close proximity to St. Joseph, notably at Logan Barrio (Garcia 2007). These Mexican residents could have continued at St. Joseph, yet they worked to establish a parish focused on serving the Mexican community. Many of the parishioners of St. Joseph were white, some European immigrants. Our Lady of Guadalupe, on the other hand, became a center of the Mexican community.[11] At one point in the late '30s, the parish even welcomed the appointment of Fr. Charles Logan, one of the few black priests in the entire nation (Murray 1947), highlighting the salience of a white/non-white color line at this time.

Protestantism and Latinx Religious Boundaries

Within Protestant missionary circles, discourses highlighting Catholics as religious "others" were prevalent and were especially meaningful for how Mexicans were perceived. Mexicans, as a predominantly Catholic population, were seen as a population to be reached with the Protestant message. Catholic work among Mexicans in the southwest was seen by Protestants as either deficient theologically, or deficient in resources (Martinez 2011). Santa Ana, with its emerging Mexican population, soon became a focal point of Protestant missionary activity. Records of Protestant outreach aimed at Santa Ana's Mexican population indicate that one Reverend Antonio Diaz established Protestant missionary efforts to local ethnic Mexicans in the 1880s, under the sponsorship of the Methodist Episcopal Church (Cal-Pac UMC 2014). The following decade, the California Spanish Mission Society, founded by Yale Divinity School alumnus Alden Case, conducted

[10] For extensive analysis of how these intra-religious boundaries operate along ethnic distinctions in a Catholic parish context, see Hoover (2014). Hoover notes the entrenched nature of these boundaries once they are accepted by parishioners.

[11] This parish has continued to function as a de facto national parish, in accordance with the typology provided by Palmer-Boyes (2010), given its commitment to the local Mexican-origin population.

missionary work among Mexicans in Santa Ana c. 1897 (Case 1902).[12] A 1902 issue of *The Pacific*, a Congregationalist newspaper, mentions a Spanish language parish in Santa Ana founded by Case's Mission Society (Case 1902). Because Case was a Congregationalist, the work of his interdenominational Protestant mission society would ultimately be subsumed under the Congregationalist church. Case's motivation was rooted in his assessment that neither the Catholic church nor the Protestant churches were effectively serving the Latinx population in the area (Case 1902). By Case's estimation, among "the old Spanish Fathers," "gospel truth was not prominent in their teaching" (Case 1902). Case's church did not continue long, perhaps taxed by a lack of consistent pastoral leadership, as hinted at by Case's own account in the *Pacific* paper (Case 1902): The church "might alone engage all the powers of an able missionary." Case is suggesting that the church needed more permanent leadership, but also indicating that Mexicans were responding to Protestant outreach. The Protestant presence among Santa Ana's Mexican residents lay bare the possibility of intra-ethnic religious boundaries early in the city's history.

With Case's mission no longer in operation, another Protestant congregation would lay claim to being Santa Ana's first Mexican Protestant church. The Mexican Methodist church, so named in 1912, was founded by the joint efforts of various Protestant groups that shared desire for outreach to ethnic Mexicans. As one Protestant historian notes:

> The people of Santa Ana, realizing that the Mexican people in the city were in need of some kind of religious privileges, organized a Mexican Mission in 1910. The churches united in supporting this mission for about two years. The meetings were held in a small building on South Main street. (McArthur 1948)

Two years after its 1910 founding, the Methodist Episcopal Church denomination was handed charge of the fledgling congregation. This church is likely the county's oldest Spanish-language Protestant church

[12] Case himself indicates in a report that the Presbyterians were the first to conduct outreach to Mexicans in the region, but it is unclear if Santa Ana specifically was a site of outreach.

still in operation. The church would be headed by Rev. Ambrosio Gonzales, a Mexican minister known as "the hero of God" (Hoiles 1939). Rev. Gonzales's grandfather was arguably the first Hispano convert to Protestantism in New Mexico (Harwood 1910). Gonzales was succeeded by a Mexican national, Rev. Vicente Mendoza, who became one of the most prolific hymn composers in the Spanish-speaking world. Mendoza's most famous hymn, "Jesus Es Mi Rey Soberano," was penned during his ministerial appointments in Santa Ana and Los Angeles. He returned to Mexico soon after. Walker (1928) suggests that a concentration of Mexican Protestants, a Protestant enclave of sorts, was forming in close proximity to Santa Ana's Mexican Methodist church. Perhaps as minorities within a minority, Mexican Protestants sought opportunities to strengthen their support network through spatial proximity.

A report published by a Protestant missionary agency illustrates how outreach to Mexicans in Orange County was at times motivated by a negative opinion of Mexicans:

> In Orange County the Mexican is the greatest problem in many ways. To the county probation officer, he presents a most difficult problem. Emotional, stubborn, often illiterate and handicapped by generations of inefficient living, the Mexican is difficult to handle and hard to teach. The county has separate schools for Mexican children up to, and including, the sixth grade, largely for the reason that it has been found impossible to deal with the Mexican along with the American educationally and be fair to both races. (Brunner and Brunner 1922:96)

The authors go on to note that many Mexicans were Catholic, revealing an underlying opinion that the Mexican population was to be reached with a Protestant message because the Catholic church had not sufficiently helped to better their position in life.

Emergence of Pentecostalism

Another form of Protestantism, Pentecostalism, would early on take root in the Mexican barrios of Santa Ana and reinvigorate intra-ethnic religious boundaries through its experiential, conversion-centered focus. The Azusa Street revival in Los Angeles is considered the birth of US Pentecostalism. The revival was known for its multiethnic participation, led by a Southern black preacher named William Seymour and attended by a variety of ethnic groups in the Los Angeles basin. Robeck notes (2006), in this regard, that in the year following the Azusa St. revival in Los Angeles, churches had been founded in other cities along the Pacific Electric streetcar line. Santa Ana was on this line, and was one of the cities that Robeck indicates had a church established as a direct outgrowth of the revival. Latinxs were present at the revival in Los Angeles from its inception, as noted by religion scholars such as Sanchez-Walsh (2003), Espinosa (2014), and Ramírez (2015). The family members of one AC Valdez were among the early adopters of this movement of meteoric rise.

In his autobiography, Pentecostal evangelist AC Valdez relates walking from his job of picking oranges in Tustin, California, to a Santa Ana chapel, c.1914. In Santa Ana, one city over from his job, Valdez had a transformational experience that he claims left him healed physically and spiritually (Valdez and Scheer 1980). Valdez thereafter launched into public ministry, helping to start Pentecostal ministries throughout the United States and abroad. He is one of the founders of Pentecostalism in Australia and New Zealand (Hutchinson 2009). Sporadically, Valdez would return to preach in Santa Ana, once being jailed there for "disturbing the peace" (Valdez and Scheer 1980). Religion provided Valdez with an impetus to cross boundaries near and far. It appears Valdez had the freedom to cross ethno-racial lines in both his professional and personal life. His first wife, Lottie May Gage, was white, as was his second wife, Evelyn, whom he married after being widowed. He identified as "Spanish," tracing his lineage to a Spanish soldier that settled in Spanish rule California during the Catholic mission era. In spite of salient Catholic and Protestant distinctions, Valdez on occasion spoke sympathetically of Catholicism, communicating that his family had encountered God through Catholicism prior to becoming Pentecostal (Valdez and Scheer 1980).

In the decades following the emergence of US Pentecostalism in 1906, Pentecostal churches were founded in Santa Ana to serve Mexican communities. Established in 1925, Micion Pentecostes moved to several Orange County locations before settling in central Santa Ana. Changing its name to Templo Calvario, it would affiliate with the Assemblies of God denomination and grow to become one of the largest Latinx congregations in the United States. An early convert of the ministry, Gilberto De Leon, and his new bride, Santa Ana native Rosaura Benites, would return to Gilberto's native Texas. Empowered by a newly found Pentecostal message, they worked in Texas as pastors. Their son, Daniel De Leon, would decades later return to Santa Ana and serve as pastor of Templo Calvario for over thirty years. Cases such as those of the De Leons and the previously mentioned family of Ambrosio Gonzales highlight the manner in which geographic connections were forged across the US southwest by ethnic Mexicans, with religion being an important linchpin of shared culture.

The initial wave of Protestant outreach activity to Mexicans was primarily spurred on by white Mainline Protestant leaders. The work of Congregationalists, Presbyterians, and Methodists among Mexicans, for example, largely arose as an extension of existing mainline Protestant institutions, which at the time were primarily white. An important wave of Protestant outreach quickly emerged through the work of ethnic Mexican leaders who were themselves Protestant. Leaders such as Ambrosio Gonzales and Vicente Mendoza played critical roles as they were not recent Protestant converts but rather had deeper Protestant roots. The rise of Pentecostalism presented an additional layer of Protestant outreach to Mexicans. Here, some of the leaders, themselves ethnic Mexicans, were newer converts to Protestantism. These two latter streams of Protestant leadership, constituted of co-ethnic leaders, played an important role in the sustaining of a Protestant presence among the Mexican population of Santa Ana.

Sustained Patterns of Exclusion

Moving through the 1930s and beyond, Mexicans continued to experience marked levels of social exclusion, and often faith would empower Mexicans to face insurmountable obstacles toward their social incorporation. The repatriation of Mexicans, for example, was a direct assault on people of Mexican descent in the United States. In documenting the growth of Apostolic Pentecostal churches, Ramirez (2015) notes that many Apostolic congregants were deported under US repatriation efforts. Ramirez indicates that repatriation trains passed through the Santa Ana train depot c. 1931, picking up locals there en route to Mexico. In this case, the faith that was acquired in the United States would be passed on in Mexico, forging transnational faith networks. Though Ramirez does not specify that Apostolics from Santa Ana were on those trains, records indicate that several apostolic churches were established in Santa Ana, and that in the 1930s, Santa Ana was a preaching point for Latinx Apostolics (Holland 1974).

The decades to follow would bring other contests of boundary negotiation to the Latinx communities of Santa Ana related to labor and education. The Bracero Program initiated new waves of Mexican migrants to the United States, including to Orange County. While these were temporary migrant workers participating in the US agricultural industry, the program had effects beyond the immediate labor contribution of these workers. As I would discover from several interviewees, some immigrant families in Santa Ana had fathers that came to the area first, as braceros. That is, the permanent migration of some families was preceded by seasonal labor provided by the Bracero Program. This program sparked a longstanding dependency on Mexican labor, particularly in the agriculture sectors. The Bracero Program lasted from 1942 through 1964. Some local churches, such as Our Lady of Guadalupe and Templo Calvario, would serve these migrant workers.

During the time of the famous Zoot Suit Riots, Santa Ana experienced a similar incident of aggression against Chicanos. As regional newspapers broke the story of the Zoot Suit Riots, famous Chicano organizer Bert Corona was stationed at the Santa Ana Air Army Base. In García's (1994) biography of Corona, Corona recalls the way some white community leaders characterized Chicanos during the riots; for example, Corona recalled "Captain Duran Ayres of the L.A. Sheriff's Department, who commented that Mexicans were a violent people because of their bloodthirsty Aztec ancestors." A negative association between Chicano identity and indigeneity still surfaced periodically in the white media. Corona conjures up tense moments during his stay in Orange County:

> [W]e had some similar incidents in which some of our Anglo servicemen beat up on local Chicanos. It caused much concern among the fairly large number of Mexican-American soldiers in our camp and in surrounding camps also. After one incident involving the beating of some young Chicanos, hundreds of Chicano kids from the nearby communities advanced on our base and waited for servicemen in the areas where the buses took us into town. That weekend, almost no servicemen ventured out to take the bus. (Garcia 1994)

Within the time span of the Bracero Program, in 1947, another restrictive social barrier for ethnic Mexicans was overcome locally. That year, the *Mendez v. Westminster* lawsuit took place wherein Mexican families in the area banded together to demand that local districts invest in the educational equity of their children. Most Mexican children at the time were receiving subpar education in segregated schools, though some lighter-skinned Mexican students were allowed into white schools (Arriola 1995). As Sylvia Mendez, daughter of plaintiffs Gonzalo and Felicitas Mendez, tells it, "I was so dark that they told me I couldn't stay in the white school and my cousins were light so they could" (Ocaño Perez 2011). Mendez describes her experience of the trial decades later saying, "to me it was like going to church. I'd have to sit in the front row and listen. All this time that they're fighting and I'm all excited about going to court and getting all dressed up. All you're thinking as a 9 year old is, 'they're doing this so I can go to that beautiful school'" (Ocaño Perez 2011). Mendez's comparison between court and church signals that she had familiarity with church, as it functioned as a reference point for her courtroom experience.

The '50s, too, were fraught with incidents of exclusion. As Agius-Vallejo (2012:32) notes of the time period, "Regardless of generational or class status, people of Mexican origin continued to be considered foreign, alien, and inferior." As the Korean War concluded, the United States faced a recession. Support was drummed up for "Operation Wetback" where approximately 1.1 million Mexicans were deported by the INS in 1954. Some were unauthorized braceros, but some were US citizens (Massey, Durand, and Malone 2003). The threat of deportation loomed overhead throughout the southwest, including in Orange County. As

Mitchell (2012:86) documents, "Some—like those who ended up in the guarded Orange County camps—were made to understand their propertied status viscerally."

Religious Presence in the City

The Latinx population of Santa Ana was still proportionally small through the 1960s, barely topping 15% of city residents (Harwood and Myers 2002), but religious opportunities for Latinxs had increased as the city's overall population had grown. The number of Latinx churches was held to roughly nine Protestant churches (Holland 1974), and by then, eight Catholic churches were in operation in the city (Krekelberg 2016), with seven of the parishes offering masses and/or programs that specifically served the local Latinx population. While Latinxs were a presence in local Catholic parishes, not all Catholic churches were dominated by Latinxs. Many parishes in Santa Ana welcomed Latinx residents, but as some interviewees noted, Latinxs were still the minority in several of these parishes into the '60s. The two Our Lady of Guadalupe parishes, and the Our Lady of the Pillar parish, established in 1965, were three of the primary parishes frequented by the Latinx community. Our Lady of the Pillar had initially been a mission of Our Lady of Guadalupe on Grand Ave. In the '60s, as it was established as a full parish, it would grow to become "the official parish church of the Mexican-Americans in Santa Ana and the 'mother church' was now a mission of her vigorous daughter" (Iribarren 1974:n.p.). This was an important era for the Catholic church, following the Second Vatican Council (1962–1965). During this new season, to a greater extent, "[b]ishops and pastoral leaders could innovate, critique, and experiment; Catholic laity could offer greater input in pastoral affairs." (Adler, Bruce, Starks 2019:30). These forms of innovation were indeed applied within Santa Ana's parishes.

With the Latinx presence in Catholic parishes increasing for several decades, Catholic leaders provided a critical voice of advocacy for Santa Ana's Latinx residents. Not all of these leaders were themselves Latinxs, but they were committed to serving the Latinx community. Msgr John Coffield, known as Padre Juanote, played a pivotal role in Santa Ana's religious communities. Appointed to Our Lady of Guadalupe Delhi, Padre Juanote served there between 1967 and 1973. As noted in a tribute, Padre Juanote "marched with the Rev. Martin Luther King Jr. in Selma, Ala., and supported Cesar Chavez's drive to unionize migrant farmworkers in California" (McLellan 2005). Msgr Coffield was known for being outspoken on issues of race and even imposed an exile upon himself from the archdiocese of Los Angeles over disagreements related to civil rights issues. Coffield also "helped found the Santa Ana Organizing Committee, which lobbied the city for better services for its Latino community" (McLellan 2005).

Fr. Allan Figueroa Deck, a renowned Catholic scholar, conducted much of his early ministry in Santa Ana, continuing on at the same parish where Msgr Coffield labored. Ina Rosenthal-Urey (1984), a migration scholar, references crossing paths with Deck in 1979, while Deck worked among migrant populations, a substantial portion of which were reportedly undocumented. Morris-Young notes that Deck's "official Hispanic ministry started at the grassroots level as administrator of Our Lady of Guadalupe in the Delhi Barrio of Santa Ana, California, and as the first director of the Orange Diocese's Hispanic Ministry" (2008). While much can be said about Fr. Decks impressive scholarly contributions, in regards to local history, Deck's advocacy for inculturated forms of worship has significantly advanced the emergence of a homegrown Latinx Catholic culture.

The work of several other leaders is worth mentioning. Fr. Matthias Ho was an ethnic Chinese priest who founded the Spanish mass at St. Anne, a church that some interviewees described to me as an "Anglo church." Fr. Ho also directed the Hispanic Committee through the 1970s. Fr. Ed Poettgen, raised in the Santa Ana neighborhoods that he would later serve, sustained a close tie to the barrios of Santa Ana. Fr. Ed served at St. Josephs, St. Anne's, St. Barbara's, and eventually at Immaculate Heart of Mary, where I would meet him. While at St. Anne's, in 1980, he was instrumental in the founding of SANO, a community organizing group that became affiliated with the Pacific Institute of Community Organizing. SANO would eventually be known as OCCO, and is still a strong voice of advocacy for a variety of marginalized communities, including Latinxs (Spencer and Carty 2017).

Becoming a Latinx City

The 1970s witnessed a major boom in the Latinx population of Santa Ana and the religious landscape experienced drastic shifts in light of this expansion. After the Hart-Celler act, immigration from Latin America to the United States expanded. From 1970 through the 1990s, Santa Ana became a Latinx-dominant city. During the beginning of this period, the center of the city had largely fallen into disrepair. The patronage of Latinx consumers and the entrepreneurship of Latinx business owners and those catering to Latinx consumers in the area began to revitalize the downtown district of Santa Ana, raising the regional fame of the area known as "La Cuatro," or Fourth Street (Gonzalez 2017). This is a story of working-class Latinxs revitalizing the core of a city (Harwood and Myers 2002). Yet the emergence of a "Latino City" was coupled with significant levels of white flight (Harwood and Myers 2002). Some white majority churches from the central religious district moved out while several others made ostensible commitments to stay in the city.

An article from the *L.A. Times* captures a snapshot of how local churches engaged Santa Ana's demographic shifts. The article details the plight of a faithful community church, Church of the Brethren, at the twilight of its institutional life:

> The church leaders tried busing. They tried recruiting some of the area's Spanish-speaking residents to services in English. They tried everything to bring children, who symbolized the promise of a future, into the small church on Ross Street. But in the end, they failed, victims of changing demographics that kept the Church of the Brethren, in the heart of what is now a Latino neighborhood, from replenishing its aging, Anglo membership. (Reyes 1995)

The article goes on to point out that a Latinx church affiliated with the Brethren denomination would be taking over the church facility. The Latinx church is still there today. A time of mourning for one group, was a time of rejoicing for another group that would now have the freedom to steward a facility they previously rented.

In the period of the '70s through the '90s, Latinx church life in Santa Ana began to grow exponentially. What was once a cluster of nine Latinx Protestant churches, and several masses serving Latinx Catholics, expanded to Latinx-dominant Catholic parishes throughout the city, and dozens of evangelical churches dotting the city grid. The growth of Latinx churches, both in terms of more churches and larger congregations, is not completely a surprise, given the growth of the Latinx population in the city. In the span of three decades, from 1960 to 1990, the Latinx population went from being 15% to being 65% of the city population (Gonzalez 2017). To put things in perspective, the city population itself grew exponentially, from 100,350 residents in 1960 to 293,742 residents in 1990. Santa Ana was, by 1990, a city of over 190,000 Latinxs (Gonzalez 2017).

What used to be a city with several barrios, became an ethnic enclave unto itself. This carried important implications for the religious life of Santa Ana's faithful: Latinx church life was now far more visible throughout the city. As some interviewees described, precursors to the large-scale acts sponsored by religious institutions already existed. The Catholic church, for example, would sponsor *jamaicas*, Latinx festivals that helped to raise funds but also to provide opportunities for recreation and community interaction. On the other hand, some of the older residents remembered a time when public acts of devotion were less visible, and more contained within specific Latinx barrios. They observed that as more Latinx immigrants settled in Santa Ana post-1965, so too religious symbolism and ritual became more prominent in the public arena. Processions and pageantry became part and parcel of community life in Santa Ana's neighborhoods. The growth of the Latinx population and the growth of Latinx dominant churches, was accompanied by an expansion of public acts of faith. Particularly among the city's Latinx Catholics, public acts of devotion constituted an important form of community building.

The diversification of Latinx immigration in the early 1980s especially left a mark on the religious landscape of Santa Ana. As immigrants from Central America came to the region, new religious institutions began to emerge. Central Americans are a minority in Santa Ana, but they are an influential minority, with religion providing an important node of influence. Several churches established in the area were tied to movements in Central America, such as the Elim movement originating in Guatemala. Compared to Mexicans, a much higher proportion of Central Americans are evangelical Christians (Cooperman et al. 2014). Many Mexican-dominant churches in the area drew from Central American neo-Pentecostal styles of worship and attended conferences in neighboring Los Angeles County, where their Central American coreligionists shared their gifts of music and preaching.

Other parts of Latin America and the Caribbean also left an imprint on the city's religious ecology. The Iglesia de Dios Pentecostal Ministerio Internacional based in Puerto Rico, for example, established a local congregation in 1981. After several decades, the congregation raised enough funds to purchase the historic grounds of a once thriving United Methodist church. The well-known Iglesia Universal based in Brazil founded a successful church on one of the busiest streets in the city. Famous Argentine evangelist Alberto Mottesi established his headquarters in the city as well. Latin America broadly, not just Mexico, was leaving a mark on Santa Ana's religious ecology.

This era also marked the rise of independent Pentecostal churches. The city already had independent Pentecostal churches, but their numbers multiplied during this phase. While denominations of all stripes were represented in the roster of Santa Ana Latinx churches, independent churches began to sprout up throughout the city. Some of these were tied to independent *concilios*, but some were also independent of any governing body, other than that contained within each respective congregation. In some cases, churches were birthed out of church divisions, with some congregations splintering from denominational churches and from denominations altogether. As one parishioner revealed about her church, "we split from the denomination because our pastor started preaching about the baptism in the Holy Spirit." These types of independent churches were almost always Pentecostal or charismatic in their orientation.

Latinx-majority Catholic churches were also experiencing a diversification all their own. While Catholic church expansion is enacted within leadership structures more centralized and hierarchical than their evangelical/Pentecostal counterparts (Adler, Bruce, Starks 2019), notable growth was still taking place in the constellation of Santa

Ana parishes. Eventually, two new parishes were founded in the city. Christ our Savior Catholic parish was founded in 2005 in the South Coast Metro area, a part of the city appealing to young upwardly-mobile households, and Our Lady of Lavang opened its doors in 2006 in a working class neighborhood, especially serving Vietnamese and Latino parishioners.[13] Within existing parishes, the rise of numerous types of lay ministries drew many Latinx participants. The importance of the Catholic Charismatic Renewal cannot be overstated (Espinosa 2017; Matovina 2017). In some cases, Charismatic groups within parishes seemed to function as congregations within a parish, often outsizing some of their Pentecostal neighbors around the way. Other lay ministries, particularly those focusing on Catholic outreach, such as La Legion de Maria, grew in their ranks. The Cursillo movement would likewise draw a sizable following from Santa Ana's Latinx population. These ministries also gave the Catholic church a more visible presence in the community, often organizing neighborhood-based events and sending representatives to make house visits on a regular basis.

The growth of faith-based nonprofits has made a significant impact within Santa Ana's Latinx neighborhoods. Founded by Sr. Eileen McNerney in 1995, Taller San Jose provides educational and job-training resources to young men and women (McNerney 2005). Sr. McNerney was motivated to start the nonprofit while living in a neighborhood with salient gang activity. Other faith-based non-profits strongly grounded in the community would also emerge. What initially started as an afterschool program, Kidworks, was founded by Larry and Jayme Acosta, evangelical ministers dedicated to youth leadership training. Kidworks would expand to various Latinx neighborhoods in the city, providing services for children and adults, and collaborating with both Catholic and evangelical churches. Templo Calvario would found its own community development corporation, which has engaged everything from job training to food distribution to the

[13] The opening of Our Lady of Lavang was not without controversy, as it involved the closing of Our Lady of Lourdes a small, predominantly Latinx parish, among other things. The name, Our Lady of Lavang, refers to a Marian apparition in Vietnam. Ninh (2014) explores the marginalization of Vietnamese Catholics in the Diocese of Orange, despite their substantial representation in the pews.

launching of its own charter school. Several churches and organizations in the city would also establish drug rehabilitation programs, such as Victory Outreach and Teen Challenge. Finally, operating for over four decades, Catholic Charities of Orange County works primarily from Santa Ana as a social service arm of the Diocese of Orange. It offers services related to food and nutrition, immigration and citizenship status, counseling and therapy, and disabilities assistance. These and other nonprofits function as important nodes of collaboration for congregants from a variety of different church traditions, and of different ethno-racial and socioeconomic backgrounds, all within the Latinx neighborhoods of Santa Ana.

Boundaries of the Latinx City

With the expansion of the Latinx population largely through the central corridor of the city, Latinx-majority neighborhoods were framed through racialized lenses both by key stakeholders in the city, and by people outside of the city. Gonzalez in his study of the emergence of Santa Ana as a Latinx City, notes the implementation of a discourse that cast in a negative light the growing working-class Latinx population in the city's central core. The popular discourse in local planning circles, one of "urban degeneration," was intended to catalyze new developments attracting "white and economically well-off patrons":

> For city officials, Downtown Fourth Street and the downtown in general were in a major urban crisis and they needed to redevelop the core immediately. The consistent message was that the city needed to act quickly to revive the once glorious downtown because it was blighted, had been doing economically very poorly, and had been socially undesirable for way too long. The discourse and practice of spatial alienation that evolved over urban space were comprehensive and the basis to erase or minimize distinctive and affirmative cultural and working-class qualities of the downtown commercial character and local neighborhoods that were on the rise. (Gonzalez 2017:25)

In the local context, such opinions were especially aimed at "Fourth Street," or "La Cuatro," which had become the heart of the Latinx and Mexican community in the region. Latinxs were allegedly the primary cause of this urban blight, and some leaders vowed to restore the clientele of the city center to its former demographics, and to alter current residential demographics of the city center. Gonzalez traces these particular discourses through several decades, noting the diverse array of policies intended to see this plan come to fruition.

Beyond the borders of the city, Lacayo documents how discourses about Santa Ana similar to those of "urban degeneration" recorded by Gonzalez have permeated the broader Orange County region. Lacayo's research specifically focuses on whites' opinions of Latinxs in Orange County, tracking especially opinions related to residential patterns. Santa Ana is cast in a negative light, especially for its working-class Latinx neighborhoods. Lacayo (2016:9) summarizes the rationale of some white respondents in the following manner:

> When explaining why they stayed away, they spoke at length of how they regarded people in that area [of Santa Ana] as culturally deficient and how they perceive Latino areas as unsafe due to crime and gangs. Even though Santa Ana is filled with many Latinos who are middle-class and are homeowners, most respondents characterized it as an unfavorable area.

The reductionistic, negative opinions offered by some white respondents indicate that Santa Ana is viewed by at least a segment of the Orange County population as a place to be avoided. Such perspectives have contributed to a social boundary being developed around the city. That is, Santa Ana has been constructed by many as a racialized space.

The framing of Santa Ana along racialized lines has also been bolstered by law enforcement maneuvers, according to Davis (2001). Davis describes how following a controversial murder case that took place in the South Orange County city of San Clemente, law enforcement agencies took part in a highly visible gang sweep: "The largest criminal taskforce in local history swept through the sprawling 'superbarrio,'—centered on Santa Ana but also straddling Anaheim,

Fullerton, Orange and Garden Grove—that segregates two-thirds of Orange County's almost 800,000 Latino residents." The Latinx population of Orange County today is closer to 1.09 million (U.S. Census 2018). Davis's commentary suggests that high-profile enforcement patterns of this nature contribute to broader regional perceptions about Santa Ana as a site of urban degeneration.

Even in noting the Latinx-majority population of Santa Ana, it is unfortunate that more people have not primarily associated the city with its history of resisting racism and of fighting against unjust social boundaries. The place of Santa Ana in civil rights history and key leaders of the past and present who are advocating for the rights of Latinxs and immigrants locally and beyond merit far more attention. Likewise, regardless of religious inclinations, residents of the region would do well to note the work of religious leaders in the Latinx communities of Santa Ana. Much of this religious advocacy has empowered Latinxs to contribute to the production of ethnic space. Finally, the work of everyday Santaneros should not be ignored. Santaneros' engagement within their communities of faith have proven to be particularly significant, often making an impact within broader society.

The Importance of Context

The history of Santa Ana's Latinx religious ecology demonstrates how ethnic and religious identities have intersected locally. Residents identified ascriptively as non-whites, particularly those identified as Mexican, have had a long history of actively negotiating the labels of ethnic identity placed upon them. Religion at times offered a space and a resource of negotiation, though it also functioned as a marker of difference along ethno-racial lines. Negotiations of ethnic boundaries were not merely matters of label preference but matters of life opportunities and of social trajectories, as seen through the life history of Della Molina-Cruz. The sustained patterns of exclusion among ethnic Mexicans in Santa Ana would create a space of co-ethnic collaboration, wherein a critical mass of co-ethnics sought ways to work together for the sake of their livelihood. Communities of faith especially provided platforms of co-ethnic collaboration. As Latinxs became the majority of Santa Ana's population, faith communities serving Latinxs significantly expanded. Racialized perceptions of the city would keep some Orange County residents away from the city, but many spiritual seekers would continue to travel into the city to participate in its faith communities. More importantly, residents of the city would themselves contribute to the expansion of this central city sanctuary—a space where many Latinxs now find a home to worship and where echoes of the past continue to inform Mexican ethnic identity.

Through both external opinions and internal participation, central Santa Ana functions largely as an ethnic space. Religion continues to be a major part of the edifice that upholds this ethnic space. The diversity of the religious ecology that thrives in this ethnic space has given rise to both innovation and competition and the socially contained nature of this ethnic space makes the negotiation of ethnic identities that much more salient among co-ethnic Catholics and Protestants. As I present in the chapters to follow, negotiations of ethnic and religious identities are enlivened as Santaneros encounter religious others in their midst.

3
The Authentic Ethnic Self

Carmen Gomez was proud of her ethnic heritage. When asked what ethnic label she preferred to be identified by, she resoundingly responded, "Mexican!" Carmen's expressed commitment to ethnic identification was of little surprise, given the ways her life mirrored the life of her Santa Ana neighbors. Like many in her community, Carmen's narrative of migration into the United States involved unauthorized entry. Carmen reported, "My parents drove across the border with false documents when I was four years old. They cut my hair short. I was brought as a boy, my sister as a girl, so we matched with the papers my parents were using." Two years later she and her mother returned to Mexico. Not until age twelve would she settle in the United States permanently. That was twenty-six years ago. Carmen was now highly invested in the ethnic communities of central Santa Ana. Her job as a local preschool teacher and her role as a lay leader in her Pentecostal church, Templo de Alabanza, provided her with strong institutional anchors to central Santa Ana. Her social world was substantially populated by co-ethnics from Santa Ana.

Meeting Carmen at her school, she could be observed engaging in friendly banter with parents as she handed out paperwork at the end of the school day. She would keep up with the life of many of her students even after they completed preschool. A key impetus in this investment was Carmen's understanding of her job as part of her spiritual calling—her vocation. She explained,

> I've always been drawn to kids and they follow me. And in working with kids, I also get to work with families. When I see families in need in the community, I can see myself reflected in them and I ask God to let me be useful in their lives. I said, "Lord, if you're going to allow me to get a career, that it wouldn't only be for me to feel better

The Saints of Santa Ana. Jonathan E. Calvillo, Oxford University Press (2020). © Oxford University Press.
DOI: 10.1093/oso/9780190097790.001.0001.

> as a person, but that it would be a way to help others be better, for me to be a bridge, and to guide them as one resource more."

Templo de Alabanza, Carmen's church, was another important space of social connection in central Santa Ana that shaped Carmen's ethnic identity. Interviewing Carmen at her church provided a glimpse into her church's congregational life. The Thursday night service had just let out. Carmen and I stopped to observe four young men engaging in a musical jam session in the church sanctuary. A young woman, Carmen's teenage daughter Sarai, heroically joined the band, pouncing on the drums. Carmen provided some background information on the band members: One young man recently migrated from Honduras, one was from Nicaragua, and two were from Mexico. The drums, bass, guitar, and keyboard were played intermittently as makeshift band members coordinated their impromptu performance. Byron, Carmen's husband, greeted me through the clamor with a hearty handshake and a bright smile. Like a number of his co-parishioners, Byron was an immigrant from El Salvador; he and Carmen met at church where they steadfastly volunteered as lay leaders. This was Carmen's primary social world, a blend of Mexican and Central American church members.

The demographics at Templo de Alabanza uncovered an unexpected point of tension in relation to Carmen's ethnic identity: Carmen perceived that people at work read both her evangelical identity and her marriage to someone from El Salvador as signals that she was not Mexican, or perhaps not Mexican enough. As she explained, "I don't know if they focus on me like that because my husband is from El Salvador and they think that most people from El Salvador are evangelical. Right away you get labeled like this. Then they find out I'm Mexican and they say, 'Oh!'" Carmen indignantly added that "Even if they know where I'm from, some people forget that I am Mexican." Whether or not the individuals initiating these interactions with Carmen intended to be subtle, to Carmen these were salient experiences.

The questioning of Carmen's ethnic identity in light of her faith and her marriage was amplified by how these two facets were intimately intertwined for her. Carmen viewed her marriage and faith as closely linked not only because she met her husband at church, but because her marriage to Byron fulfilled a prophecy given to Carmen at her Pentecostal church. As she recounted, "Through prophecy I was told, 'you're going to marry someone that has a missionary heart and that is involved in worship ministry.' That's Byron." Picture collages on a rear church wall indicated that most of the missionary work Carmen and Byron were involved in took place in Mexico. Ethnic investment, household ties, and faith commitment, were closely linked for Carmen. She wished more of her co-ethnics would understand this.

When among co-ethnics, Carmen was particularly wont to assert her ethnic identity. She declared, "when I'm around other Mexicans, I let them know I'm from the capital, 'el DF,'" which stands for Distrito Federal. Carmen emphatically proclaimed, "I like to be called 'Chilanga,'" the nickname for people from Distrito Federal. "Whoo hoo!" she cheered with arms uplifted, after brandishing her regional provenance and designation. Carmen carried a burden to prove that she was legitimately Mexican, and she deployed various resources from her background to make her case. In Carmen's estimation, what could be more Mexican than being from the capital of Mexico?

Religion and the Negotiations of Self-Identification

The manner in which evangelical affiliation was a mark of difference for Carmen illustrates a broader trend in the religious communities of Santa Ana. Subtle yet important differences manifested in the discursive strategies of ethnic belonging employed by Catholics and evangelicals. In comparison to Catholics, evangelicals employed a more varied arsenal of discursive tools to assert the legitimacy of their ethnic membership. That Catholics were less involved in verbally signaling their ethnic membership was not due to a categorical deficiency in Catholic respondents' sense of ethnic identity; I argue that it is the opposite. Catholics experienced less of a burden in asserting their Mexican ethnic identity because they were more likely to view Mexican ethnic identity as a default identifier. Catholic respondents demonstrated variation in regard to self-identification, but they generally reflected a sense of confidence in affirming a Mexican ethnic identity. This confidence was less prevalent among evangelicals. The way that individual informants constructed their sense of ethnic identity points to the types of ethnic boundary markers most salient to them in their local, day-to-day experience.

Mexican and Latinx Identities

An exploration of recent US trends in the construction of Mexican identities through legal-juridical and socio-cultural means offers a helpful starting point for discussing Mexican ethnic self-identification. Under the Treaty of Guadalupe Hidalgo, Mexicans were granted the de jure status of "white." Mexican de facto status, however, was largely one of isolation from whites, particularly for working class Mexicans, as noted in Chapter 2 of this volume.[1] Mexicans have not experienced the solidifying of ethno-racial labels experienced by other ethnic groups, particularly European immigrants, or immigrant groups primarily identified with the African diaspora.[2] Mexicans continue to confound categorizations of race in the United States, circumventing the black/white binary (Almaguer 1994; Lee and Bean 2007), yet being shifted into varying categories by the state (Dowling 2014; Mora 2014; Rodríguez 2000). In fact, research shows that Mexicans themselves, along with other Latinxs, have understandings of racial categories that diverge from what state-sanctioned definitions purport to convey (Dowling 2014; Rodriguez 2000). As Emeka and Vallejo note (2011), many Latinxs, including some Mexicans, struggle with how to respond to questions of racial identification in the United States. While some neatly place themselves into census categories of "white," or "black," based on ancestry (Emeka and Vallejo 2011) and/or affiliative identities

[1] There is evidence that not all Mexicans were racialized in the same way. Those that were seen primarily as Spanish were more readily integrated into white US society. Many Californios, particularly women, intermarried with European immigrants to the region, for example. However, such individuals did not constitute the majority of US Mexicans, and many would likely pass as white, particularly the children of Californio/European unions.

[2] More research is needed to understand how Santa Ana's Afro-Mexican immigrants from Mexico are constructing their identities in comparison to the broader mestizo identified Mexican population.

(Jimenez 2010), others prefer to identify themselves as "Other" (Emeka and Vallejo 2011). Given the confusion and variability around racial categories, it is no wonder that many first-generation Mexicans find more value in identifying primarily as "Mexican" (Emeka and Vallejo 2011; Dowling 2014; Taylor et al. 2012). In other words, for many ethnic Mexicans, ethnic categorization is a more salient identifier than the racial categories put forth by the state.

Pan-ethnicity offers a self-identification alternative that has provided some degree of legitimacy for Mexicans as a label accepted by the state, by the media, and by activists (Mora 2014). Pan-ethnic identities for Latinxs may be a result of aggregate level racialization from extra-group sources and/or intra-group desires for coalition building (Alcoff et al. 2006; Rodriguez 2000; Itzigsohn 2004). Perceptions of a shared culture and history may help to fuel pan-ethnicity among Latinxs, even if such a frame is externally imposed (Mora 2014). Instrumentalist motivations such as political mobilization have also been posited by various scholars as being central to the emergence of Latinx pan-ethnicity (Padilla 1985; De Genova and Ramos-Zayas 2003). Yet, as Dowling (2014) contends, pan-ethnic labels are used in disparate ways and hold inconsistent meanings regionally.

Migratory status and citizenship have also shaped Mexican ethnic self-identification. Mexico has been the most prolific source of unauthorized migration to the United States in the last century. In the current era, so prevalent is the association between "illegality" and the Mexican-origin population, that even Mexicans residing in the United States legally, including some of later generations, are labeled as "undocumented" (De Genova 2004; Ponce 2014) and actively combat this stigma (Hall, Greenman, and Farkas 2010; Yoshikawa and Kalil 2011). A cultural threat narrative projected onto Mexican and Latinx populations has been predicated upon expectations of cultural unassimilability (Chavez 2013; Huntington 2004). Some ethnic Mexicans have made conscious efforts to counteract perceptions of unassimilability by distancing themselves from co-ethnics (Dowling 2014; Jimenez 2010; Vila 2000). For Mexican immigrants who have obtained some form of legal status, highlighting this status may function as a salient form of identification. While this may be additive to ethnic identity, for some it comes to function as a master status.

Mexicans, then, aggregately, have vacillated between varying state-imposed ethnic categories and have flouted state-imposed racial options of identification. In Santa Ana, labels of self-identification were largely constructed in relation to the local social context. Particular labels signaled particular relationships to the broader ethnic community. Points of insecurity, I argue, are suggestive of the points at which boundary negotiations are taking place.

Ethnic Labels and Self-Identification

Mexican-origin Catholics and evangelicals in Santa Ana shared much in common in regard to preferred labels of ethnic self-identification. Many gave similar responses when asked the question, "What label would you use to describe your ethnic background?"[3] As discussed subsequently, the majority of respondents, regardless of religious affiliation, identified as "Mexican." On the other hand, subtle yet perceivable differences emerged across religious affiliations. Catholic and evangelical informants' preferred ethnic labels varied in similar proportions, yet the ways they qualified their preferences varied in salient ways. Moreover, though the majority of respondents, regardless of religious affiliation, identified as "Mexican," novel patterns emerged from the justifications provided by respondents regarding preferred labels.

Emotive Expressions of National Origin

Among informants who selected "Mexican" as their primary label of ethnic self-identification, many Catholics expressed their choice in a

[3] Subjects were allowed to answer in an open-ended manner but were also allowed to respond as succinctly as they desired. The terms that respondents indicated as their preferred ethnic labels fell into one of the following five categories: (1) National origin label: Mexican, Mexicano/a; (2) National origin label modified by a regional qualifier: Mexican from Oaxaca, for example; (3) Pan-ethnic label: Latinx or Hispanic; (4) Legal status label: Ciudadano/Citizen [of the United States]; and (5) US-oriented label: American, Mexican-American.

cool and collected manner. The grand majority of Catholic informants that selected "Mexican," simply made their selection and provided little explanation. Some provided a cursory explanation but did so in a nonchalant manner. Such was the case with Jose Luis Vargas, for example, who highlighted the importance of nation of birth as central to ethnic identification. Jose Luis sat back calmly in his chair and explained, "I've always seen myself in the same way. I've never really been asked to describe myself. I guess if someone were to ask me, 'I was born in Mexico' so Mexican." Jose Luis was a twenty years old Catholic parishioner who grew up in a densely populated neighborhood within close walking distance of his family's parish. Brought to the United States as a minor in unauthorized fashion, Jose Luis identified as a "dreamer." Jose Luis made his statement with very little emotional expression.

Another pattern that emerged among Catholics was that several Catholic informants, when talking about their preferred ethnic labels, made a direct link between devotion to La Virgen de Guadalupe and Mexican identity. Jesus Ibarra, an employee of the local school district, expressed this sentiment regarding the tie between Guadalupan devotion and Mexican ethnicity. Jesus identified as Mexican, but he elaborated, "In the way that I was raised, I was told that I'm not one hundred percent Mexican if I'm not Catholic. There's a term we use—'the Guadalupan Mexican' (Mexicano Guadalupano). If you're Mexican and you don't believe . . . I don't know about you. For me, the Catholic church is like my culture, they go together." Rodrigo, introduced in Chapter 1, shared a similar perspective to that of Jesus. To revisit Rodrigo's words, "I don't really see how someone can be really Mexican and not be *Guadalupano*." Rodrigo and Jesus spoke confidently about the interplay between their faith and their ethnic identity. It was difficult for them to separate the two. Their responses also suggested that they considered the ethnic identity of Mexicans who were not Catholic to be suspect.

Saúl Nieto, a retired carpenter, elaborated on this theme as well, as he discussed his identity as "Mexican." Having trained for the diaconate within the local diocese, his response hinted at his theological education:

> The Virgen of Guadalupe came and became inculturated within Mexican culture. For me, I am 100% devoted to La Virgen de

> Guadalupe. When you come into my house, the first thing you see is a painting dedicated to La Virgen de Guadalupe. When it's the twelfth of December [the feast day of Our Lady of Guadalupe], it doesn't matter if we get together at 4 a.m., in that moment, there is no tiredness.

Saúl demonstrated knowledge of inculturation, a concept highlighted in Catholic scholarship which speaks to the close relationship between Christian faith and local culture (Doyle 2012; Garces-Foley 2008; Starkloff 1994). As evident in Saúl's remarks, part of the potency in the relationship between Guadalupan devotion and Mexican ethnic identity rests in the understanding that Guadalupe "came" and "became" inculturated; that is, she revealed herself in such a way that the Christian gospel became intelligible to the local culture and conversely the local culture would shape Christian teachings. Saúl's description denotes a sense of direct action—divine intervention—not merely a passive association of ideas and symbols. Saúl's explanation emphasizes divine intentionality.

Evangelical Mexican Self-Identification

Sixto Nuñez, an evangelical food processing plant worker, gave a response that also indicated "Mexican" as his label of choice, but he delivered his response in a manner that differed from his Catholic co-ethnics. Sixto proclaimed, "Well I always say that I'm Mexican. I live in this country, but . . . 'where am I from?' I'm from Mexico, and I take pride in that!" Sixto pounded the table before him as if to drive his statement home. Usually speaking in calm, drawn-out syllables, Sixto uttered these words with firmness, his voice elevating, his posture straightening up as he spoke. I was taken aback by Sixto's agitated response, as throughout most of our interview he was calm and demonstrated little emotional expression. Sixto's social life was tightly enveloped within the activities of his Pentecostal church. He rented a room in a large house, close to his church, along with other co-parishioners. He explained that some of his housemates "are Central American, from Honduras and El Salvador." Like Carmen, he was connected to pan-ethnic social circles, but he hoped to be identified as Mexican.

Yolanda Herrera, who worked as a preschool teacher and converted to evangelical Christianity in young adulthood, also emphasized a national origin-based response. Yolanda insisted, "I've been in this country. I've learned to love this country! I know that when I die, I want to be here. But I know, I'm Mexican. I'm Mexican!" Yolanda reflected determination as she repeated her final phrase, the volume and pitch of her voice rising. In similar fashion to Sixto, she became more rigid in her body language as she asserted this particular response. For Yolanda, being Mexican would not to be erased by love of her receiving country. She further stressed that her two daughters were born in the United States and that they too would continue to be Mexican. She relayed that, "my daughters, if you ask them, they say, 'I'm Mexican American,' because I've influenced them in this." In other words, she believed that her two teenage daughters were retaining an ethnic identity because of her influence. Her emotive responses revealed a labored, emphatic approach to stressing her preferred ethnic label. Both she and Sixto differed in this regard from their Catholic counterparts.

Catholic respondents in this case demonstrated confidence in their responses through either offering little explanation, or through stressing a natural connection between their faith and their ethnicity. Jose Luis admitted that he had not thought of his preference much, but still processed questions of ethnic identity with confidence and poise. Jesus, Rodrigo, and Saúl appealed to the authority of their faith to bolster their preference for identifying as "Mexican." On the other hand, the evangelical respondents appealed to a more generic authority. They appealed to their place of birth and punctuated their responses through a demonstration of emotion. The confidence shown by some Catholics was not mirrored by any evangelicals.

Regional Legitimacy

Several respondents preferred to be identified as Mexican from a particular region, and here too, Catholics demonstrated higher levels of confidence. Margarita Luna, a Catholic parishioner who served as a caretaker to extended family members, provided a helpful point of comparison to the evangelical responses. Margarita identified ethnically as "Mexicana de Oaxaca" (Mexican from Oaxaca). In her sixties, her weathered yet robust brown skin and stark black hair hearkened to her ancestry in a region that is home to a high proportion of indigenous communities. Margarita frequently referenced aspects of her home state of Oaxaca, noting how much she missed her home region. In Santa Ana, immigrants from Oaxaca were historically a minority, outnumbered by Mexicans originating from states such as Guerrero, Jalisco, and Michoacan. Nonetheless, more recent migration streams from Oaxaca had expanded in recent decades (Kresge 2007). The presence of two Oaxacan restaurants close to Margarita's neighborhood indicated local demand for Oaxacan delicacies.

Margarita volunteered in various ways at her Catholic parish, including helping to organize El Rosario de la Aurora prayer gatherings as well as participating in a home visitation ministry. Having been in the United States for about thirty years, she resided in one of Santa Ana's barrios since her arrival. Within her community, she expressed her Mexican regional culture through cooking and participating in religious festivals, among other things. I initially met Margarita at a Rosario de la Aurora gathering during which she and her husband described to me a special ceremony centered on an image of La Virgen de Juquila, an iteration of the Holy Mother that first appeared in the Mexican state of Oaxaca (Higgins 1990). An image of La Virgen de Juquila was unveiled at this ceremony and she was adorned with new clothing. This ceremony, emulating a practice from their homeland, was organized by a group of Oaxacan devotees in Santa Ana.

While Margarita was nostalgic about her maintenance of Oaxacan customs in the United States, she was not forceful about expressing her commitments. Again, she spoke in a matter-of-fact manner, framing her current practices as a natural extension of her upbringing. Margarita spent much of her time among co-ethnics who shared her religious beliefs and practices, and she valued the fact that she could contribute to the faith experience of others via her regional expertise. The population of Oaxaca includes a high proportion of indigenous residents. Nearly half of the residents of the entire state identify as indigenous.[4] Socioeconomically, the state is known for having high rates of poverty. Still, poverty and homeland distinctions may be imbued with an added sense of ethnic authenticity and legitimacy by the broader co-ethnic community. It is a type of intra-ethnic hypodescent (Waters 1990), wherein ethnic authenticity is attributed to people of lower social status and individuals experience this as their most salient identity. Margarita understood her regional identity to be recognizable and that it was valued by co-ethnics for the resources she provided through this identity. Margarita had nothing to prove. She had already been authenticated.

Carmen Gomez, whose story was introduced at the start of this chapter, also chose a regional Mexican identity as her primary label, but unlike Margarita, she expressed it in a compensatory manner. There was a marked difference between the way that Carmen and Margarita presented their regional Mexican identities. For Carmen, regionality served to overcome the added burden that being non-Catholic placed on her. For Margarita, regionality actually amplified her Catholic religious identity. Margarita's regional identity provided an added legitimacy within her religious community as she was someone able to properly lead others in particular homeland traditions, something I witnessed on several occasions. Carmen, on the other hand, chose to deploy her regional Mexican identity to counterbalance the suspicion aimed her way due to her religious identity. For Carmen, regional identity was compensatory whereas for Margarita it was additive.

Expanding Boundaries through Pan-Ethnicity

Several respondents expressed preference for pan-ethnic labels (i.e., Latino, Hispanic), and here too discursive differences emerged. Miguel Luna, for example, stressed that "Latino" was a term that he preferred to use because it was more inclusive of other Latin Americans. He compared the tendency to label all Latinxs as "Mexican" with a tendency he observed in co-ethnics to refer to all Asians as "Chinese."

[4] Only the Mexican state of Chiapas has a higher percentage of indigenous people than Oaxaca does.

He summarized his views by alluding to a conversation he had with a coworker:

> I use Latino because it is more general and not all Latinos are Mexican. I can refer to people from Asia as Chinese, but not all of them are Chinese, as I was telling one of my co-workers. In the same way, not all Latinos are Mexican.

Miguel, a Catholic parishioner, was heavily involved in neighborhood-based activities organized by the church. More than emphasizing his involvement at church, Miguel stressed that his religious devotion was centered on practicing religious customs in the community. His use of a pan-ethnic label did not indicate that he was attempting to distance himself from other Mexicans or from clearly identifiable aspects of his culture. Even after thirty years in the United States, he was more than happy to talk about the regional feast days observed in his Mexican hometown which he worked to maintain in the United States. Nevertheless, in using a more inclusive label, he felt that he was able to emphasize solidarity with non-Mexican Latinxs. His stated reason for making this decision was that in his work context as a landscaper, he had Latinx co-workers from different regions and countries, and he saw value in building solidarity with non-Mexican Latinxs.

Juanita Vargas, a Catholic parishioner in her mid-forties who held a janitorial job, explained her preference for the pan-ethnic label in the following manner:

JUANITA: I believe that I am Mexican, but here what is used is "Latina." Over there [in Mexico], it's not used. Hispanic isn't used [there] either. Here we are Latinos. I came to learn this here.
JONATHAN: So you use this term to interact with others here in the U.S.?
JUANITA: Latina, now it's Latina. I no longer say Mexican. I know that being Latina includes being Mexican.

Juanita emphasized how "Latina" identification marked a break with how she identified in Mexico, though she believed herself to be "Mexican." She admitted that it was a term she used because she had been exposed to it with more frequency in the United States. She too recognized that Latina/o was a term that was more inclusive, and she implied that this was important; she used Latina/o not merely because it was generally inclusive of all Latinos but also because it included "Mexican." The final acknowledgment of inclusion may seem redundant, but to Juanita this was central to her conceding to a pan-ethnic identification.

Several evangelicals also preferred pan-ethnic labels, but they offered reasons that distinguished them from Catholic co-ethnics. Maite Barrera specified "Hispanic" as the most appropriate label for herself. Having arrived in the United States at the age of six, Maite fit into the category known as the 1.5 generation. She also identified as a "dreamer," denoting that when she entered the United States as a minor, she was undocumented. Her recollections of Mexico were sparse, as she spent most of her childhood in the United States. Now in her early thirties, Maite worked as an administrative assistant. "Normally I usually do Hispanic," Maite admitted, explaining that she did not like to be identified in more particular ethnic ways:

MAITE: I tried to be part of . . . what is that? . . . it's a club that's in high school and goes into college.

JONATHAN: MEChA?

MAITE: Yes, I tried to be part of MEChA, and I was like, "I don't get you." But it's also because I wasn't brought up to have my culture mixed in with my heritage.

Terms such as Mexican, Mexican-American, and Chicano, for Maite, did not capture her experience. She attributed her side-stepping of more particular ethnic labels to her attenuated cultural exposure at home which largely began when Maite was ten years old and her single mother began attending an evangelical church. Attending church quickly became a central component of their week and became one of Maite's primary spaces of social interaction with co-ethnics, in a Latinx majority church. When Maite's mother converted to evangelical Christianity, there was a distancing from many of the social events that would have provided Maite with exposure to the broader co-ethnic community. The fact that Maite migrated at the age of six years old is also important, since most of her life had been lived in the United

States. Though general socialization likely influenced Maite's choice of ethnic labels, a moral boundary rooted in religion that distanced her from certain ethnic spaces was paramount within her narrative. Pan-ethnicity, for Maite, was a way to differentiate herself from co-ethnics.

Federico, an evangelical warehouse worker in his late forties, also preferred a pan-ethnic label so as to distance himself from the more particular label of "Mexican." He explained his preference for Hispanic above Latino, stating, "I do not like the term Latino, but all of us are Hispanic." In similar fashion to others that subscribed to the pan-ethnic label, Federico emphasized the inclusivity of Hispanic: "all of us are Hispanic."

It is notable that several evangelical respondents who preferred a pan-ethnic label chose the term "Hispanic" over the term "Latino." The term "Hispanic" was part of the institutional vocabulary in at least two of the evangelical churches I sampled from, and I heard the term in several evangelical church settings. One possible explanation is that high-level leaders at these evangelical churches had generational ties to the southwestern United States, including Texas, New Mexico, and Arizona. Arguably, the term "Hispanic" has more history in regions occupied by Mexican origin populations for multiple generations. Texas, for example, has long shown a strong inclination toward usage of the term "Hispanic" (Dowling 2005; Lopez 2013; Mindiola et al. 2002). Perhaps the term "Hispanic" in the vocabulary of these Mexican and Mexican-American church leaders trickled down to their parishioners.[5]

The most significant difference in the use of pan-ethnic labels across religious affiliations was not so much the label itself, Latino versus Hispanic, but the meanings Santaneros imbued upon these terms. Catholics tended to emphasize that for them, pan-ethnicity did not exclude "Mexican-ness," but rather was capacious enough to include being Mexican. Evangelicals, on the other hand, used the pan-ethnic label as a way to highlight their distance from homeland labels and from co-ethnics broadly. Maite chose Hispanic because it allowed her to retain a sense of difference from society, but also differentiated her

[5] To be fair, the Catholic Diocese of Orange also employs the term "Hispanic" in some of their literature, but I did not hear the term being used by leaders in the local parishes.

from co-ethnics who preferred more particular labels. Federico, while highlighting the inclusive nature of being "Hispanic," also indicated perceptions about Mexicans that he did not want to be associated with. For evangelicals, then, the pan-ethnic label was a way to highlight intra-ethnic difference. Simultaneously, it provided a way to claim a legitimate place in society as people of color.

Legal Status as a Marker of (il)Legitimacy

The question of legal status provided a counter-current to discussion of ethnicity based on national origin, but only evangelicals drew on legal status as a discursive strategy of ethnic belonging. Leo and Patricia Martinez, both evangelical respondents, initially focused on their national origin when asked about their preferred ethnic label, but they modified their terminology by inserting a statement regarding their legal status. Leo, a landscaper, and Patricia, a homemaker, both in their early fifties, responded in the following manner:

JONATHAN: How do you identify yourself when it comes to your ethnicity?

PATRICIA: For me, Mexican and Latina. I don't have papers. I'm neither from here, nor from there.

JONATHAN: And you use the term Latina also?

PATRICIA: Yes, I am from Mexico.

LEO: I am Mexican, and I opened up my legalization process when amnesty opened up.

PATRICIA: He's a resident.

Initially, Patricia selected the label of "Mexican," along with the modifier "Latina." The subsequent interjection of legal status marked parameters she perceived as constraining the labels available to her. "Mexican" coupled with "Latina" was a way for Patricia to emphasize her descent-based understanding of ethnicity, but also to signify her otherness and her liminality. Patricia was from Mexico but expressed that since she was no longer in Mexico, she could not merely belong to Mexico. Her legal status limited the extent to which she could travel to

Mexico and caused her to live a more restrictive life in the United States for fear of deportation. Patricia still had close family in Mexico, though she had lived in the United States for nearly thirty years. Patricia's legal status held her back from feeling more "American," but also limited her ties to Mexico in practice. "Mexicana y Latina" paralleled her expression, "Ni de aqui ni de alla."[6] As "Mexican," she was "not from here"; as Latina, she was something different from compatriots in the homeland. She was especially differentiating herself from co-ethnics in Mexico. Patricia's legal status magnified her perception of "otherness" on both sides of the border.

Leo, Patricia's husband, made mention of his legal status by explaining he had "papers," which his wife clarified to mean that he was a legal resident. Contrasting with his wife's statement, Leo was emphasizing that he did have legal standing in the United States, but still was Mexican. Mexican was not merely what he called himself; it was what he believed himself to be. "I am Mexican," he asserted, looking at me sternly and nodding his head up and down. Unlike his wife, he did not need a broader pan-ethnic term to emphasize his otherness. It was notable that though Leo's legal residency could have given him more legitimacy in asserting a United States–based identity, it actually allowed him to feel more at ease about asserting a Mexican identity than his wife did. For Patricia, liminality cut both ways.

Two other respondents brought to light their citizenship status in connection to their ethnicity, and both were evangelical. Federico Reyes, introduced previously, stated that he would use the term Hispano because he did not like the term Latino. Federico, having an energetic, outgoing personality, explained further how he felt about the term "Mexican."

FEDERICO: If I identified as Mexican . . . we are American citizens also! A lot of times there's controversy, like, "are you Mexican or are you an American citizen?" We can't call ourselves simply Americans, though, because we don't have blue eyes.

JONATHAN: What about those [Latinos] that call themselves American?

[6] Patricia's words are reminiscent of Gloria Anzaldúa's definition of the term Nepantla, as a liminal status (Anzaldúa 1999).

FEDERICO: I've met some of those. I tell them, "I'm also an American citizen, but I don't identify myself in the same way as you."

For Federico, the term Mexican was closely intertwined with having Mexican citizenship. He valued his US citizenship, and hinted that he did not want his status to be questioned. He recognized the rights his status afforded him. His response reflected the influence of US citizenship on his understanding of ethnicity. Adding "Hispanic" allowed Federico to affirm ethno-racial "otherness." Federico hinted at an experience of racialization by pointing to a physical characteristic: He stated that he and his wife did not have blue eyes. Perhaps he meant to include me in this statement as someone of Mexican origin whom he shared general physical features with. Blue eyes served as a proxy for whiteness. As a person of color, he did not feel comfortable solely identifying as an American or as a US citizen. As people of darker skin tone, and dark hair, it would be highly unlikely for him and his wife to be racialized as white. Furthermore, Federico was undocumented for a number of years. His discursive strategies reveal attempts to counteract the marginalization he was all too familiar with.

Pedro Perez, an evangelical employed in an administrative role at a non-profit organization also introduced citizenship status into his discussion of ethnic identity. When I interviewed Pedro, he wore black slacks and a neatly tucked in, long-sleeved, buttoned shirt. As a church leader who would at times preach and teach at his Pentecostal church, Pedro carried himself in an authoritative manner, speaking with confidence. While Pedro readily described himself as "Mexican," he nuanced his ethnic identity with notions of citizenship:

> Being a Christian means being a follower of Christ. I want people to see me as a follower of Christ. The term Christian was first used in ancient Antioch to identify followers of Jesus. I don't mind if they identify me as a Mexican, or as a Christian. I don't have a problem with one or the other. How people see me, how they identify me, really depends on the context. When I'm around Christians, they know that I'm a Christian and that's how they identify me. I want non-Christians to also know that I'm a Christian. When I'm out in public,

people are going to see me as Mexican, but first they have to see me as a citizen.

Pedro's inclusion of citizenship into his discussion of ethnic identity suggested that this was an aspect of his identity that he situated in juxtaposition to ethnicity. In some ways, his life as a citizen was paralleled to his life as a Christian. Citizenship may not have been something that could be ascertained by his physical appearance, but he hoped others would recognize it when enacted in the public arena.

Pedro had formerly been undocumented. A man of brown skin and stark black hair, Pedro would hardly be confused for being white. He was aware that his phenotype signaled Latinx ethnicity. Faith and citizenship, by Pedro's estimation, required performative expression. According to Pedro, this was important because, "my legal status influences the place that I have in society and also how I am viewed by others." Pedro's discourse presents the other side of the coin to what Guzman Garcia (2016) posits as "spiritual citizenship," a religious appeal to avoid deportability. In the case of Pedro, he had avoided deportability given his current status, but he still wanted to be recognized for having achieved citizenship, which he understood as being paralleled by his Christian devotion.

American Identification

For several respondents, the preferred term of self-identification included the word "American." These responses consisted of American, Mexican-American, and Hispanic-American. While these three terms do not all mean the same thing, they do all make reference to the United States as an integral aspect of identification. To be fair, these three terms each take a particular angle on "American-ness." Given the context and reference points expressed by the respondents that used these terms, I have chosen to group these responses together.

Two respondents, Abel Lopez and Delia Carrillo, referred to themselves as "Mexican-American." Both Abel and Delia were brought to the United States at young ages. Delia came to the United States in the early '60s while Abel came to the United States in the late '60s, both as children. They both arrived in Santa Ana on the cusp of the major boom in Santa Ana's Latinx population (Gonzalez 2017). They were raised in contexts inhabited by Chicanos and others who had lived in the United States most of their lives. These were generally racialized contexts, with high degrees of segregation.

Abel, for example, was labeled as a cholo because of how he dressed and carried himself. Prior to his religious conversion into evangelical Christianity, his appearance drew others to judge him as a gang member. Moreover, Abel had an experience of belonging to a subculture, Chicano street culture, that carried with it a certain level of marginalization in broader society (Flores 2014). It is, nonetheless, a subculture characterized by many cultural elements originating in the United States, such as its music, its car culture, and its style of dress.

Delia recalled a number of experiences where she was discriminated against in salient ways. Like Abel, Delia had very little memory of Mexico. Like Abel, she too emphasized her "American-ness," in conjunction with an experience of being the "other." Delia was Catholic, and she explained that much of her spirituality was lived out among co-ethnics. She recalled a time when her local parish offered few services for Latinxs. During that time period, about fifty years ago, Mexicans clung to their faith through community and home-based practices, according to Delia.

For Obed Herrera, a term denoting a broader pan-ethnic identity, coupled with the label "American," seemed most fitting; Obed referred to himself as "Hispanic-American." Obed was the sole respondent that was not born in Mexico, though he was a migrant in the sense that he grew up in Mexico for part of his youth and then migrated back to the United States as an adult. Through the course of my research I found that in Santa Ana patterns of circular migration were common, even for some US-born ethnic Mexicans; with the fortification of the border and of immigration policy in recent decades, such patterns had grown less common. Obed completed several years of his high school education in Mexico. He clearly recalled the experience of moving between cultural worlds, a case that illustrates the borderlands reality that many of Santa Ana's residents experience and the manner in which rigid labels of generation do not always capture the lived realities of individuals. Now in his late forties, Obed's wife was a Mexican immigrant. Much of Obed's ethnic connection was maintained via his involvement in his Latinx congregation but he had also had access to educational and employment resources that others did not have. His response, that of "Hispanic-American," highlighted his free-thinking personality, and gave a nod to pan-ethnicity while simultaneously acknowledging his partial upbringing in the United States.

For Beto Flores, a real estate agent in his late fifties, the preferred term of ethnic identification was "American." Having come to the United States as a toddler, Beto had little to no recollection of Mexico. In my interview with Beto, he recalled many memories of growing up in the San Diego area, and soon after in the Artesia-Pilar neighborhood of Santa Ana, one of the city's oldest Mexican barrios. Beto recalled the demographic shifts that were taking place in Santa Ana in the '60s and '70s. During my interview with him, he conjured up memories of an era when Mexican immigrants and Chicanos were viewed as outsiders and as a minority. With an entrepreneurial spirit, Beto fought his way up the pay scale having begun work as a grocery checker in young adulthood.

Beto retold with detail a number of stories indicating the racial stereotypes and structural disadvantages that he had to overcome to achieve some level of financial stability. Contrasting the marked outsider status he and his family endured throughout his childhood and early adulthood, Beto's life now reflected a semblance of middle-class status.[7] He spoke in articulate, standard English, but could also code switch to Chicano street slang. His thoughtful vocabulary was consistent with his narrative of having performed well in school despite being tracked into lower tiers of academic rigor, arguably because of his ethnicity. Being able to call himself "American" was an achievement more than an ascribed status for Beto.

Those that used the term "American" in their identification shared several important characteristics: They all had lived in the United States forty to fifty years, had worked in settings with ethnic, racial, or socioeconomic diversity, had experienced being a minority in their community and/or job setting, and had also achieved a high level of

[7] See Vallejo (2012) for a discussion of middle-class Latinxs with ties to Santa Ana and their continued relationship to the barrio.

structural assimilation into the workforce. Moreover, they had employment opportunities where they worked in non-blue-collar jobs, expressed a sense of job stability, and had other career options available to them if a particular job did not work out. This group tended to be among the most assimilated. Even still, these respondents also demonstrated a desire to sustain ethnic identification, both through co-ethnic networks and through cultural practices. Indeed, for all of these respondents, their support network consisted entirely of co-ethnics. The boundary that was brightened by these respondents' responses contrasted their higher levels of structural assimilation with that of their local co-ethnics. This is relative, however. It is possible that in other contexts, their ethnic identity would have been far more salient.

Discussion: Negotiating Boundaries

Prominent patterns emerge across religious affiliations in regard to ethnic self-identification: Generally, Catholics were far more confident in their choices of ethnic labels and felt little need to elaborate on their responses. When Catholics did elaborate on their responses, they often shared about the linkages between Catholic devotion and Mexican identity. For these Catholics, Mexican ethnic identity had been divinely authorized by the inculturation of La Virgen de Guadalupe. Some Catholics also tended to emphasize their commitment to a particular Mexican region, in some cases punctuated by religious practices tied to their region of origin. For Catholics who selected a pan-ethnic label, the tendency was to emphasize that pan-ethnicity was inclusive of Mexican identity. Moreover, those that identified pan-ethnically stressed the solidarity that pan-ethnicity signaled to other Latinxs. Catholics did not speak of legal status in relation to ethnic identity, suggesting that for them legal status did not alter or affect their prospects of identifying with a broader ethnic community, even if it did affect their prospects of US incorporation.

Evangelicals, on the other hand, either claimed to be Mexican in a more forceful, emotional manner when compared to Catholics, or articulated label preferences that discursively differentiated them from the broader co-ethnic community. The use of a regional Mexican identity was done in order to gain credibility among co-ethnics. The use of a pan-ethnic label—Hispanic—was a way to be differentiated from other co-ethnics who were more likely to use Latina/o and to emphasize its inclusion of Mexican ethnicity. Legal status was spoken of as either a hindrance or as an entry point into US society, an important accomplishment that had ramifications for ethnic self-identity claims. The strategy of seeking legitimacy through the state is similar to Vila's finding about evangelicals in Mexico who "detach their *religious* identity from their *national* one, and then they reattach their national identity to the most important *secular* elements of it" (2005:64). What Vila is intimating is that many evangelical Mexicans attempt to show their legitimate ethnic identities through "secular" means, knowing that religious pathways of legitimacy are dominated by Catholic expression among co-ethnics.

In the United States, among Latinxs, non-Catholic religious identities may provide a perceived pathway of societal legitimation (Chavez 2013; see also Ammerman 1997) but may simultaneously constrain immigrants' options in ethnic self-identification among co-ethnics. Some evangelicals, it seemed, experienced authenticity policing at the hands of the Catholic majority. However, among those who were more structurally incorporated into US society, co-ethnic authenticity policing was less potent, as suggested by those who responded as "American." It seemed that those that had achieved some degree of social mobility were less invested in asserting Mexican ethnicity, perhaps signaling that their social circles placed less weight on this identity or perhaps seeking legitimacy through embracing an "American" identity.[8]

Given the historical marginalization of ethnic-Mexican peoples in the United States, discursive strategies of identification often provide potent forms of self-affirmation and signal ties, whether real or desired, to legitimized segments of society (Sears et al. 2003). For those of unauthorized status in the United States, for example, alternative

[8] 7% of Latinx immigrants select "American" as their primary label of choice, over and above other ethnic labels, according to Lopez et al. (2017).

pathways of legitimacy become crucial (Coutin 2013; Fishman 1968; Sassen 2002). Asserting an "American" identity, or a pan-ethnic identity, may provide members of marginalized populations a sense of legitimacy based on state and/or societal promotion of these labels (Omi and Winant 2014). On the other hand, identifying with a particularistic ethnic label may facilitate legitimation from co-ethnics but denote social distance from whites. While evangelical identity would have been legitimized within a broad segment of US society, in central Santa Ana, it was looked upon with suspicion in terms of ethnic membership. It was Catholic identity, in this case, and especially Guadalupan devotion, that was more broadly embraced for signaling Mexican identity. The ethnic space of central Santa Ana, it seemed, was segmented by religious affiliation.

4
Altar Encounters

"¡Muchacho! ¡Muchacho! ¡Muevete! ¡Muevete!" (Young man! Young man! Move out of the way! Move out of the way!) In the midst of the celebration at the apartment courtyard on Myrtle Street, I looked around and realized that these words, spoken faintly yet firmly, were directed at me. Amid the buzz of conversation and music, I nearly missed the elderly woman, likely in her late seventies, sitting at a table a few feet away from me. I stood at the end of a row of tables, one of two rows, with the other lined up about ten feet away. The rows cut through the courtyard between two apartment buildings, visually directing new arrivals toward the centerpiece of the celebration—La Virgen de Guadalupe. An expansive portable canopy of white canvas and metal rods sheltered the tables and temporarily nestled the feast day scene within its larger concrete context. As I conversed with several local residents, at the edge of the last table, I was awakened to the fact that I was blocking the elderly woman's line of sight to the Blessed Mother.

A provisional altar of sorts had been set up with three images of La Virgen de Guadalupe placed side by side at the end of the table rows. The images, in statue form, had processed into the neighborhood alongside devotees after the feast day mass at the local parish. The images stood atop metal carts, each adorned with an abundance of flowers at their feet, shiny robes draped over their shoulders, and spotlights affixed at their bases. Each image had been accompanied by a sign denoting the neighborhoods they were typically stationed at. These images had homes, after all, and were cared for. "Viva la Virgen de la Myrtle de Santa Ana," read one sign, handwritten on orange poster board, indicating that this particular image belonged on Myrtle Street. This image was distinguished from among the rest by a crown of flowers floating atop her head. A more permanent altar stood a few feet away at the corner of the apartment courtyard and this temporary

The Saints of Santa Ana. Jonathan E. Calvillo, Oxford University Press (2020). © Oxford University Press.
DOI: 10.1093/oso/9780190097790.001.0001.

display functioned as an extension of that permanent space. The altar had reached outward, occupying more of the neighborhood.

I was taking in the sight of the altar as the elderly woman implored me to move. I took three steps back and asked for her pardon. "Disculpeme," I uttered, somewhat embarrassed. Ensuring I understood why she had directed me away, she added, "¿Que no ve que quiero estar aquí viéndola?" (Can't you see that I want to be here seeing her?) As she ended this statement, she breathed a sigh of relief. There was no question as to the "her" she was referring to. Her eyes readily locked onto the countenance, the very eyes, of that particular image of la Virgen de Guadalupe, the one that resided in her neighborhood. The woman's momentarily rigid facial lines quickly softened into an expression of tenderness as she contemplated the Holy Mother. Despite the movement and noise occupying the surrounding vicinity, this woman shared a special moment with La Virgencita (Castañeda-Liles 2018). Her concentration remained fixed to the altar to La Virgen de Guadalupe.

Altars, I would come to observe, could offer life-changing moments for Santaneros, moments to affirm something new, or moments to acknowledge rootedness. They could be spaces of marked redirection, or spaces of re-centering upon what was long assented to. The altar, it seemed, was a space where time stood still—where space itself took on a different meaning, apart from the mundane. More than physical structures or physical spaces, altars were characterized as spaces of encounter, and as moments of altered awareness. These moments were bases that believers returned to, to find a sense of focus. They functioned as the ritual practices that Swidler (1986) describes as forming part of the "tool-kit" individuals draw from during unsettled times. From these springboards, believers would begin to believe for the first time—or for the first time in a long time. If ever a moment of transformation occurred away from the altar, the altar was often sought out as a space to affirm or confirm that what had taken place was real. People seemed to find their way to the altar, or the altar would find its way to them. For a significant number of my subjects, altars were of utmost importance.

An observable divergence between Catholics' and evangelicals' notions of altars related to the temporal-spatial interpretation given to these spaces. There was a temporal reality to altars related to the before and after of divine encounters that was prominent in the accounts of evangelical converts (Winchester 2015). The encounters that took place at the altar forced people to take account of who they had been and who they would be. For evangelicals, altars were especially a place that marked breaking away from the past. For Catholics, altars were often a place to reaffirm what they had known to be true. Scholars have grappled with questions like these—questions of how religious experience spurs continuity or discontinuity in the lives of spiritual seekers.

For immigrants, questions of continuity and discontinuity are compounded because the change experienced in migration is not only temporal, a process experienced through the progression of time, but also spatial, a process experienced through the movement across geographies. In the words of Thomas Tweed (1997), diasporic expressions of religion are "translocative" and "transtemporal."[1] Immigrant believers encounter strong motivators in their very experiences of movement and in the passing of time to interpret punctuated faith encounters in relation to changes in geography. Altar moments for immigrants are best understood as temporal-spatial realities.

Discontinuity at the Altar

Jorge Alvarado could not quite figure out what was wrong with his body. His sense of fatigue and occasional pain was starting to hinder his ability to work. Running his house painting business required him to both engage in physical labor at a rapid pace and to employ administrative acumen, tasks that were becoming increasingly difficult. After a number of medical consultations, a definitive diagnosis was yet to be had. It occurred to Jorge, that his problem was more than physical. He believed someone was inflicting a spiritual curse upon him.

[1] Tweed argues that religions in essence should be understood as spatial practices with temporal implications. He writes, "As spatial practices, religions are active verbs linked with unsubstantial nouns by bridged prepositions: *from*, *with*, *in*, *between*, *through*, and most important, *across*. Religions designate where we are from, identify whom we are with, and prescribe how we move across" (Tweed 2009:79).

He decided to go to a local *botanica*,[2] a shop that offered customers a blend of herbal and spiritual cures for their ailments. In Santa Ana, storefront botanicas rest alongside of businesses like liquor stores, tax offices, check cashing centers, restaurants, etc. Some botanicas double as other types of businesses, such as a print shop, and not in clandestine fashion. Jorge visited one such shop to seek assistance for his physical pain and returned multiple times once the *curandera*[3] confirmed his suspicion that indeed someone had inflicted evil upon him.

After several unsuccessful consultations with the same *curandera*, Jorge received an alarming prescription. The *curandera* told Jorge that he should find an evangelical church where he could be prayed over. They would be able to help him, she assured. Jorge was taken aback by this suggestion, but in his desperation, decided he had nothing to lose by following this plan. Until then, he considered himself Catholic. One of his brothers had visited a nearby evangelical church, and he decided to visit that particular congregation. After several visits to the church, his pain completely disappeared. One of the turning points took place when Jorge was prayed for at the church, just as the *curandera* had said. Within the church, Jorge was prayed for at an important place—at the altar.

In evangelical churches, altars were partially denoted by physical markers, and partially denoted by the activities that took place within them. Evangelical altars were less physically contained than Catholic ones. For evangelical churches that had a stage, the altar was most typically the space before the stage. For churches or spaces that did not have a stage, the altar would have been the space directly in front of where the primary speaker would speak. Altars were characterized as spaces of prayer, most typically occupied after a preacher gave some sort of "altar call," to people in attendance. Some churches used altars for more regular prayer spaces outside of larger church services.

[2] Botanicas are shops that fall into the realm of folk or popular religion, often selling amulets, relics, incense, candles, and a variety of hands-on procedural services dispensed by spiritual healers or *curanderos*.

[3] *Curandera/os* are healers that employ a variety of folk medicine techniques to cure clients or assist them with difficult situations. Mull and Mull (1983) indicate that in the 1980s Orange County may have had about one thousand practitioners of *curanderismo*.

For Jorge, his quest to find relief from his physical pain brought him to a place of religious change at the altar. Jorge's spiritual orientation was altered. Soon after, he began to attend the evangelical church regularly with his family and involved himself more fully in the church, joining a choir and volunteering as an usher. He credited his physical illness with leading him to spiritual wholeness. Jorge now identified as an evangelical Christian. He expressed no need to return to a botanica or a *curandera*, and neither to reconnect with a Catholic church. Jorge now served as a lay minister within his church and one of the characteristics he most appreciated about his church was the way that people "seek the presence of God" during the services there. He saw himself as a man that had been thoroughly transformed. He had left the past behind.

Continuity at the Altar

Catholics had much to say about altars. The partaking of Holy Communion at the altar was indeed of utmost importance to many Santaneros that I spoke with. Even for several Catholic informants that hesitated to partake of the Eucharist, their reluctance was marked by a disagreement about how it was being administered, a phenomenon noted by Matovina (2011). When my Catholic informants mentioned communion, they most typically spoke about it with reverence. Moreover, in participation or non-participation, Catholics gave importance to the Eucharist. Communion was most typically an act of quiet devotion for them, not an act of braggadocio. Yet, in the neighborhoods, Catholic Santaneros spoke more effusively about a different type of altar—home and community altars. Certainly, the Eucharist was of utmost importance to my Catholic informants, but there was something distinct about the altars that they themselves fashioned and presided over within their own personal spaces. These home and neighborhood altars were the spaces that most typically operated in contrast to the evangelical altar.

For Gerardo Zamora, for example, the prominence of his home altar was fused to a trying experience that he and his family endured. Gerardo's eyes welled up with tears as he recounted the time that his brother was kidnapped by lower-level drug cartel operatives. He explained, "That was a very tough moment for my family. This was my youngest brother who was living in Tijuana. They kidnapped him so that they could make some money. They put out a ransom for him and they wanted us to pay for it. We don't have a lot of money, but we got together what we could. Everyone was worried because he's the youngest out of all of us. We're all married and have families and he's the only one that lives with my parents." Gerardo described how he became exceedingly focused on an image of La Virgen de Guadalupe that they had at their home. He said that he, "asked and asked of the *virgencita* that she would answer our prayer." The kidnappers communicated with family members that they would murder the young man if they did not receive the amount of money they were requesting.

Gerardo triumphantly described how his prayers were answered: "We couldn't get the amount of money that they were asking from us, but we got close to it. We offered them what we had, and they accepted it. Then, when it came time for them to let my brother go, something happened. They had some kind of mix up. It seems that they didn't plan the handover correctly. Then one of the kidnappers abandoned the other one. The police were able to catch them. Our prayers were answered! My brother was free!"

While Gerardo and his family had images of the Virgen de Guadalupe at their home, it was after this moment of crisis that he put together a more ostentatious altar within their living room. This was a spiritual revival of sorts for the Zamora family. The altar became a central part of their family life. According to Gerardo, "the kids respect the altar. They sometimes point out when something on the altar needs attention. My daughter especially pays attention to this, more than my son. They take care of it." Gerardo's facial expression reflected a sense of satisfaction and pride when he described his children's attentiveness to the care of the altar.

The minimalist altar initially present in the Zamora home became a central space of devotion to them during and after their family crisis. Now, Gerardo and his wife, Araceli, would more frequently participate in neighborhood processions or posada celebrations. In the trailer park where they lived, a community altar had been set up next to the communal laundromat. The Zamoras would sometimes come together to pray with neighbors there. While they were not previously consistent in their faith involvement, tragedy brought them to more regularly participate in acts of devotion. Because they both worked multiple jobs, they were sometimes forced to miss their preferred Sunday mass. Nevertheless, they now attended Sunday mass nearly every week. Devotional practices at home remained all the more important as the altar grew, both figuratively and literally, in the lives of the Zamoras.

Gerardo Zamora immigrated from the Mexican city of Guadalajara, and Jorge Alvarado migrated from Mexico City. Both households, in this case, had their roots in urban centers in Mexico, unlike many of their rurally rooted neighbors. For both the Zamoras and the Alvarados, Catholic devotion was something that they brought from Mexico. Gerardo and Jorge both followed pathways wherein dealing with a moment of crisis drew them to seek a faith-centered solution. One sought a solution that drew him away from the faith he held in his homeland and the other sought a solution that reinforced his existing faith. In Jorge's case, his seeking help from a *curandera* already drew him beyond the boundaries of the traditional Catholic church. For Gerardo, too, his focus was not within the institutional church, per se, but was at least centered on practices that were encouraged by the parishes of Santa Ana. For one, crisis drew him to a moment of punctuated continuity, and for the other, crisis drew him to a pathway of discontinuity.

Continuity at the Altar: Faith through Migration

While for some, altar moments broke into their lives in unexpected ways, for others, altar moments were routinized. Indeed, routinized altar moments were often sought out when all else was unpredictable. The space of the altar here was less about change and more about confronting change. For some, the altar brought stability in the face of change. The altared habitus (Bourdieu 1984),[4] when the altar

[4] Manglos-Weber (2010) argues that conversion is both about belief and behavior, but is critical of frameworks that overly emphasize belief. Premawhardana offers a similar critique, downplaying a logocentric thrust and arguing for more focus on "corporeal

was embodied, compelled the individual to seek, to recreate, and to share the altar experience. Such was the case with many migrants. It is no surprise that altars dot the path of many a migratory journey (Hagan 2008).

The story of the Delgado family illustrates the propensity of Catholics for establishing altar moments and spaces for altars in their lives. "I am Catholic to the core," Francisca Delgado broadcast proudly while conversing with me at her Santa Ana home. From the corner of her living room, a conspicuous altar to La Virgen de Guadalupe silently echoed her declaration. Born into Catholicism in their native state of Michoacán, both Francisca and her husband Ricardo indicated that their Catholic faith was a dominant aspect of their lives together. The role of faith in the lives of the Delgados became central to them soon after they were married and prior to migrating to the United States. Certain practices that they learned in their household setting in Mexico would come to signal the authenticity of their faith and would provide stabilizing effects as they migrated to the United States.

During a season of their lives when the Delgados rarely went to mass, Francisca recalled feeling troubled, as if "something were missing." The devotion of Ricardo's mother, Doña Tomasa, was instrumental in nurturing devotional consistency in Francisca and Ricardo. "My mother-in-law showed us how to pray the rosary. She would go to the via crucis, and she would prepare our children for their first communion." Tomasa not only modeled faith to her son and daughter-in-law but also actively instructed her grandchildren in the faith. Catholic faith, for the Delgados, was largely cultivated through following the rhythms set forth by Doña Tomasa. Their family history reflects a localized, intergenerational faith. Efforts of constructing continuity through familial practices would assist the Delgados in the process of settling into Santa Ana's urban spaces.

The Delgados' faith prominently punctuated their migration narrative. Venturing to the United States alone in 1980, Ricardo's first US passage marked an important milestone in the Delgados' faith

dispositions, mundane metaphors, and quotidian practices" (2018:15). I frame this experience as a habitus, in agreement with these scholars, to emphasize the embodied nature of these conversion and conversion-like experiences.

journey. Ricardo's Catholic faith provided a sense of security as he migrated to the United States; he believed he would be unscathed on his trek across geographic borderlands, and that his family would be safe back in Mexico. An undocumented immigrant unsure of the duration of his US sojourn, Ricardo eventually accumulated twenty-four years residing stateside apart from Francisca. For nearly two decades, Ricardo adopted a circular migration pattern, undertaking an annual faith-filled journey back to his family, then returning stateside. Three of Ricardo's four children were born while he was away. Before every journey, Ricardo followed a routine of spiritual exercises. Francisca paralleled these through her own prayers. Ricardo recounted: "I would pray a novena to El Santo Niño de Atocha or to La Virgen. I also had faith that when Francisca prayed for me, well, I would arrive here." Ricardo's work in construction was grueling, but his spiritual practices motivated him to persevere. As heightened border vigilance made circular migration increasingly implausible, concerted prayers shifted focus to Delgado household unification. Through this transitional period, faith provided a sense of continuity and groundedness in an otherwise alienating experience.

In 2004, with Ricardo now a US citizen, Francisca and her two youngest children left Mexico and joined Ricardo in Santa Ana. Walking distance from their new apartment, the Delgados began attending mass on a weekly basis at Immaculate Heart of Mary, a Latinx majority parish with over five thousand households on its membership rolls. Parish participation bolstered family cohesion, though Ricardo sheepishly admitted to skipping mass during heavy work weeks. The neighborhood provided a site of religious community as well, with the Delgados often participating in neighborhood-based activities related to their faith, such as processions, and feast days. Soon after settling into their densely populated neighborhood, neighbors of shared faith proved a source of support for the Delgados and vice-versa. Even recently, Francisca, who identified as an *ama de casa*, or housewife, made money providing childcare for neighborhood children at her home. According to Francisca, "the faith brings unity in the community for those of us who are Catholic."[5] The Delgados especially appreciated the

[5] "La fe trae unidad en la comunidad para los que somos católicos."

way that practices from Mexico had been reproduced in their neighborhood. The practices were not identical to those in Mexico, but the semblance was sufficient to be appreciated. These forms of communal continuity had been central during the season following their family reunification.

Catholicism offered the Delgados important avenues for constructing continuity, or maintaining ties with their past. The familial link provided through Catholic devotion was an aspect of constructed continuity that highlighted the personal ties embodied in these practices. Continuity on one level was perceived and imagined, mostly symbolic. Actions and objects proved to be strong symbols, such as devotion to La Virgen de Guadalupe. At another level, the continuity related to actual intergenerational interaction, wherein traditions and customs were being passed on within a household. Maintaining tradition in collaboration with living family was arguably one of the simplest, most concrete ways to construct continuity. The practices themselves, in this case, were potent forms of constructed continuity because they pointed to not only an honoring of family tradition in an abstract sense, but also to an honoring of specific family members. Whereas in Chapter 1 I introduced the notion that religion links people to an ancient past, the Delgados' story in this chapter highlights that ties to the past may be embodied through intergenerational linkages merely one or two generations removed.

Secondly, Catholicism aided the Delgados through periods of transition. Experiences of crossing borders and of being apart from each other were perhaps the most taxing of transitions experienced by the Delgados. Catholic ritual provided a certain toolkit that had a stabilizing effect on the Delgados emotional well-being. While this contribution of faith also related to beliefs about divine protection, and was not reduced merely to continuity, the experience of continuity provided the Delgado's with an added sense of wholeness. That is, there were aspects of the Delgados' identities that persisted, even through the most treacherous and humbling moments. In this case, continuity was less intergenerational, and more individual. Still, these components functioned together, ancient, intergenerational, and personal continuity.

Finally, there was a temporal-spatial dimension that was prominent in the story of the Delgados. In moving to a neighborhood that provided them with communal experiences of Mexican Catholicism, the Delgados were able to communally construct a sense of continuity. Constructing continuity beyond the bounds of the individual or the household in a spatially situated community made these efforts all the more significant by reproducing a sense of shared peoplehood within a spatial location. Likewise, the homeland was the place of previous habitation. Though it continued to be home for family members and old neighbors, and though transnational ties allowed for vibrant cultural and religious exchanges across borders, within the personal narrative of the Delgados, the homeland was now in the past. The spatial and temporal in this sense were interconnected. The chronology of the immigrant narrative was by its very nature a fusion of temporal and spatial elements. Even in cases where US immigrants maintained a desire to return to the homeland, there was still a desire to maintain what they "temporarily" had given up. Ricardo, for example, toyed around with the idea of retiring in Mexico, but knew that he would not be able to completely uproot his family. His adult children were now well established in the United States. Mexico could still have been in his envisioned future, but for the time being, it was a past that he labored to bring into his present.

Evangelical Faith and Reformative Ruptures

The story of migration and settlement told by Xochitl and Vicente Garza was less about continuity and more about change. In the mid-1980s, a few years after Ricardo Delgado came to the United States, Xochitl and Vicente migrated to the United States from their native state of Guerrero. Born into Catholicism, Xochitl and Vicente were now committed to their Pentecostal church, Templo Calvario. Yet, they certainly had much to say about their past experiences in Catholicism. Indeed, much of their descriptions of their religious participation in Mexico emphasized why they believed they needed to distance themselves from the Catholic church. The Garza's narratives were largely about breaking with the past.

Xochitl and Vicente were married by the Catholic church and both stated that they identified as Catholic in Mexico. Vicente, for example, asserted that "I was one of those Catholics that goes to church every Sunday." Yet, Vicente was especially emphatic about why he disavowed the Catholic church. He explained that, "I knew priests that would drink, that had women, and carried guns. I walked away when I saw that there were representatives of God in the Catholic church that were doing wrong. When I was a child, I believed in God very strongly, but with what I saw, I left the church and I distanced myself from God." Interestingly enough, Vicente claimed God was already present in his life in his early years, while he was Catholic, but he blamed the wrongs he witnessed in the Catholic church for weakening his faith. Despite his criticism of the Catholic church, Vicente's account nevertheless suggested that his belief in God was nurtured by his initial upbringing in the Catholic church.

Xochitl's story highlighted a different type of rupturing with the past. For Xochitl, a distancing from the Catholic church was secondary to a distancing from a dysfunctional past.[6] Similar to the Delgados, the Garzas experienced periods of separation after migration to the United States, but in this case it was due to Xochitl leaving Vicente periodically to go back to Mexico. According to Xochitl, "I had left him. We had a lot of problems and we couldn't live together anymore." On three separate occasions, Xochitl left Vicente for several months at a time. She would return to her family in Mexico during these times. For several years, this cycle of separation and pseudo-reconciliation went on. "We kept trying to work it out, but we couldn't," Xochitl reflected. Vicente described the situation by placing the blame on both of them, but then zeroing in on his own guilt: "We had strong personalities. Both of us did. Neither of us would give in. But, you know, in Mexico, men are macho and can't allow a woman to control you.[7] So that was

[6] Mayrarque effectively encapsulates conversion in the following manner: "The language of rupture is twofold: The break with former beliefs and practices and the break with the life led until that moment with the two breaks linked as one" (2001:286). Several scholars characterize this shift as a bridge-burning experience, drawing from Goffman (Brenneman 2011; Alvarez 2015). Meyer (1998) goes so far as to say that time itself becomes an epistemological category. In Meyer's estimation, converts hold the past in tension. They recognize themselves as products of the past, but also recognize the past as a burden.

[7] See Brusco (2011) for a discussion of machismo and conversion in Latin America.

my problem." Their situation appeared hopeless to both of them, and Xochitl admitted that "we were at the point of divorce."

Xochitl explained that in a period of marital despair, "I cried out to God. There was a Christian radio station that I would sometimes listen to, even before I ever went to a Christian church. I put on that station and listened to it. The words, the music, and the sermons, spoke to my spirit. I prayed that night. I asked God into my heart. I felt the presence of God that moment." A friend had invited the Garzas to her home for a home Bible study, and soon after Xochitl's prayer incident, Xochitl and Vicente accepted the invitation. Both of them felt the need for some sort of intervention. Xochitl had a much stronger sense of needing spiritual intervention. Vicente accepted the invitation mostly because he was curious to see what evangelicalism was about. For about two months, they visited the Bible study. The host friend was a member of Templo Calvario and had been an evangelical Christian for several years. After two months of visiting the Bible study, they accepted their friend's invitation to attend a church service at Templo Calvario.

Xochitl quickly found a spiritual home in the evangelical church, understanding that the experience she had after listening to the evangelical radio station was a declaration of faith and finding commonality in what she experienced at church. She took the initiative in opening her house to a home Bible study sponsored by Templo Calvario. According to Xochitl, "When we opened up our home to the Bible studies, we started seeing healings in our home." For Vicente, these testimonies of healing were the tipping point for him to make a commitment of faith within an evangelical community.

> At first, I went to church just to see what it was about. I thought it was corrupt like the Catholic church in Mexico. I started to like it, but I wasn't convinced. I expected to see something bad, like pastors getting rich from the church offerings. One whole year passed, and I was attending. It was then that the Lord touched me. I couldn't resist more. I didn't believe in miracles, but when I saw what God was doing in people's lives, that took the doubts away.[8]

[8] Chesnut (1997) groups conversion factors into three helpful categories: Crisis, Contact, and Cure. He argues that conversion narratives often begin with an experience

At a fateful church gathering, Vicente prayed a prayer to "give [his] heart to Jesus," and had been committed since then. It is notable that for Vicente, in describing his conversion experience, differentiating his current experience from his perceptions of the Catholic church was important, but within Xochitl's personal narrative, this was not a dominant theme. Much of Xochitl's hardship, it seemed, originated with Vicente's obstinate attitude, not with her issues with the Catholic church.

The Garza household was now comprised of two parents, two teenagers, and one pre-teen. The Garza children had largely grown up in the evangelical church. Xochitl and Vicente prided themselves in being consistently active at their church. Xochitl was active in church activities up to five times a week, on a regular basis. She was involved in everything from Bible institute courses, to church Bible studies, to volunteering at a food pantry program. Vicente lamented that he was currently only a "*dominguero*," someone that only attends church on Sundays. Previously, he was more involved, but his work schedule as a truck driver kept him away. Much of Vicente's musings about the future had to do with him not only thinking about prospering at his job, but also being able to return to more extensive church participation. He and Xochitl seemed to have left their conflictive history far in the past.

For evangelicals, the past was a catch all category characterized by experiences that inhibit spiritual flourishing. This may have included hardships and vices that had been or should have been left behind. It may have included religious and spiritual practices that were now deemed to be erroneous. While distancing from the past may have taken time, there was nearly always a definitive point within evangelicals' timeline that they would point to as signaling their internal transformation. The experience of conversion, of being born-again, was a point at which a rupture with the past took place. Those things which categorically belonged in the past no longer marked the person. Certainly, evangelicals may have struggled with a variety of vices and hardships post-conversion. The lives of these working-class

of crisis, and at some point, many a narrative is punctuated by an illness or social malady being cured through supernatural intervention.

evangelicals were far from worry-free; still, there was a sense with which these experiences no longer fractured the integrity of the evangelical Christian. They had been made whole through breaking with these things.

In the interview process, it was clear that conversion was an orienting frame around which evangelicals structured their personal narratives. In alignment with what Vila proposes in his study of Mexicans at the Juarez-El Paso border region, conversion becomes the primary "narrative plot" around which all other aspects of life are situated. Vila argues that "these kinds of interviewees are somehow taught to accept the hegemonic discourse advanced by their church as their unique narrative framework" (2005:11). In other words, Vila situates this reorientation within the institutional context. Sanchez-Walsh (2003) also argues that these narratives are highly influenced by ideal types enshrined within institutional spaces (see also Winchester 2015). That is, converts construct and shape their narratives based on the ways in which they are socialized to discuss their personal experiences. I agree with Vila and Sanchez-Walsh in that churches play a powerful role in socializing members within their respective institutions. Such discourses are reinforced time and again through testimonies, sermons, and Bible studies. I witnessed these efforts as I visited evangelical gatherings.

However, there are additional components to conversion narratives of people such as that of Xochitl that are not fully encompassed within the institutional sphere, or at least not within the sphere of institutional membership. For example, for Xochitl and several of her evangelical peers, the experience of conversion was spurred by contacts with the evangelical message outside of the institutional context. That is, potential converts interacted with friends or even media outlets that espoused an evangelical message. While it is difficult to measure the degree of influence that these external contacts exercised over "future" evangelicals, it is clear that such elements were present and active in the broader community.

An additional extra-institutional element surfaced when evangelicals reported some type of emotional and/or "supernatural" encounter that motivated them to identify within the evangelical faith tradition. Xochitl's experience of "crying out to God," was one such example, but I encountered others that were more dramatic. In other words, it is possible that a strong affective connection to something that is understood as conversion precedes an institutional socialization process. Certainly, it should be noted that these experiences in a study of this nature are reported in retrospect, at a point from which they have already interacted with institutional influences. Nevertheless, my observations suggest the presence of socializing mechanisms that permeate the social milieu, and which work in concert with strong affective experiences, so as to move some individuals toward a more regulated conversion narrative. The institution may solidify and streamline the conversion narrative, but the socializing process often begins before institutional affiliation has been cemented. The evangelical message has so permeated places like Santa Ana that socialization occurs "pre-conversion."

An emphasis on breaking with the past via conversion functions as an important diacritical marker for evangelicals. It is an authenticating marker of membership within the evangelical community, and likewise a sign for those that are outsiders.[9] That is, the potency of this shared narrative among evangelicals is pronounced, not only because of its unifying effect internally, but also because of its propensity for highlighting difference with outsiders. While this is not the sole marker of evangelical membership, in the making and unmaking of social boundaries, this particular marker plays a central role in the performative fortification of the Catholic and evangelical boundary. True evangelicals have a testimony. The truest evangelical testimonies leave the past behind.

Evangelical Continuity

Among the evangelical cases presented so far, individuals exhibited religious change post-migration. According to Cooperman et al. (2014), however, nearly half of all Latinx converts to evangelicalism experienced change in their countries of origin. Is it possible then, that some evangelicals in Santa Ana were actually exhibiting a continuity

[9] Espinosa (2014) argues that, historically, for Latinx Pentecostal converts, conversion is marked by a breaking away from popular Catholicism.

of religious identity, rather than a rupture with the past? The cases of evangelical congregants Patricia and Leo Martinez demonstrate variation in the location of religious change. So too, they demonstrate the cross-border nature of evangelical affiliation, especially in Patricia's case.

Patricia and Leo Martinez's residence rested in the shadow of Immaculate Heart of Mary Catholic parish, but Patricia and Leo were members of Templo Calvario, a Pentecostal church two miles away from their home. One of the largest Latinx Protestant churches in the nation, Templo Calvario was established in Santa Ana over eighty years ago. Faithfully attending Sunday services, the Martinezes also frequented weekly midweek services and home Bible studies. Patricia had undergone church training to lead a women's Bible study group, and Leo volunteered as a church security guard. Special church events provided added allure. The Martinezes' involvement in church activities was an important source of support for them and their shift toward this pattern of participation was narrated alongside a shift away from what they described as a less desirable past.

As with the Delgado family in the opening vignette, the Martinezes also communicated the centrality of faith while sharing their migration narrative. Leo migrated to the United States in 1980, close to the same time as Ricardo Delgado. In similar fashion to the Delgados, Patricia stayed behind in their native state of Guerrero, Mexico. Leo also made return visits to Guerrero. After one of those visits, the couple's eldest daughter was born. After one of those visits, Patricia herself was "born again." Patricia testifies that, "By the grace of God I'm a Christian, a child of God. I became a Christian when I was in Mexico, and I've still remained." The evangelical message was conveyed to Patricia through an aunt and uncle that returned to Mexico from Santa Ana.[10] According to Patricia, "they took the gospel to our pueblo because none of that existed there. We were very Catholic. We believed all that

[10] Perhaps the case of Patricia illustrates an extension of the proposition made by Ramos et al. (2017:136), who suggest that, "in places Protestants gained an early foothold, other Latinxs are more likely to convert regardless of the social context." Here, the "early foothold" was actually transplanted back to Patricia in Mexico, altering her context.

stuff about La Virgen. But the Lord touched my heart."[11] This aunt and uncle helped establish an evangelical church at the ranch home they left behind in Patricia's hometown. Her uncle became the pastor. "[Her relatives] became Christians at Templo Calvario, when they were in Santa Ana," Patricia explained. Another aunt and uncle stayed in Santa Ana and continued as members at Templo Calvario.

The Martinezes, unlike the Delgados, initially painted a portrait of a disjointed family. As part of a migration stream from the Mexican state of Guerrero, Leo encountered in Santa Ana numerous *paisanos* from his pueblo, including Patricia's evangelical relatives. Leo's life contrasted with the message Patricia's relatives preached, as evidenced in the narrative of Patricia's eventual arrival to Santa Ana; enmity, not joy, characterized Patricia and Leo's initial reunification. Patricia described her husband as a drunkard. "Since he would drink so much, he would forget about me," Patricia complains. Leo was able to obtain his green card in the '80s under the Immigration Reform and Control Act, but he confesses that "When I got my papers, I didn't have enough money because I was always drinking. I would get money and I would waste it." Through the nine years he lived in the United States without Patricia, his visits to Mexico grew sparse, as did his remittances. Patricia's aunt and uncle, not Leo, eventually drew her to Santa Ana. They offered her the support that Leo could not, and invited her and her daughter to live with them in their Santa Ana home. Patricia accepted their offer, and recounts that "when I got here to their home, they were really into the word of God." Patricia's aunt and uncle allowed her to live rent free, and were wary of her desire to move in with Leo. "They would tell me, 'For what? He doesn't even have money and he drinks too much,' " Patricia recalled.

Church became a primary space of support for Patricia as she and her daughter would attend various activities per week. Eventually, Patricia and Leo moved into an apartment together, close to where the Delgados would live. Though Leo had no desire to attend church, Patricia asserted her plan to stay active at Templo Calvario. She described her struggle with Leo in the following manner:

[11] Ellos llevaron el evangelio al pueblo porque no había nada de eso. Eramos bien católicos, creíamos todo eso de la virgen. El Señor toco mi corazon.

> I would go to church alone. I thank God that [Leo] would let me go. He would drop me off and he would pick me up, but he would still get home very drunk. I would ask God to touch him, and touch him, and God changed him! It was the prayer. Leo waited for like fifteen years. It took some time. He would start going into church but he would come drunk. I would hold onto him so he wouldn't fall over. Very drunk. I would tell him, "you better sit down," when we were all standing.

Leo explained that during a physical altercation at work, a coworker brought him to task for his drinking habit. After this fight, Leo stated, "I made the decision. I asked God to change me." Leo believes that after this declaration, circumstances started to change for the family. Evicted from their apartment for sub-leasing to unauthorized tenants, the Martinezes experienced an unintended consequence. Patricia proclaimed, "God is so good. The doors to rent an apartment were closed, but the opportunity to buy a house opened up. [Leo] had bad credit, but when they went to check his credit, they said, 'the gentleman has good credit!' We said, 'Wow!'" The Martinezes now lived about three blocks from their old apartment in a single-family home they owned. Leo ran his own landscaping business, abstained from alcohol, and attended church with his family. Patricia was a housewife and served as caretaker for her grandchildren. She was still undocumented. Patricia and Leo had three adult children, and one pre-teen son, all active in evangelical churches.

On the one hand, Patricia's case points to a dimension of change that has already been touched upon: That of discontinuity with family tradition. She made clear that she no longer believed "all that stuff about La Virgen." She attributed this change to how "The Lord touched [her] heart." In other words, she saw this change as guided by supernatural intervention, and not solely by a choice to let go of these past traditions. She referred to many of the traditions of her former neighbors in Mexico and Catholic family members as "puras fiestas paganas," or "only pagan parties." These no longer occupied a central part of Patricia's life.

On the other hand, Patricia's commitment to an evangelical faith was a form of continuity. She became evangelical while in Mexico, and in her own words, she had "still remained." Furthermore, it was her family that shared "*el evangelio*" (the gospel) with her. Though she broke with the traditions of some family members, she had actually maintained commonality with other family members. Still, it is notable that her family members became evangelicals while in Santa Ana, and took their message back to Mexico. They established a church there, but there was still a reorienting experience in that the catalytic conversions of her family members originated in the United States. In Patricia's case, migration would bring her closer to the very institution in the United States where her family members had an evangelical conversion. That is, migration spatially brought her into close proximity to where the evangelical message was first planted in her family. This was not the case for all, as I address subsequently, but is significant nonetheless in the case of Patricia.

In framing a storyline wherein conversion is a temporal-spatial rupture, conceptualizing experiences like Patricia's as a reorientation towards a US-based faith is an easy, but oversimplified way to streamline the conversion narrative. That is, asserting that evangelicals are merely embracing a US-based faith flattens out much of the lived experience of evangelicals in Mexico and Latin America. While evangelicalism certainly has strong links to US-based institutions, its prevalence among working-class Latin Americans means that it often develops its own distinct spaces. In Santa Ana, for example, there are many independent Pentecostal churches that are not tied to US-based denominations, and even some congregations that are tied to movements in Latin America. Pentecostalism has especially been adept at developing indigenous forms of practice. Latin American evangelicalism is both/and. It is susceptible to influences from US institutions, but it is also innovative enough to create expressions anchored in Latin American soil. Denying the former proposition ignores historical evidence of US involvement in spreading evangelicalism in Latin America, while denying the latter proposition ignores the growing masses of leaders and institutions in Latin America that are independently forging a Latin American evangelicalism.

In addition, many of Santa Ana's evangelicals had ties to an older history of Protestantism among Mexican origin populations (Ramos et al. 2017). Pastor Adolfo Solis, for example, pastor of La Gran

Cosecha Sobrenatural, spoke of his generational ties to Protestantism in Mexico. An immigrant from the Mexican state of Chihuahua now in his eighties, Pastor Solis explained that his grandfather became Methodist as a young boy, over a century ago, and eventually became a Methodist pastor. Carmen Gomez, an immigrant from Mexico City, indicated that her grandfather was a Protestant pastor in Mexico. Julieta Esparza, an immigrant from the Mexican border town of Tijuana, now residing in the United States over fifty years, indicated that she grew up in an evangelical home as her parents "became Christians when we were still in Mexico." Mexican Protestantism is certainly not a new development, and neither is it new to Santa Ana, a city where the first Mexican Protestant congregations were founded over a century ago.

Conversion, then, was not interpreted by converts as a reorientation to a US religion. It was primarily seen as a reorientation to a new moral freedom, typically mapped onto a geographic journey. As Vila (2004) notes, converts that remained in Mexico had very similar conversion narratives but had no need to reinterpret a migration narrative through the lens of a conversion experience. Vila does present a fascinating argument that among evangelicals in the Mexican border town of Juarez, there is a perceived spatial hierarchy in regards to where in Mexico people are from; those from southern Mexico are seen as more obstinate in their rejection of evangelicalism, given the intricacies of Catholic spirituality practiced there. The reigning paradigm for evangelicals though, was that new life in Christ superseded all else, and everyone necessitated such a life-changing encounter. Those who were born into an evangelical home also required a life-changing encounter. All needed to be born again. No one received a pass for being a generational evangelical. Even those that have not lived a life of ostentatious sin, needed to admit that the possibility of being controlled by sin had been broken away from.

Catholic "Conversion"

Contrasting the conversion of evangelicals with the continuity of Catholics runs the risk of erasing an important pattern exhibited by some Catholics: Some Catholics also recounted experiences that paralleled the evangelical conversion experience. David Soto, for example, an immigrant from the Mexican state of Michoacan who had been in the United States for two decades, enthusiastically related a story of how he "encountered salvation" through one of the ministries at his church, Our Lady of the Pillar Catholic Church. He credited the "couples' ministry" with saving not only his marriage but also, he proclaimed, "the couples' ministry saved my life!"

I met with David at the small business that he ran. As I entered the business, a small electronics repair shop, I noticed he was playing evangelical praise music in the background. I inquired about the music he was listening to. "Oh, I really like this music. It brings me encouragement to listen to this while I work!" I pointed out that it was evangelical music and he responded, "Well it's the same God anyway!" As I asked him about his church involvement, he immediately directed the conversation to a discussion of the couples' ministry he was a part of. A lean and lanky fellow, David gestured with his hands as he explained, "My wife and I are leaders in this ministry now. We go on retreats, and we help plan gatherings. I wish I would have gotten involved sooner, before my problems got to where they were. I almost lost my marriage!" This would have been devastating for David, who was proud of his family and of the small business that he maintained to sustain his family. His description of previously being caught up in alcohol abuse and mismanaging his funds sounded similar to some of the evangelical testimonies that I heard. Like many of his evangelical co-ethnics, David's testimony was one of hitting rock bottom. He quipped, "sometimes we don't look for God until the Devil doesn't want us anymore. That's what happened to me."

David's "conversion" story was not as rigid as that of the evangelicals I interviewed, but it still shared many key elements with these narratives. On the one hand, as with evangelical accounts, there was a clear breaking away from social vices and a restoration of important relationships, namely that of his marriage. On the other hand, David's story was less centered on one specific conversion moment. David, after all, was already Catholic. He did not understand himself as having converted to another faith. He did, however, frame his involvement in the couples' ministry as a life turnaround. The turnaround may have been gradual, as perhaps it was for some evangelicals as well, but there was less impetus to identify one point of transformation as was typical of the evangelical narratives. David's narrative seemed less scripted than those of his evangelical co-ethnics. The narrative came across as less rehearsed and less developed than those of evangelicals, despite sharing common elements with this conversion genre.

Alicia Suarez, an immigrant from Guerrero who had been in the United States since the early '90s, talked about how she had a surge of religious faith in her own life. As she described her previous life,

> I used to say, "I'm Catholic" just because I was baptized. But I wasn't really. I didn't attend any church events. Maybe only on baptisms, when I would get invited I would go. But a lot of personal things have happened where I had to say, "Ok!"

Alicia lifted up her face during her last exclamation, revealing a glimmer of resolution in her eyes that on occasion flashed through her typically guarded facial expressions. Alicia went on to say, "to have my own faith, I had to go through a lot of things. I had a lot of trips and falls where I would fall and get up again. That is what drew me closer to my faith, more than anything, the falls of life." Some of the falls Alicia spoke of referred to the relational challenges she had faced, raising her four daughters as a single mother, once her husband left her. In her late fifties, with three of her children now adults, Alicia presently experienced more times of respite than she had in previous years. Her oldest daughter and son-in-law, with whom she lived, helped to sustain her. Her hands revealed her years of working on a ranch in Mexico and eventually working extensive hours in retail. Nostalgically, during our interview, she recounted a childhood story about life on her family's ranch; with a smirk on her face she recalled how she and her siblings were tasked with caring for their family farm's livestock but they would "corral the animals into an abandoned house and play on their own."

Alicia's story of religious change did not emphasize one specific moment of transformation, but rather an ongoing and increasing awareness that faith would sustain her through her difficult moments. Alicia's narration situated her growing reliance on faith within her increased participation at church activities and within specialized church ministries. She said that whereas initially she would only attend

Sunday mass, she now was taking Bible study classes through her church. In addition, she sometimes stayed after mass for a special time of "oracion y alabanzas," or prayer and praise. She emphasized the variety of activities she was now active in:

> On Thursdays I would go to prayer at church, and that was a time specifically only for prayer. Right now I can't go other days but Sunday, because I'm going to school. Anyone can go, Mondays and Thursdays. We are the same ones that go on most days, it's as if we were divided into different duties and everyday a different one of us is in charge. Our group is called Pescadores de Hombres [fishers of men].

I inquired more about the group and prayer time that Alicia was involved in. This prayer group, as Alicia explained to me, was tied to an important movement, which also intersected with David's story: Both Alicia and David indicated that they participated in ministries related to the Catholic Charismatic Renewal. Alicia's prayer group was a charismatic prayer ministry. Along with the couples' ministry, David for a season would regularly visit a ministry that was part of the Catholic Charismatic Renewal. The prayer and worship music were particular elements that David pointed to as central to his spiritual renewal. Alicia, too, emphasized these as aspects of her spiritual renewal. Other Catholic interviewees that I spoke with were also committed to ministries of the Catholic Charismatic Renewal within their parishes. These ministries, in fact, had many parallels to the evangelical, and particularly the Pentecostal, gatherings I visited in Santa Ana.

Charismatic Renewal

A parishioner from Our Lady of the Pillar, Jesús Ibarra, invited me to accompany him as he attended a Charismatic renewal gathering. The salient imprint left on Santa Ana by the Catholic Charismatic Renewal reflects the broader growth of the movement in the Catholic church, particularly among Catholics of Latin American origin. Jesús, a facilities maintenance supervisor at a high school in Santa Ana, had one of the longest residential stints in the United States and in Santa Ana from among my respondent sample. He had been in the United States for over forty years, hailing from the Mexican state of Michoacan. The charismatic group that he belonged to met at a hall across the street from the parish's main sanctuary. The gathering was led completely by lay leaders, most of whom were women (see Matovina 2011).

A distinguishing aspect of the Charismatic services that Jesús attended was the energetic worship experience, less restrained than a traditional mass. The service incorporated lively music, unscripted prayer, a casual sermon, and a call to the altar to receive additional prayer. Special occasions may have included testimonies, and even dramas. Invitations to go to a retreat also appeared to be a staple of the group gatherings. Expressions of emotion were acceptable during these services, in contrast to the more traditional masses taking place across the street. Attendees were jubilant and gleeful as they sang and motioned along with the worship band on the stage. One of the song leaders, a jovial man in his early fifties, swayed and twirled, his feet moving in cumbia-step fashion as the rhythm of a new song kicked off. He wore faded jeans and his shirt was partially untucked, perhaps a result of his movements. He called out to attendees to "worship God with freedom." Attendees followed suit, as various songs involved coordinated steps and motion. I recognized a number of the songs as songs sung in evangelical churches. I noted that these were songs from an older evangelical repertoire, *coritos*. The room was electrified, filled nearly to capacity with more than one hundred people. The gathering felt like a congregation unto itself, where people greeted each other as "*hermana*" or "*hermano*" and warmly inquired as to whether they would see each other at the next event. This was one Charismatic gathering at one parish, but some parishes in Santa Ana had multiple Charismatic ministries of varying sizes, offering spiritual retreats, prayer groups, and *congresos*, or conventions.

About 52% of Latinx Catholics identify with the Catholic Charismatic movement in the United States (Cooperman et al. 2014). The Charismatic belief system places an emphasis on experiential manifestations of God's power through spiritual gifts such as speaking in foreign and/or unknown tongues, spontaneously sharing words of prophecy, and exhibiting exceptional amounts of faith in regard to the healing of diseases or other miraculous possibilities. Believers from this tradition have an expectation that God can be experienced in both a spiritual and physical sense. The time of open altar that I observed bore witness to this belief, as leaders and attendees engaged in times of prayer for particular needs and situations. These practices have many parallels to evangelicalism and Pentecostalism, and the branch of the Catholic Charismatic Renewal most prominent among Latinxs was in fact founded by US missionaries to Latin America that were Pentecostal and converted to Catholicism (Espinosa 2017). Within the Catholic church, this movement has gained an inordinate amount of Latinx followers (Deck 2015).

Though the charismatic service shared a significant amount of similarities to its Pentecostal church neighbors, there was never doubt that the service was Catholic. Even ignoring its location in a Catholic church, the visual elements employed within the service reminded participants of their Catholic faith. At the front stage, on opposite ends, statues of a crucified Christ and of the Holy Mother faced the audience. The placement of the two images evoked a sense of gender balance, a male image and a female image, which was also represented in the participation of those speaking, singing, and reading from the stage. Some of the songs that originated in evangelical churches had been adapted to include Catholic lyrics. For example, one song, "Que viva Cristo," contained a stanza not found in the evangelical version, repeating the phrase, "Viva Maria madre de Dios." Such a lyric was never heard in the evangelical churches I visited in Santa Ana.

The Charismatic renewal exemplifies an important instance of boundary negotiation between Catholics and evangelicals. On the one hand, it generated common ground in practice and belief between the two groups. Several of the respondents I interviewed that were part of Charismatic groups exhibited a vocabulary and conduct very similar to evangelicals.[12] On the other hand, the Charismatic renewal is known to energize Catholics in some of their distinctively Catholic traditions, such as veneration of the Virgin Mary (Suro et al. 2007). So, while it provides points of dialogue and mutual admiration between

[12] Matovina (2017) notes that some Latinx Pentecostals have been drawn to Catholicism through the Charismatic movement.

groups, it also brightens the boundaries of difference, suggesting that complete blurring will not occur.

Catholic Renewal through Tradition

Some Catholics described renewalist types of experiences tied to more traditional elements of Catholic practice. For example, Jose Luis Vargas, a college student in his early twenties, described several moments in his life that stood out as points of spiritual renewal. Jose Luis was a leader for a youth Bible study group at his Catholic parish called Jovenes de Esperanza. A recent event which solidified his Catholic identity was a youth-oriented concert that he attended. On the surface, the event seemed anything but traditional. The event, called "The City Lights: God Among Us," was sponsored by an organization called Young Catholic Professionals and took place in Santa Ana. The Yost Theater, a historic theater in downtown Santa Ana, provided the site of the event. For several years, the theater had been used by a Pentecostal church, but it had fallen into disrepair and the church relocated to another part of the city. When the venue was reopened, it was rented out for a variety of events including prom nights, dance clubs, and concerts. Still, it was not a typical venue for a Catholic event in the city. Also, in many ways, the event seemed similar to an evangelical worship night, given that some of the music was the type of music played at evangelical churches. The event was held in English and drew from a diverse set of participants, including many 1.5- and second-generation Latinxs. Jose Luis lamented that,

> When it happened I let my youth group know but nobody seemed interested because they said "it's probably a Christian event." I don't know. It's funny. Catholic churches, especially Hispanic churches, don't really have those kind of events. I was the only one that went to check it out from my youth group and when I went it was really nice.

Jose Luis emphatically described what to him was the height of the event:

> They had the whole presentation of the eucharist. When the eucharist is coming, what you're supposed to do is kneel. But there were so many people, the place was packed to standing room only. The guy leading the event said you don't have to kneel, you just have to bow your head when the eucharist comes by. Out of nowhere, people started kneeling and kneeling and kneeling. People just started to kneel! At the end everyone was kneeling! The guy was like be careful we don't want anyone to get hurt. But everyone was on their knees the whole time. 'Cause the eucharist thing lasts half an hour and everyone was kneeling for like half an hour. My knees were hurting. It was really nice.

This event helped to reinforce Jose Luis's Catholic identity. Jose Luis enjoyed the music and the ambience of the event, but what distinguished the event most for him was the Eucharist and the response of the audience to the Eucharist. As Jose Luis described the scene, he did so with enthusiasm, and with a glistening smile emblazoned on his face. Reflecting on the event, Jose Luis explained,

> I've been to a lot of Christian events. but then seeing your faith that was the most predominant faith that was there, and everyone expressing it, it makes you feel something more. It was the greatest thing, like event that I've ever been to."

Having attended an evangelical youth camp with friends in the recent past, Jose Luis was not a stranger to evangelical styles of worship and gathering. He was well aware of some of the parallels that the event had to the camp he had previously attended. Yet, the event at the Yost impacted Jose Luis precisely because he knew it was a Catholic event, and the eucharist was one of the primary indicators that the event was Catholic for Jose Luis. Certainly, Protestants also take part in communion, but the evangelical churches in Santa Ana that I visited did not place the emphasis on the eucharist that Catholics did, likely in part stemming from differing understandings about the doctrine of real presence. It is also difficult to ignore the way that Jose Luis processed the experience of pain at kneeling for half an hour on concrete floor in a crowded hall. There was an element of sacrifice in the act of kneeling, and the pain that was felt was part of the beauty of the event, perhaps echoing the *mandas* and *promesas*[13] (De la Torre 2009; Hagan 2008) that Jose Luis's family was familiar with.

Spatial and Temporal Continuities

As an extension of their differing understandings of religious experience, Catholics and evangelicals reflected differing temporal-spatial understandings of their faith. For Catholics, faith was closely linked to the maintenance of temporal-spatial continuity. That is, Catholics were much more invested in sustaining localized practices that they learned in Mexico. Moreover, these were practices that were tied to very particular regions of Mexico, and transplanted in such a way that approximated their original form as much as possible. Evangelicals, on the other hand, were invested in a more universalized, and less localized version of faith. If breaking with the past was emphasized, even if not everything in the past was bad, there was still less motivation to focus on "tradition." Spaces of past spiritual devotion were less prominent in the spiritual worlds of evangelicals.

Miguel Luna provided a prominent Catholic case of how both spatial and temporal continuities were sustained. Miguel's Catholic practices, and the objects of his devotion, closely linked him to his region of origin in the Mexican state of Oaxaca. Central to Miguel's faith was his devotion to La Virgen de Juquila, a Catholic saint revered in Oaxaca. Her original image is found in Santa Caterina de Juquila, in the state of Oaxaca. Images of La Virgen de Juquila could be found in Miguel's home, and for Miguel these images triggered memories of devotion to la Virgen in his home region. He described witnessing devotees "riding their bikes from far away cities, such as Puebla to honor La Virgen de Juquila. Many would perform *mandas* for things that would cause them pain, or make a sacrifice, to ask something of La

[13] Hagan (2008) characterizes *mandas* as "a debt for a favor granted" typically by a spiritual personage. These become mandates that a devotee promises to follow through with. *Promesas* are the promises made to spiritual personages in response to favor that devotes are granted.

Virgen [de Juquila]." Miguel first left Oaxaca forty-five years ago, but had a period of two years where he went back and forth in "la frontera," specifically the borderlands of Arizona and Sonora, before settling in Santa Ana. His maintenance of devotion to La Virgen de Juquila had sustained a sense of continuity between Oaxaca and Santa Ana, and during his liminal time in the borderlands.

Now settled in the United States, Miguel gathered with other devotees at various points throughout the year to commemorate la Virgen de Juquila. Such gatherings increased in the LA basin throughout the last decade, as the population of migrants from Oaxaca in the United States had grown. Reporter Soudi Jimenez (2015) documents these gatherings in various parts of Los Angeles. Miguel explained that, "La Virgen de Juquila is admired throughout many regions of Mexico. She is known in many places and many come to see her in Oaxaca." Miguel had invested in making sure that his children maintained the faith of their ancestors. As a testament to this, his granddaughter Adriana, a college student, followed in his footsteps of devotion. She considered "the times when we have gone to Oaxaca and visited the site of La Virgen de Juquila" among her best memories of religious devotion.

The group that Miguel was a part of was certainly not the only one that worked to sustain spatial ties to their homeland region through faith. I met a number of individuals who participated in diasporic communities and hometown associations that celebrated the patron saint of their region, in some cases partnering with a local parish to do so. One such community that caught my attention was a network from the Mexican state of Guerrero who migrated from the region known as la Costa Chica. La Costa Chica is known as one of two concentrations of Afro-Mexican populations in Mexico, starting South of Acapulco, Guerrero and moving partway into the neighboring state of Oaxaca.[14] One of the focal events of this diasporic community is the feast day of Señor Santiago Apostol, or Saint James the Apostol, on July 25. Many of the immigrants from that region

[14] The other Afro-Mexican concentration can be found in the Mexican state of Veracruz. Additional black communities are found in northern Mexico where fleeing African American slaves known as Mascogos settled.

were from the town of Cuajinicuilapan, where Saint James is the patron saint.

Close to the end of July, immigrants from the Costa Chica region convene upon Santa Ana and celebrate their patron saint. I noted that one year, masses in honor of St. James the Apostol were hosted on different days by two different Catholic parishes in the city, St. Joseph and Immaculate Heart of Mary. Throughout the celebrations, there are many opportunities to remember the towns devotees came from. At the celebrations following the mass, masters of ceremonies recognize particular towns and villages in the region that are represented by participants. Dancing is a typical activity that takes place during festivities, including music that is popular in the region, and also more "folkloric" styles of music and dance. The danza de diablos, or dance of devils, is one such dance, wherein performers wear costumes with larger protruding ears and horns, intended to signify faces of devils. These traditions are a blend of African, indigenous, and Spanish traditions. Where devotees came from is brought front and center, and fused with devotion to Señor Santiago Apostol.

Father Ed Poettgen, parish priest at Immaculate Heart of Mary, encouraged the maintenance of localized faith practices, including some that were labeled as "folk" or popular practices.[15] He was aware that some colleagues did not agree with practices that migrants brought to local parishes from their homelands (see Badillo 2004). Yet, during an interview, Father Ed emphatically told me that he wanted his parishioners to know that the "traditions they bring from their homeland are good and equal to what they learn here in the U.S."[16] Many of these were traditions surrounding veneration of Our Lady of Guadalupe. Due to the increasingly strong presence of the Mexican community, as another local priest put it, "we're making a big effort to be inclusive with the Virgin of Guadalupe" (Reiff 2006). Many of the practices surrounding veneration of Our Lady of Guadalupe were not only Mexican, but rather tied to a specific part of Mexico.

[15] Espín (2006:16) presents a compelling description of "Popular Christianity" as "an epistemological womb within and through which all of daily reality is produced and reproduced."

[16] Fr. Ed essentially wanted his parishioners to embody "ownership" of their parish as discussed by Hoover (2017).

Evangelical Spatial Ties

Evangelicals did at times make references to spatial ties to Mexico, but often these were cast in a negative light. For example, Berenice Lopez, member of a Pentecostal church, considered the views espoused by people like Miguel to be idolatry. Berenice described her own spiritual orientation, and that of other evangelical converts from Catholicism like herself, along temporal-spatial lines but centered on an experience of rupture. According to her, "It's as if people that cross the border, there's a veil that falls from their eyes. They go back to Mexico later, and they can testify. They no longer have that strong idolatry[17] that they used to have." Berenice was essentially communicating a version of the theologizing thesis that posits migration as an experience that increases the religiosity of migrants. Specifically, though, she was proposing an evangelical theologizing experiencing, arguing that migration increased people's predisposition to move away from Catholicism and towards evangelicalism. In her estimation, the very crossing of the border was a spiritually transformative experience.

Federico Reyes introduced a different temporal-spatial element to his testimony, that of acculturation to his US context. Federico, who came to the United States from Mexico City thirty years ago, recalled not completely fitting in to his new context. As a migrant from an urban area of Mexico, he quickly learned to navigate the city systems in Santa Ana and promptly enrolled in night school. However, there were still some cultural and aesthetic markers which Federico believed highlighted that he was not quite adapted to the United States. He felt that his difference was particularly pronounced when he first started visiting an evangelical church that his brother invited him to. He explained that he was motivated to visit his brother's church after he asked his brother, "van a haber hermanitas?" (will there be women/sisters?). His brother responded that yes, there would be, and food as well. In describing his first visits, he focused on the appearance of he

[17] This account parallels Freeman's description of Pentecostal conversion wherein converts attempt to "break off from any form of traditional religion or ritual practice" (2012:14). Freeman also argues that such converts classify these forms of religion and ritual as part of "the past."

and his friends: "I had long hair, like in Mexico. And we dressed—we didn't dress right! Like over there in Mexico. People looked as us like strange bugs [bichos raros]." One of Federico's hopes was to draw the attention of someone of the opposite sex, but while there he realized he might be drawing attention to himself for the wrong reasons. Federico made it clear that in part, his aesthetics were unappealing because they were like "over there in Mexico."

Federico's conversion came when he hit rock bottom. The turning point was an incident where he drank so much that he had no recollection of how he returned to his apartment. He awoke to find himself laying on the floor, asleep in his own vomit. At that point he began to take his brother's invitation to go to church more seriously. Soon after, he asked God, "If it's your will, I need to stop smoking, but I need your help." He testified that from then on he never smoked again. This was the moment he gave his life to God and was born again. He also stopped drinking, though it is unclear if that was sudden or gradual. Some of his roommates were also experiencing change in their lives. He recalled asking himself, "how can we be hungry for God? God started to deal with us then. We used to get together and drink and smoke. Now we're so much better. When the dog returns to his vomit, that's how I saw myself back then." Federico makes clear his reorientation from how things were "over there in Mexico." Indeed, when speaking of the future that he desired for his children, one of his comments was striking: "I hope that they would not continue to be a reflection of all those Mexicans, that they wouldn't just be one of the bunch."

Conclusion

When comparing moments of heightened spiritual awareness among Catholics and evangelicals, altar moments, it is clear that within this sphere Catholics are more invested than evangelicals in sustaining temporal-spatial ties to the homeland. Catholics generally experience moments of religious revivalism as moments of reinforcing the tradition that they are already connected to. This is not to say that Catholics cannot make note of past mistakes and have criticisms of their ancestors or of where they came from. Nevertheless, they do generally express more positive outlooks in relation to their linkages with ancestors and with places of origin. Moments of heightened spiritual awareness for Catholics are often accompanied by rituals, habits, and practices that point back to the homeland, contributing to an identity that inhabits ties to the homeland. Evangelicals, on the other hand, are more invested in drawing distinctions between who they were in the past and who they are in the present; their place of origin is by extension fused with their past, undergirding a dynamic of temporal-spatial distancing through conversion. So important is the evangelical temporal-spatial distancing as a marker of evangelical belonging, that even those that had been raised in an evangelical household conveyed a similar narrative. These evangelicals, too, had *testimonios* of being born-again. Essentially, those who were born into evangelicalism were also "converts." Heritage evangelicals were not converts from a religion that differed from that of their parents, but they were converts away from the possibility of being ruled by sin. Turning to Jesus Christ in the evangelical sense involved an active turning away from a potentially sinful past for the evangelical.

Altar moments, experiences of deep spiritual reflection, for some Catholics may have separated the faithful from acts of sin, or may have energized them in a time of trial, but these experiences did not lead to the forceful temporal-spatial distancing that was present among evangelicals. If anything, Catholic altar experiences led to a stronger sense of Catholic devotion rooted in past traditions, and a generally more hopeful outlook toward the past. Moments at the altar, even forceful moments, were moments of re-centering, of returning to the base. Perhaps the words of Elizondo best capture this sentiment: "Conversion takes place not against one's tradition but within it" (1997:86). While evangelicals, too, could have these recurring altar experiences of returning to their foundation, they were ultimately founded on an initial, forceful rupturing with the past.

How did these distinct forms of engaging temporal-spatial aspects of spirituality affect notions of ethnicity? The Catholic experience of renovation strengthened ties to a long line of ancestors, at least in perception, and heightened affect to the homeland, from whence the traditions of lived religion had been birthed. Evangelicalism, as a tradition of converts, tended to emphasize distancing from one's past. For those of evangelical ancestry, this heritage was at times celebrated, but was not elaborated on as in depth of a fashion as the traditions that were common among Catholics. On this count, Catholicism seemed to provide more resources for maintaining the plausibility (Berger 1967) of ethnicity. Catholicism offered more material for sustaining a community of memory, for cultivating a sense of membership in a community that was passing on ways of remembering and ways of being. This is not to say that evangelicals could not commemorate the past, and that Catholics could not work towards personal change, but merely that the two groups were disproportionately engaged in one endeavor or the other, respectively.

This chapter has argued for a foundational difference in the lived religions of Catholics and evangelicals, which has implications for their understandings of ethnic identity; it has not, however, settled the question of ethnic identity maintenance among Mexican immigrant Santaneros. After all, from a social boundary perspective, the maintenance of ethnic identity is more than the maintenance of ethnic traditions. The question of ethnic identity maintenance resides in the processes of social boundary maintenance, which ensure that an identifiable category remains not just a symbolic label, but rather a social category with members that operates with a degree of social closure and exhibit network viability. In the chapter to follow, I consider how Catholics and Protestants move about within their social ecologies to seek out religious experiences that best meet their needs and how these processes solidify distinct religious identities intra-ethnically. Forms of continuity and change are largely reinforced through the religious communities that parishioners encounter throughout the city; parishioners are able to construct ideal blends of religious experiences from various institutions and groups. Rather than reflecting a religious free-for-all, consumption patterns in the midst of abundant options tend to operate within particular religious boundaries. The religious boundaries established in the local religious ecology have implications for the ethnic boundaries that are maintained.

5
Defining Commitments through Spiritual Dialogue

From the church room where we were conducting our interview, Mariela pointed out the building where she and her family lived. It was visible from the church. A tan, stuccoed, block-long complex, where every unit had its own streetside balcony, her building exuded an accidental air of Mesoamerican architecture. Clayish earth tones layered numerous times upon cubic forms provided that effect. The condo complex, with rooftop tennis courts now used as soccer fields, was home to mostly working-class Latinx households like Mariela's. Conveniently, this home positioned Mariela steps away from the gatherings offered by the Pentecostal church that she had committed to. She and her church seemed like a match made in heaven. Yet, Sunday after Sunday, the sound of church bells coming from various directions, and the sight of well-dressed pedestrians crisscrossing nearby streets, spotlighted a reality that Mariela was faced with: She lived in a religious district (McRoberts 2003), an area with a concentration of numerous religious options.

The panoply of religious options in Mariela's immediate religious ecology were plainly visible, but less visible were the processes by which commitments to specific communities were deliberated. On one level, Mariela would describe how she had been invited to her current church by a friend, and how she enjoyed the music and preaching there. On another level, she would proclaim with confidence that, "God brought me here!" Mariela's narratives expressed that her deliberations between religious commitments involved being attuned to spiritual entities at work around her. More than an environment erected of concrete, bricks, and lumber, for many Santaneros the religious ecology harnessed a spiritual world, a city of Spirit, to be navigated. Contained within informants' narrations of their journeys through the religious

The Saints of Santa Ana. Jonathan E. Calvillo, Oxford University Press (2020). © Oxford University Press.
DOI: 10.1093/oso/9780190097790.001.0001.

ecology was a sense that spiritual beings, especially God, served as interlocutors. Certainly, the plethora of religious choices appealed to individual, mundane tastes and preferences, yet informants rarely spoke of their decisions solely as processes of human deliberation. This appeal to ongoing encounters with the spirit realm in navigating religious options was an important element in the sustaining of religious commitments and identities. For most of my informants, the space of Santa Ana was cartographically infused with points of ongoing access to spiritual entities. To see Santa Ana as an ethnic space, for many informants, was to see it as a space where the Spirit, and the spirits, directly engaged with Santaneros.

Dialogue and Expectation

Mariela's story illustrates how many informants understood their direct, ongoing interactions with the spirit realm as integral to defining religious commitments in the city. Born into Catholicism in her native state of Veracruz, Mariela's evangelical journey began five years after arriving in the United States. She explained, "We had been thinking of going back to Mexico, because it was so tough here. People speak so nicely about coming here, but never tell us how we'll suffer here." Mariela considered separating from her husband, whom she had met in town. When it came to employment, Mariela proudly declared herself "una mujer mil-usos" (an all-purpose woman). Her work consisted of cleaning homes and selling cosmetic products on the side. Still, working to provide for two children from a previous marriage, with little help from her alcoholic spouse, Mariela was losing hope. She explained that regularly, "I sought help from what I knew—card readings, fortune tellers. One has their eyes closed. And since that's what I knew from family, I continued to seek it." Mariela reflected on how she hoped that these spiritual consultations would guide her through her difficult seasons.

Mariela's facial expression brightened when she began to describe her introduction to an evangelical church. At one point, Mariela described, "things were getting worse, our money didn't last, and my husband was drinking even more." Then, Mariela's friend invited her to an evangelical church. As she recalled, "My friend told me, 'let's go to church.' I asked, "What time is mass? Because I go to mass at twelve.' She said, 'No, the service is at ten here, and it's nice.'" Mariela trusted her friend, who had already been supportive of her during her time of need. After attending church with her friend, she told her husband, "I don't want to go back to the Catholic church!"

Mariela's friend would speak about God, to God, and for God, in an authoritative manner. Mariela began to speak in a similar fashion. During Mariela's time of need, she was grateful for these moments of encouragement from her friend, describing one especially memorable interaction: "My friend that had invited us to church said, 'I declare that in your house you will never need bread and will not hunger. You are a daughter of the king and he will always keep your refrigerator full.' That same friend brought us food from a food bank and said, 'take what you need.' I took so much." Mariela reminisced, "when I started serving God. I began to see a difference. It was when I began to tithe, that the Lord began to bless us. I declared, 'Satan you liar! My money lasted!'" Mariela understood the shift in her financial trajectory as a direct response from God; her action was a type of communication, and the stabilization that she experienced was God's answer. God was not the only one involved in the conversation, though, as Mariela was quick to fire verbal shots at Satan, whom she understood as holding back her success. These exchanges would guide Mariela through her process of selecting her community of worship.

Interviewing Mariela at her church, La Gran Cosecha Sobrenatural, I assumed that her story was centered on experiences there. I was surprised when she clarified, "this happened at the other church we used to go to. That's where I got to know the Lord." Surprisingly, Mariela and her husband had been members of two other churches prior to the one they currently attended. Evangelicals for five years, they had already belonged to three congregations. All of these congregations were walking distance from their home. Conflict and disagreement within the congregations had spurred them to look elsewhere while at their two prior churches. Amid these experiences, Mariela found guidance as to where she and her family would go next. She recalled that in one moment of discerning her options, "I would call out to God and God would say to me, 'I've been here, and I'm not going to let you go.'"

These perceptions of assurance from God would allow Mariela to settle in, even if just momentarily.

As Mariela encountered distinct expressions of church, her ongoing sense of spiritual dialogue helped her articulate what she looked for in a church and what it meant to be evangelical. In reference to her first visit to an evangelical church, she recalled, "When the pastor preached, I thought, 'who told him my life?'" Mariela felt that God was speaking to her through the preaching. Music, too, played a notable role in Mariela's evangelical commitment. She recalled enjoying the *alabanza*s that she first heard and preferring evangelical worship music to what she took as a more solemn approach in traditional Catholic masses.[1] Through the evangelical praise music, she "felt something very special," she recalled. She described an increased awareness towards the appropriate attire to wear at evangelical churches, explaining that, "I started to look around and ask myself, 'why are they so elegant?'" Mariela tied the outward appearance of the evangelical congregants to their testimonies: "I would hear the *testimonios* they were sharing. God was giving me understanding of how he was operating in their lives and I could see it in them." Mariela's consciousness shifted from an awareness of personal opinion to a perception of God-infused knowledge.

Rather than waning in her evangelical commitment after witnessing organizational conflict, her experiences at distinct, unrelated evangelical churches seemed to cement Mariela's evangelical identity. In moments where she was unsure about what to do, as she visited churches, she explained that she would talk to God: "I said, Lord, where are you that you're not at my home? Why am I not seeing you? The Lord said, 'here I am, you're just not seeing me.'" Through these conversations, Mariela claimed, her faith began to grow, her evangelical identity solidified, and decisions were made about the congregations she would link herself to. She perceived herself as having greater awareness of God's presence and guidance and developed conversational practices with God through certain styles of prayer practiced in her now Pentecostal church. She asserted during our interview, "Now I identify as a Christian," using the broad term

[1] See Manglos-Weber (2018) for a helpful discussion of how music plays a significant role in the conversion testimonies of some Pentecostals and Charismatics.

"Christian" to denote evangelical Christian as other Santaneros did. Because of a friend's invitation, Mariela and her family landed at La Gran Cosecha Sobrenatural, their current church. Mariela expressed assurance in her current church affiliation: "I say 'God, it's for a purpose that you have us here.'"

Seeking the Spirit

Faced with a plethora of choices, informants often navigated the religious ecology with a sense of divine guidance. As informants engaged distinct religious communities in the religious ecology, their articulations of religious identities were shaped by their perceptions of ongoing spiritual encounters. The distinct experiences these Santaneros had in the religious ecology also helped them to map particular religious boundaries onto the city. The religious taxonomies that informants mapped out were made clearer through their practices of engaging the spirit world. Whereas altar encounters were significant in helping people to solidify broader religious identities, altar encounters did not always solidify the particular spaces that Santaneros ultimately chose to participate within. For some, altar encounters actually opened the door to more options, rather than cementing their allegiance to one religious community. Ongoing practices of engaging the spirit world provided important discursive tools for navigating the boundaries of belonging.

In talking about their interactions with distinct congregations and with religious others in the religious ecology of Santa Ana, a significant theme that emerged in informants' accounts was their desire to maintain dialogue with God and other spiritual entities. The notion of ongoing dialogue with the Spirit/s especially influenced informants' patterns of spiritual commitments. In part, these informants reflected a pattern noted by Luhrmann (2012), that practices and perceptions of spiritual dialogue were shaped by the religious communities that adherents belonged to. Yet, what I found indicated an additional pattern that worked in the opposite direction: Many informants selected the churches they participated in based on their practices and perceptions related to spirit engagement. Yes, informants were socialized by specific institutions into particular practices of engaging spirit beings, especially God, but cultural traditions, and interactions with the broader religious ecology also socialized people towards spirit engagement. The plausibility structure (Berger 1967) upholding understandings of the spiritual realm was more than institutional. Unlike in Luhrmann's study where subjects dialogue with God while moving through a world inhabited by skeptics, the world of working-class, immigrant *Santaneros* was generally far less skeptical of the supernatural. Thus, even as institutions helped informants to better articulate their sense of spiritual dialogue, institutions also did the work of harnessing informants' existing beliefs and practices related to the spirit world. Informants engaged the religious ecology through maintaining a delicate balance of seeking both spaces that confirmed their existing notions of spirituality, and experiences that challenged them to encounter the spirit realm in novel, helpful, self-fulfilling ways.

Various informants recalled ongoing experiences perceived to be direct communication from God which influenced their ties to particular churches. Such experiences were, in some cases, sensational, and in other cases more subdued. Various Catholic informants expressed having developed particular patterns of exchange with God or with saints. The case of Saúl Nieto was quite memorable in this regard. I met Saúl during a gathering to pray the Rosary in the neighborhood of Townsend St. A Catholic deacon, Saúl was leading El Rosario de La Aurora, a morning prayer gathering where participants prayed the Rosary at different stations throughout the neighborhood. Neatly dressed in black slacks and a white, buttoned-up shirt, Saúl was treated with respect by the group of thirty or so participants in the neighborhood. This introduction to Saúl allowed me to observe a particular posture that he took in relation to God being present around him.

I had been to several gatherings of El Rosario de la Aurora, and noticed how this one was especially embedded within the public spaces of one Santa Ana neighborhood. One of the makeshift prayer stations was set up directly on the sidewalk, for example, necessitating that participants spread out along a narrow sidewalk in front of apartment buildings as they prayed the rosary. That particular station was made up of a small coffee table, draped over by a white tablecloth, and holding two images of *La Virgen de Guadalupe* that reflected an aesthetic reminiscent of "Precious Moments" figurines. That is, the images had a child-like appearance to them, in both countenance and their proportions, and their pink pastel coloring also projected a child-friendly representation. Saúl moved comfortably through the community and treated each prayer station with utmost care. I would later come to understand that much of his outlook was reflective of the Catholic imagination, a perspective that "sees created reality as a 'sacrament,' that is, a revelation of the presence of God" (Greeley 2000:1). God was in the child-like image of La Virgen de Guadalupe as much as in the more permanent altars, and Saúl treated them with the same reverence that he treated images at the church sanctuary with. This space on the sidewalk, sometimes occupied in the evenings by women hawking freshly made tamales out of grocery carts, and neighbored by an oft-stationed grocery truck, became a space to commune with the divine.

The seventy-year-old Saúl, during a later interview, explained that he had served as a Catholic deacon for fifteen years. He recalled that in his childhood, in the Mexican state of Michoacán, he wanted to be a priest because he had a high appreciation for the life of Saint Francis. In his late teens, he talked to his parish priest about his desire to become a Franciscan. His priest told him to take a year and contemplate his future, and then to approach him again to talk about the matter. During the year of contemplation, Saúl met Eugenia, the woman who would become his wife. After a year, he conversed with the priest about his future and sheepishly told him he wanted to get married. His priest assured him that there were many ways that he could serve the Lord. The idea about serving God in a more concerted fashion stayed with Saúl even after he migrated north, first settling in Tijuana, then in Santa Ana.

Years later, in the United States, Saúl explained that the desire to serve began to well up in him again. Saúl attributed his desire to the following experience and pattern:

> I had an encounter with God on a retreat, that in those days was called Cursillo de Cristiandad. A compadre, rest in peace, invited me. He told me about it, that "it was so nice and you'd have an experience so close to God." "No compadre, I'd rather have a beer. It sounds

> nice but it's not for me." But I ended up going and I had an experience with God. I had that experience at the cursillo, where they make you conscious of the presence of God in your life, and I continued to be aware of how God was present around me.

While Saúl's encounter with God had some similarities to an altar encounter, what was pivotal in his formation was what he described as his developed awareness of the presence of God in his life that emerged from that initial experience. Saúl reported experiencing a heightened sensitivity toward the divine. He already had a high view of "the holy mass and the Eucharist, which is the most special thing we have as Catholics," according to Saúl.[2] Yet, this awareness of God became heightened as he navigated through life and through various religious commitments. It was during a season that he was helping to found a new parish in Santa Ana, initiating meetings at a local park, that he was encouraged to consider the diaconate. Two separate priests approached him, on unrelated occasions, after observing his leadership, and told him that he would make an excellent deacon and should consider going through the required courses offered by the diocese. At first, Saúl did not take their suggestions seriously, but this ongoing awareness of God helped him to ultimately consider that God wanted him to become a deacon. Both he and his wife, Eugenia, believed that if God wanted him to be a deacon, he would be successful through the rigorous training process. Saúl described a moment of discouragement during the start of his training to be a deacon:

> When I went, and they introduced all of us, people talked about the colleges and universities where they had gone. Most of them were "Americanos." They asked me, "And you, what school did you go to?" I was hesitant to tell them that I had only gone to sixth grade [in Mexico]. I told them, "I went to La escuela de la vida [the school of life]." I had to take so many classes [at the diocese school]. "You and I don't have the proper preparation for this," I told my wife. She responded, "If the Lord needs you as a deacon, you'll be a deacon.

[2] Wilson argues that Latinx Catholics have distinct ties to the sacraments (2008).

> And if not, just as he has you now, he will indicate it." And thank God, that's how it went. God showed me that he wanted me to be a deacon and I completed the course.

Saúl was able to persevere because of his conviction that God had indicated to him that he would be a deacon. This notion of communicating with God, and this awareness of God's presence, were cultivated in his early involvement in the Cursillos movement. As I reviewed notes from my interview with Saúl, it was clear that this perception or awareness of God was a thread that permeated his life narrative, especially after his exposure to the Cursillo movement (see Nabhan-Warren 2013). As he helped to found a new parish by gathering people at a local park several decades prior, as he now gathered people in various neighborhoods throughout Santa Ana, and as he met with ill parishioners in hospitals to administer communion to them, Saúl understood that he was in constant divine dialogue. He likewise understood that he was helping others to experience a dispensation of God's grace through the sacraments and through partaking of the Holy Mass. In large part, Saúl saw it as his mission to bring people into God's grace through helping them to fulfill the sacraments that they had never completed.

For some informants, this divine dialogue took on a more sensational tone. Lourdes Vasquez, a single mother in her early sixties who attended a Pentecostal church, vividly recounted a series of experiences also of remarkable nature. Lourdes had been an evangelical Christian for several years, but had stopped attending church regularly because of her work schedule; the long hours at her manufacturing job were taking their toll on her. During that time, some of her children were invited to a nearby church. Lourdes related the series of events that followed:

> My kids were invited to a church pastored by a Salvadoran woman. This was a small Pentecostal church. They would go and learn about the word. I had never gone, but the woman, the pastor, started to look for me at home. I hated it. It would drive me crazy! I wasn't going to church at that time. I told her I didn't want to go but she wouldn't listen! Why did she keep looking for me? It was only one time that I went, and that's where the Lord got a hold of me! From there on,

> God started to give me dreams. I started to have supernatural things happen in my life. The third time I went, I remember the scriptures that were read. I'll never forget them. The pastor was reading the scriptures and I heard a trumpet. Then, when another scripture was read, I heard a waterfall, and that sound of the water drowned out the voice of the pastor. I then heard a voice that said to me, "be strong and courageous!" That voice would follow me, and it was the Lord. There's just so much love that the Lord has had for me!

Lourdes was greatly encouraged to continue in her commitment to this particular church as she engaged in divine dialogue. As someone who had, for a season, waned in her commitment, this series of experiences energized Lourdes's faith, and raised her expectations. She had already become an evangelical several years prior to the season she described but during this particular season she developed an expectation of ongoing spiritual conversation. Though at the time of our interview she no longer attended the church described previously, she continued to seek out Charismatic experiences, ultimately ending up at Templo Calvario, a Pentecostal church. She attended other churches along the way before visiting Templo Calvario; she found her place there, with teachings and worship that affirmed the possibility of God working in supernatural ways.

While Lourdes and Saúl's accounts of communicating with God appear dramatically different in terms of style and form, their experiences denoted some commonality as they both shared the expectation that God communicates with people in an ongoing fashion. For Lourdes, the voice of God broke into her life. For Saúl, hearing the voice of the divine was a process of learning to discern God's voice. Though Lourdes's experiences appeared as less of a process, she needed to develop a pattern of interpretation and response as Saúl had. Her confident claim to knowing God's voice required a level of interpretation that she was socialized into.

For both Saúl and Lourdes, there was a salient notion that one could learn to listen and to respond in accordance with the message interpreted. Generally, these experiences fell under the description provided by Cassanati and Luhrmann (2014:334) as "named phenomena without fixed mental or bodily events." They alone perceived them, even if they talked about them with others. These were personalized experiences. The ongoing practices of communication were particularly influential in the lives of Lourdes and Saúl for defining belonging and roles within particular churches. Their decisions about religious commitments and about religious investments were discursively reliant on these expectations of divine guidance.

Only When We Need Something

Several experiences recounted by informants, both Catholic and evangelical, emphasized that divine dialogue was a two-way street. What was novel to this set of informants was not only their expectation that God would speak to them, but also the importance they gave to understanding how to speak to God. Moreover, a sense of awareness about God was important for listening to God, but informants also stressed the importance of communicating back to God. These practices of spiritual engagement were often framed as communication of needs and wants. Specifically, informants brought forth these experiences of divine dialogue around needs and wants when they discussed their religious commitments. Miguel Luna, for example, a Catholic informant, discussed how he believed that one's involvement in church was itself a way to communicate with God about needs. He explained that,

> God responds to people's lack of involvement in church. God sees us and says, "Well, you must not need anything from me." If we're not involved, he might not talk to us. He doesn't tell us what we have to do. And then some people show up only when they need something! But we need to learn to tell God what we need more consistently not just when we are in major need. We have to talk to him. Talking to God!—that's how we find the solutions that we're looking for!

To Miguel, not being involved in church sent a message to God that one needed nothing in particular. Inconsistent involvement would translate to not receiving valuable resources from God. Likewise, as attending church was a form of communication, doing so only when in need reflected a weak spiritual commitment. Church involvement to Miguel was part of an ongoing dialogue. People asking God for what they needed was fine, as long as people did it consistently. As part of an ongoing give and take, a request embedded within a larger ongoing life of devotion merited God's attention. Indeed, to Miguel, for people to ask God for particular needs was an act of devotion, when it was done consistently as part of a larger commitment to the Catholic sacraments. When it was only done as a last resort effort, God would see through such an act.

Miguel was advocating for a particular understanding of faithfulness characterized by a more consistent communication with God. Showing up in times of dire need was not enough. Interestingly enough, slight variations of the phrase, "We shouldn't go to church only when we need something," were repeated almost verbatim by three other unrelated Catholic informants. The notion that church participation, and in particular attendance at mass, should be a regular occurrence was a pervasive notion among Catholics. The fact that the phrase "Only when we need something," in some cases attributed to clergy, was familiar to Catholics, suggests that the phrase functioned as a discursive tool among local Catholics to encourage attendance at mass among those that attended infrequently but also rested on an understanding of the need for ongoing engagement with God.

Some informants described scenarios where their requests made to God were personalized to the point of seeming superficial (Luhrmann 2012). Berenice, for example, a member of a Pentecostal church, described the process by which God allowed her to meet her husband. Dressed in office attire, in slacks and a blazer, Berenice was part of the pastoral leadership team of her church. When I first crossed paths with her, she was a church member, but after a handful of years taking night classes at a local Bible institute, and through years of mentoring by her local pastor, she was now involved in preaching and leading at her church. Berenice met her husband, Abel, when she was suddenly taken to the hospital for an emergency health issue. The man who is now her husband was working as a medical assistant at the hospital, and they met while he was assigned to assist her.

Berenice described that when she was a young woman, she had an affinity towards young men that were characterized by a particular street aesthetic. According to her, "I was drawn to young men that were cholos." "Cholo" is a term in Chicano street slang denoting someone who embodies Chicano gang culture aesthetics. In fact, during the time that she was taken to the hospital, Berenice was in a relationship with a young man that was considered a cholo and that happened to be in prison at that time. Her pastors had warned her not to date the man she was currently dating, and in hindsight Berenice attributed her dating choices to being "new to the things of God and still immature." Having doubts about her boyfriend, Berenice felt something different when she saw Abel, the man who would become her husband. Berenice continued: "When I saw him I immediately liked him. See, I had already told the Lord, 'I want a young man that looks like a cholo—but that isn't actually a cholo.'" The man before her, Abel, fit the description, as he looked the part aesthetically, but was not actually a gang member. While Abel attended to Berenice, she told him about her church.

Berenice went to visit her boyfriend in prison for what would, unbeknownst to her, be the last time. Her pastors, a husband and wife couple, accompanied her for moral support, as they had done before in the past. She recounted that they had been praying for her relationship, and had even told her that when her boyfriend got out of prison that he would be on "probation" with them, having to check in with them so they could monitor his participation at church. She shared the pastors' instruction with her boyfriend, and he became agitated. He told her, according to Berenice, "I'm not going on probation! Te voy a robar" (I'm going to kidnap you/ we're going to elope). Berenice explained that, "then and there I knew that I needed to break up with him. It's as if God opened my eyes. I was able to get free seeing that he wasn't what I needed. From that experience I learned that if something is not of God, God can take it away from you."

In the meantime, Berenice's new acquaintance, Abel, began to visit the church that Berenice attended. Her ex-boyfriend had not attended the church with any frequency, but her new friend became a regular. After she broke up with her boyfriend in prison, her pastors advised her to not make any relational decisions with haste. She heeded their advice. After Abel attended the church for several months, Berenice was informed that he would attend even when she was absent due to her work schedule. She asked him why it was that he would attend church when he knew that she would not be present. His response stood out to her: "What? Can I only go when you're there?" Berenice then felt that, "God was showing me that I could start a relationship with him." With the guidance of their pastors, they started dating and were married soon after. Berenice summed up the situation by saying that, "I was praying for a husband, and God brought him to me."

This communication of needs was an important part of the divine dialogue that Catholics and evangelicals developed. An underlying element of the communication seemed to be that the person asking something of God needed to demonstrate faithfulness characterized by consistent devotion. Asking was important, and it needed to be backed by acts of religious faithfulness. Likewise, this consistent devotion was understood by people such as Miguel and Berenice as a mode of sensitizing individuals to the responses that God would provide. Service signaled faithfulness, and it also shaped spiritual sensitivity.

These exchanges of communicating needs and wants, and of waiting for responses, was an important dimension in the solidifying of commitments to particular spiritual communities. When informants interpreted divine responses as being linked to their involvement in a particular community, their commitments to that place were generally solidified. At the same time, if informants interpreted involvement in a particular space as obstructing their sense of divine connection, they could look elsewhere. In such cases, evangelicals were more likely to look beyond their current church to other churches. Catholics were less likely to immediately explore other parishes. Catholics often had various options within their own parishes, though some did ultimately look to other parishes.[3] Finally, especially for Catholics, there were often options outside the traditional parish, such as involvement in neighborhood-based devotional acts which could function as their primary means of dialoguing with the divine. In many cases, these practices resulted in people constructing "customized routines of belonging" (Eiesland 2000:15).

[3] Badillo (2008) argues that Catholics have become increasingly consumeristic, venturing into Protestant churches more frequently than before. From my observation, this was less likely among Catholics who were highly involved in their parishes.

Renewalist Movements

For some informants, their notions of divine dialogue and their understandings of interacting with the spirit world emerged specifically through exposure to renewalist movements (Miller et al. 2013; Mulder, Ramos, and Martí 2017); these were movements which emphasized having experiences of the Holy Spirit, such as Pentecostal churches or the Catholic Charismatic renewal groups. Alicia Suarez, an immigrant from Guerrero, Mexico, who was also a single mother, found her place within a Charismatic prayer group at Immaculate Heart of Mary Catholic parish. Alicia experienced a life change several years prior to when I met her, and it largely came through her involvement with the Charismatic prayer group. This was a group that practiced praying for sick people so that they may be healed, and believed that God worked in other miraculous ways when people prayed (see Matovina 2011). Alicia had exposure to various religious traditions through family and acquaintances. Her daughter and son-in-law attended a multi-ethnic Pentecostal church in a neighboring city. They all lived together in the same apartment. Alicia also recounted interactions she had with people of other faith traditions in her neighborhood. Most of Alicia's firsthand experience of various spiritual options had taken place within her own parish, however. This experience of divine dialogue helped her to solidify her place even within her own parish.

Alicia explained that previously she only attended Sunday mass. Her parish was one of the largest in the county, and offered many different types of ministries for parishioners to get involved in. Alicia began to visit prayer groups, groups focused on singing, and even a group involved with plays. In her words:

> I started to get involved with one of the Charismatic prayer groups. And yes, I've gone on retreats. My first retreat was my initiation. And since then I have gone back many times. Not only to listen, but because I started to get a lot more involved. For example, I was in a play. This last retreat I went to, I went to serve - not just to go. But to serve.

Some of the benefits that Alicia received from the prayer group related to the social support that members of the group provided for her. Her timid voice warmed up as she explained how "They've never left me alone. They will give me a call and ask, 'how are you doing?' 'how are things going?'" She went on to explain the benefits that she received from her prayer group:

> They've helped me so much in prayer. The group has also helped me to experience God's presence. I used to say that God is everywhere saying, "Ok, I'm here!" I mean, I used to repeat that phrase before, but I didn't really have a notion of what that meant. Now I know. Now I understand it because I live it.

Similar to Saúl account of the Cursillo movement, Alicia noted that the Charismatic group helped her to become aware of God's presence. Coupled with prayer, this sense of divine perception infused Alicia with a more pronounced expectation of God's intervention in her life. By practicing prayer and maintaining a sense that the divine was present, Alicia's confidence that she had committed herself to a great spiritual community solidified. In Alicia's case, her commitment was not just to her parish, but also to her prayer group. Alicia had, after all, tried out various options within her own parish. A parish as large as Immaculate Heart of Mary, led by various pastors, fostered an environment where a diversity of spiritual practices emerged. Even within her own parish, her awareness of other options strengthened the voluntarism that she exercised by committing to her particular prayer group (Warner 1993).

Rosario expressed that Pentecostal churches had provided her with a more expansive expectation of God's presence in her life. In her early thirties, Rosario was part of the 1.5 generation, and labeled herself a "Dreamer." She worked at a social service agency and was completing her education in order to become a licensed social worker. Having grown up in Presbyterian churches, Rosario explained that her exposure to Pentecostal churches in Santa Ana's religious ecology changed her expectations of church participation. "My friend asked me, 'You grew up Presbyterian, but you pray in the Spirit?'" Rosario recalled. She laughed as she conjured up the memory. Praying in the Spirit typically refers to either an outward sign of "praying in tongues," as understood in Pentecostal theology (Mulder, Ramos, and Martí 2017), or possibly praying silently to oneself, but also in an unknown language.

Rosario explained, "I do pray in the Spirit now, at my church, or when I am out doing ministry." Rosario had connected herself to various churches in Santa Ana, doing ministry at some churches, and "getting fed" at her primary church. Praying in the Spirit was a way for her to enrich her experience. As she described her religious practices, I asked Rosario if she considered herself Pentecostal. She responded in the following manner:

> That's a tough one. I see myself as a Christian, I don't see the denomination. A lot of people do judge because I go to a lot of different churches. Like, "You can't serve two masters." Really, you're going to use that on me? When the Bible says that, it's totally different, but now I consider myself to be a mature Christian, but before I wasn't.

Ultimately, Rosario maintained her commitment to her Pentecostal church because it was compatible with her expectations of how God worked in the world. Her praying in the Spirit was a form of divine dialogue, and through this ongoing experience Rosario felt that she had become "a mature Christian." This particular spiritual practice helped to solidify her commitment at her church.

The most salient form of ongoing spiritual encounter for some informants was a direct experience of what Pentecostals call "the gifts of the spirit" (Sanchez-Walsh 2018). The gifts of the spirit are expressions understood to be supernatural embodiments of divine gifts enacted as a benefit to other congregants and as signs that God is at work in a place. The act of speaking in tongues, for example, is understood as an expression made possible through God's divine empowerment upon an individual. The act of prophecy is another gift of the Spirit mentioned by informants. This is the ability to speak of things to come, either in a sense of foretelling or in a sense of forthtelling. Arturo Esparza, for example, shared how gifts of the Spirit played an important role in helping him to stay connected at his Pentecostal church. A factory worker for many years, Arturo is now in his late sixties and sports a neatly combed slicked back hairdo, with a nicely trimmed moustache. He described the type of expectation that he developed after he started to attend a Pentecostal church:

> Little by little, the Lord began to change me. At first I wasn't changing. I began to compare my life. I'd go to dance clubs. I'd feel happy for a moment. I'd see the brothers, how they'd greet me. I began to feel warmth. No one hugged me before I came to church. The love of the brethren. They didn't reject me. There was a beautiful move of the Spirit there. Prophecy, speaking in tongues. It was a new world and seeing God move in that way really impacted me. It was that move of the Spirit that kept me there because I could feel the presence of God.

For Arturo, his process of deciding to affiliate with an evangelical church was drawn out, as he initially began to attend to get to know Julieta, the woman who would become his wife. Indeed, according to Julieta, "me lo gane para El Señor, y luego me lo gane para mi" (I won him over for the Lord, and then I won him over for myself). Arturo, nevertheless, emphasizes that the hospitality that he experienced from congregants was pivotal in drawing him into the congregation. Yet, his encounters with the practices of prophecy and speaking in tongues added a supernatural expectation to his commitment. Arturo spoke in a warm tone when he described the experiences of prophecy and speaking in tongues. These practices ushered Arturo into a "new world." Like Arturo, those informants that employed phrases such as the "move of the Spirit," often relied on that type of spiritual language to describe the confidence they had in their faith commitments. Once people acquired a taste for the "move of the Spirit," it seemed that they would commit to places that would fulfill that particular taste.

While divine dialogue as a concept implies an exchange of a propositional nature, it is better understood as an embodied experience more so than merely a perceived exchange of ideas with the divine. Individuals such as Arturo or Alicia, who developed a penchant for this move of the Spirit, did not merely seek out propositional truth but rather an experience that involved spirited prayer, lively music, with punctuated exchanges of authoritative speech spoken into the congregation or to people individually. Preaching could often be an aspect of this, but preaching alone did not typically encompass what some described as the move of the Spirit. Arturo, for example, did go on to include preaching as a facet of his encounters with the Spirit, but it seemed that these more spectacular demonstrations caught his attention and helped him tune into how the Spirit was speaking through the preaching.

Speaking also about gifts of the Spirit during our interview, Eduardo Aceves mentioned one of the members of his Pentecostal church who was considered to be a prophet. Eduardo, a restaurant worker in his early thirties, neatly dressed in a buttoned-up, collared shirt, got excited when he spoke of the gifts of the Spirit: "Do you know Bob? He is a prophet. He'll tell you things! When he speaks, he can prophesy to people about their lives. He doesn't speak Spanish, but he'll prophesy over people at our church." Bob was a member of Eduardo's Pentecostal church and was referred to by the pastors of the church as a "prophet." Members on occasion sought him out for prayer, particularly during weekly church prayer meetings.[4] I attended several prayer meetings at this church and observed Bob participating in the prayer time. The occasions that I visited I did not observe him proclaiming any type of prophetic message but did observe him praying and speaking in tongues in a quiet tone. In a predominantly Mexican church, Bob was the only African American attendee. The church held him in high regard for his gift of prophecy. The participation of Bob in the life of the church provided Eduardo with a sense of pride in being able to say that his church had a prophet. Though Eduardo spoke English, the fact that Bob did not speak Spanish seemed to amplify Eduardo's excitement about the uniqueness of Bob's ability.

At least one congregant that admitted to not enacting the gifts of the Spirit herself found a sense of value in seeing these practices enacted within her church. Yolanda Herrera worked as a preschool teacher and was a member of an independent Pentecostal church. In speaking about the gifts of the Spirit, Yolanda explained that her style of interacting in church was "more traditional." She elaborated on what she meant by traditional and how she believed that God still listened to her prayers:

[4] Hagan and Ebaugh (2003) note the significant role of prophecy in the decision-making processes of some migrants.

> I don't speak, "I shoulda bought a Honda," but the responses from God are the same and my prayers are still different. You've seen how others do in our church. When I pray I say, "Lord I don't speak like this, or pray like this, but I know you listen to me. And He does listen."

On the surface, it might appear that Yolanda was disavowing the gifts of the Spirit, speaking of them in a comical way; the phrase "I shoulda bought a Honda" was meant to imitate speaking in tongues. What she was expressing, though, was that she believed these styles of prayer to be special, and though her prayers appeared less supernatural, they were still efficacious. Moreover, Yolanda was validating prayer that involved speaking in tongues which some of her co-congregants engaged in. She was measuring the validity of her prayer alongside the more sensational style.

During my time of visiting churches, I did not witness any directly identifiable expressions of the gifts of the spirit within Catholic churches. Even at the Catholic Charismatic services that I visited, I did not see these practices enacted. That is not to say that they never happened, but that they were not made public in the particular gatherings I attended. What did take place at the Catholic Charismatic services I visited was that during times of prayer, attendees were invited to come forward and be prayed for. This time of prayer was quite similar in format to what took place at many Pentecostal churches in Santa Ana. People would come forward to the stage, stand clustered around the stage area, and someone else, usually a church leader or lay leader, would eventually stand with them and pray with them. Examining a Latin American context, Chesnut (2003) argues that the Catholic Charismatic Renewal tends to excel in providing participants with practices of inner healing, rather than some of the more ostentatious manifestations enacted at some Pentecostal churches. This would seem consistent with what I observed at Catholic Charismatic gatherings, where participants were invited to the front of the room and were prayed for in close, personal ways.

Most Pentecostal churches I observed in Santa Ana were reserved in their manifestations of the gifts of the Spirit. Moreover, even as some Pentecostals talked about experiences with the gifts of the Spirit, most of the churches I visited did not express these gifts constantly at their gatherings. Often these manifestations were reserved for smaller prayer gatherings, for church retreats, or for special revival services. Nevertheless, experiences of these gifts were integrated into the descriptions of divine dialogue provided by some Santaneros, almost exclusively Pentecostals.

Aside from differences between Pentecostals and Catholic Charismatics, what is clear is that Santaneros who participated in these types of renewalist communities tended to experience renewalist practices as signs of God's immanent presence. These were points of direct contact with the divine for those that were participating. Again, more than a propositional form of dialogue, these were embodied experiences of ongoing contact. As Santaneros looked back and talked about these practices and experiences, they integrated them into a broader framework of ongoing spiritual dialogue.

Renewalist Critiques

At various points in the data-collection process I considered that the project could focus solely on Santaneros who identified with renewalist movements, especially since I encountered so many such individuals among the churchgoers I was meeting. However, because not all affirmed renewalist movements, I decided to maintain a more expansive scope. As I discovered, some informants expressed a reticence toward Charismatic and Pentecostal worship experiences and their objections also figured into their religious commitments. Objections were often grounded in appeals to particular sources of authority, such as the Bible, or a clergy person.

The Catholic Charismatic Renewal came up in conversation when I interviewed Margarita Luna in the front yard of her single-family home. In her sixties, and dedicated to her work as a homemaker, Margarita stated, "I don't go to those Charismatic events anymore," including parish-based groups, or regional conferences, as other parishioners did. She was a member of a Catholic lay ministry at Immaculate Heart of Mary, where she participated in home visitations throughout the community with the purpose of assisting people to grow in their Catholic faith. Certain groups within her parish did participate in charismatic retreats or attend *congresos*. Margarita participated in some of those activities years prior, but was forceful in stating that she had no desire to participate in those activities currently. Initially, when I inquired if Margarita had been to events related to the Catholic Charismatic renewal, she responded with a resounding, "No!" Maintaining a frown on her face, she elaborated on her response in the following manner:

> We used to go to the *congresos* [conferences] in the convention center. One of the padres told me that it was all a business to make money. I had gone like ten times to those before. Many singers would show up to sing. They would bring their CDs to sell to the people. The padre said there are a lot of people that are hypocrites.

Margarita did not identify with the revivalistic tendencies of the charismatic movement, but more specifically, she was dissuaded to attend because of criticisms mounted by one of her parish priests. Margarita's response suggests that the priest had a strong influence over her opinions, as in her response, she discursively distanced herself from the Charismatic movement by appealing to the authority of her parish priest. Nevertheless, I observed that these events were promoted at the parish within the charismatic groups and parishioners that were members of these groups did attend. Most Catholic parishes in Santa Ana are religious ecologies unto themselves situated within the larger religious ecology of the city. While the Catholic Charismatic Renewal is wielding an ever-increasing influence over Latinx Catholicism in the United States (Espinosa 2017), the case of Margarita points to the possibility that not all are cheering on the growth of the movement. Margarita experienced the movement for herself, and made the decision to disengage from it.

Margarita's objections to the Catholic Charismatic Renewal did not mean that Margarita did not experience a sense of divine dialogue. As I observed, she was significantly focused on spiritual connection through the praying of the Rosary among other things. I also noted her participation in devotional gatherings centered on Our Lady of

Guadalupe. Furthermore, as she admitted, she was strongly committed to devotion to La Virgen de Juquila. For her, disconnection from the Charismatic movement was a move towards a more authentic experience of her faith. She continued to feel most connected "through praying the rosary and through maintaining my devotion to La Virgen de Juquila," as she articulated.

Rigoberto Bernal also recounted a negative experience at a Pentecostal church from several years prior. Rigoberto, who worked as a restaurant cook, spoke in a swift, staccato fashion during our interview. His voice quickened further as he shared his objections to renewalist movements. Rigoberto explained that a coworker persistently invited him to attend her church. Initially, Rigoberto met with her at a Starbucks, where they had a conversation about the Bible. Rigoberto "enjoyed talking about the Bible." He eventually went to church with her. Rigoberto explained his experience in the following manner:

> I didn't like it! Everyone was yelling, dancing, it was disorderly. Some people would even faint when they were getting prayed for, and I asked myself, "what is this?" After that night I told my friend that I no longer wanted to go to church. My friend was about to return to Mexico, so she sent her sister to pick me up and bring me to the church again. I told her sister, "No, I don't want to go!" and I didn't return.

In Rigoberto's case, he eventually committed to an evangelical church, but one that was quite conservative and did not involve itself with Pentecostal and Charismatic practices. On one occasion that I visited Rigoberto's church, a church member approached me to inquire about my study. The congregant took the liberty to tell me that he believed that many Latinx Protestant churches, "were teaching their people the wrong things. They're not teaching them what's in the Bible, but they're led by experiences that are more emotional. A lot of these churches that are supposedly growing are not teaching sound doctrine." While Pentecostal churches also appeal to the authority of the Bible, Rigoberto's church prided itself in strict adherence to Biblical teaching over and above personal experience.

According to Rigoberto's account, his exposure to a renewalist church and his articulation of objections about that church, spurred him to commit to an evangelical church that did not leave space for such outward practices. Despite Rigoberto's objections to more extreme practices espoused by some Pentecostal churches, I met several members of his church that previously had attended Pentecostal churches; these members did not explicitly disavow Pentecostal doctrine or practice, but merely focused on the approach to Bible teaching espoused by their church. Even Rigoberto himself at times used language reminiscent of Pentecostal talk. When he described his commitments to stay away from particular types of activities that he deemed as not proper for Christians, he described his decision in the following way:

> Just like anyone else, I can go dancing. I have the liberty to do that, but I have simply chosen not to do it in order to commit myself to Christ. The Spirit of God tells me, "That is not beneficial for you."

Rigoberto, too, engaged in divine dialogue, but preferred to do it outside of Pentecostal spaces.

The pervasiveness of renewalist movements in Santa Ana had brought many Santaneros into contact with renewalist practices. Some had an immediate draw to these practices, some acquired the taste, others rejected the practices altogether. It did seem, nevertheless, that renewalist practices supercharged the city with particular expectations of immediate, energized emotional experiences. The experiences of divine dialogue in these movements were often felt in gatherings where collective effervescence abounded (Durkheim 1912). The emotional authenticity that some claimed to experience at these gatherings was seen as manipulative or hypocritical by others.

Symbols and Images

For many informants, particularly Catholic informants, images were a potent reminder of God's grace and strongly shaped their devotional commitments. As alluded to in other chapters, people forged intimate connections to particular images, not because the image alone held power in their estimation, but because they understood that the image represented a spiritual personage. The use of images made the experiences of divine dialogue that much more tangible for many Catholics. This brought a divine representative into the home or neighborhood of the devotee. The use of these images served as a boundary marker between Catholics and evangelicals, but more than merely demarcating difference, awareness of difference offered an opportunity for some Catholics to further define why they believed that images were effective elements of spirituality.

Alicia Suarez explained a memorable encounter with some people at her door, presumably Jehovah's Witnesses, which involved an image she had at home. After the encounter she had a helpful conversation with the leader of her Charismatic prayer group in relation to the use of images:

> One time they came to knock on the door. Those *hermanos* that are Christian but not Catholic. I had the image of La Virgen right there where you see it now. They told me this and that. They told me that, "that picture you have framed there, that won't really do anything for you." At that time, I didn't know much about my faith. What they told me started to make me doubt. So I called my prayer coordinator from my prayer group and I told her that they had just told me that the picture won't do anything for me. She told me, "That image doesn't do miracles for you. You have a photograph of your parents, right? You have it, you contemplate it, you look at it. That image there, is not going to do miracles for you. The one that does miracles is Jesus, through Maria."

The prayer coordinator's explanation helped solidify for Alicia that it was the being behind the image that truly had power, not the image itself. In this case, Mary the mother of Jesus served as a mediator, and ultimately Jesus Christ performed miracles for the faithful. Alicia felt at ease about maintaining her prayers of devotion before the image of Guadalupe.

Catholic Santaneros owned a broad array of images of saints who served as mediators for God's grace. Besides Guadalupe, those

I spoke with made references to images such as that of El Santo Niño de Atocha, a representation of Jesus as an infant, la Virgen de Juquila, a representation of the blessed mother originating in Oaxaca, and Saint James the Apostle. Jesús Malverde, an image on the periphery of orthodox Catholic belief, was mentioned by one informant. Malverde is known to some as a "narco-saint," popular among drug cartel members. This particular informant, an immigrant from Sinaloa, had a deep devotion to Malverde, and carried his image with him on a necklace. One informant also made a passing reference to Santa Muerte as a personage revered by some individuals that felt ostracized by formal churches, noting that she knew queer people who revered Santa Muerte.

Images played a distinct role in the development of dialogue practices and in the solidifying of religious commitments for Catholics. Many Catholics felt a strong sense of communion with the divine through engaging in dialogue with the help of these revered images. The images could be held in a place of honor, signaling that the person represented in the image was held in high regard. Images offered an opportunity for personalization as individuals added personal elements to the material representations of particular personages. The placement of an image within private, personal space, the accompaniment of personal objects, indicative of individual tastes, such as select votive candles, identified a particular image as being that much more intertwined with the personal life of an individual. Images were a potent form of engagement with the divine, and for many Santaneros, images were the primary point of daily divine dialogue. I develop more extensively the place of images in Chapter 7.

The Presence of Evil

While the notion of divine dialogue encompasses communion with God, and with positive spiritual entities, many Santaneros also made references to the work of evil spirit beings. Beliefs about evil spirit beings involved a type of perception for Santaneros' which also shaped their religious commitments. Araceli Zamora, for example, a Catholic informant, referred to the devil using the term "el Chango."[5] A facility maintenance worker in her late forties, Araceli chuckled when she interjected the reference to the devil. Araceli had been speaking with joy about wanting "to retire in Mexico someday with my husband." Her description took a somber tone not masked by her laughter when she acknowledged that despite their hopes and plans, "Uno pone, Dios dispone, viene el chango y todo lo descompone" (One proposes, God disposes, the monkey comes, and everything decomposes.)

There was a fatalistic element to Araceli's description. While God was the one to orchestrate a plan, Satan had the option to sabotage the plan. I wondered if Araceli would interject a more hopeful finale to her statement, but she never did. Araceli and her husband had experienced some social mobility, moving from an apartment to a trailer park, but they had also experienced some challenges with their oldest son, a young man in his late teens who struggled with drug addiction. Araceli's dreams were currently limited by the evil that had befallen her son. A number of mothers I encountered carried these burdens for their children, but also truncated their own dreams, waiting and fighting for the lives of their children, most typically sons, against structural and personal evils.

Francisca Delgado also described a pivotal conversation involving the person of Satan that drove her to become more consistent in attending mass. In her early sixties, Francisca sported a flowered apron as I interviewed her at her home. She explained, "When I first got married to my husband, I went to a priest for confession and the priest told me 'Mija [my daughter/dear] el chango doesn't want you to be in mass.'" For Araceli, that was a sufficient point that made her reconsider her habits of mass attendance. If the devil did not want her in mass, then she needed to be in mass. This conversation took place in Mexico, but it stayed with her, so much so that she was able to recall it nearly four decades later. She had remained consistent in her participation at mass through the present. These perceptions of the evil

[5] The term "el chango" in reference to Satan has been documented by Anthropologist George Foster (1966) in Michoacan, Mexico. This is not to be confused with the Afro-Cuban Santeria practice of venerating Changó, an African Orisha, referred to by Yoruba name. Foster's research centers on a community highly influenced by indigenous culture.

one were important identity markers in terms of how some Santaneros structured their religious participation. They wanted not only to be near to God but also to safeguard themselves from Satan.

Evangelicals also referenced the intervention of Satan as factoring into their religious participation. Lourdes, who discussed hearing from God through various means, also mentioned briefly that she had been "attacked by the enemy and he has manifested to me." Lourdes had experienced a number of difficulties in her life, as a single mother who at times struggled financially, and maintained multiple jobs. Yet even outside her material hardships, she asserted that Satan had attacked her. Three of Lourdes's sons had faced prison sentences, and she had remained faithful to God pleading for her sons. She was tenacious in battling evil as she persisted in praying for her sons.

For Valeria Rodriguez, the coded term used in regard to confronting Satan was "liberacion/liberation." Valeria explained that she experienced liberation during a retreat that she attended at her Pentecostal church. In popular Latin American Pentecostal theology, liberation often refers to being liberated from a spiritual affliction or worse, from direct demonic oppression (Chesnut 1997). For Valeria, this experience was "something I told my whole family about, though they don't really understand." Most of Valeria's family, including her husband, were not evangelicals, and Valeria prayed that "they would experience the freedoms that [she] had experienced" through her faith. Liberation from evil, or the evil one, is something Valeria continued to look for others to experience through her church involvement, and as such, she volunteered to help with activities that made these experiences possible for others.

Notions of the Spirit world and of spiritual entities were not confined to the traditional doctrines of both Catholic and evangelical churches. Some spoke of situations that were beyond their respective church's orthodoxy. Often, these ideas did not focus on spirit "beings," so much as spiritual powers. Carolina Jimenez, who had started attending an evangelical church in the city, and had visited several other evangelical churches previously, shared about some of her engagement with disparate spiritual practices. I had met Carolina and her husband Bryan at a community center, and I spoke with them briefly. In speaking about her religious commitments,

Carolina explained that she and her husband had been arguing more than usual at home. She wondered if someone had performed an *amarre* on her, which is a type of spell to bind people together romantically. She decided to consult with a tarot card reader. When I spoke to Carolina, she had not gotten the results she had wanted from the card reading, given her continued tensions at home, but she continued to seek spiritual guidance, this time through evangelical churches. Her husband, Bryan, though himself Catholic, was generally tolerant of her visits to evangelical churches, and at times accompanied her; he was less at ease with her visits to the card reader, though. Both Carolina and Bryan were in their mid-thirties and were of the 1.5 generation; they both dressed in sporty attire with t-shirts, shorts, and sneakers. Both were searching in terms of their spiritual commitments, and their search had taken them to opportunities that rested outside traditional church settings. Carolina and Bryan were not part of my primary interview sample, but I include their story to illustrate that there were practices outside the traditional church systems that Santaneros engaged in.

Cases such as those of Carolina and Bryan are analytically important because several informants made observations about people close to them engaging in folk spiritual practices and their articulations of these practices were introduced discursively to fortify boundaries from such practices. Lucas Marquez, for example, a construction worker in his mid-twenties, talked about how his next-door neighbors periodically invited a healer to their home. While Lucas did not use the word *curandero* to describe this healer, from his description, the man in question was likely a *curandero*. Lucas had not observed firsthand in detail the practices this *curandero* engaged in, but he explained that he had spoken to his neighbors about these practices. Lucas stressed that he felt uncomfortable with what the neighbors had described to him and relayed the following:

> They claimed that this healer would change in age, right before their eyes, sometimes becoming younger, sometimes becoming older. He would pray over people's illnesses externally, like not having to actually operate, and he would make diagnoses regarding people's internal organs.

Lucas had become evangelical about five years prior to our conversation, and he did not find these practices compatible with his faith. He declared,

> I don't think that's right. But people come to look for this guy. And they pay him for what he does. They all have to pay him to do his procedures because he's like a doctor. They have it at my next door neighbor's house, and then they even started having it at the neighbor's house across the street. I think that people that do things like that are getting into some spiritual things that are evil.

The implications of Lucas's last statement was that both clients and healer were seeking assistance through spiritual means that could potentially harm them, as these would have been evil.

Several others indicated that they disapproved of other types of spiritualist practices. Clarisa Aceves, for example, mentioned that "My mom used to pass the egg [Mi mama pasaba el huevo].[6] She did it to my son. But I told her, 'I don't want you to do that! Please respect me!'" The practice of "passing the egg" is a folk tradition that is a type of cleansing ritual. Clarisa was furious that her mother had practiced the ritual on her son, and she berated her mother for her actions. In describing this to me, she made it clear that she would never engage in that type of practice again, but her description seemed to imply that in times past she would have partaken of this practice. Now, she saw the practice as diametrically opposed to her evangelical faith. In similar fashion, Jimena Ibarra, a Catholic parishioner, announced her disapproval during our interview of practices such as tarot card reading. She explained,

> Some people give themselves over to have the cards read. For me, the only cards that might be of significance would be ones with Saint Peter, or the Virgen de Guadalupe. But for me, it's not right. The love of God is the only thing we need. Should a Catholic person consult these things? No, it's not allowed.

[6] Robbins (2004) notes that in Pentecostalism, indigenous practices are associated with the Devil.

Among informants, nearly all, both Catholic and evangelical, spoke disparagingly of the practices that rested outside of traditional church practices. This negative view of "folk practices" was perhaps an artifact of the sampling methods I used, focusing primarily on people that had formal membership within local church parishes. Those who had at one point experienced these types of practices, talked about them as if they had discontinued them. However, informants' ongoing familiarity and awareness of these practices suggest that many people in their social circles still engaged in these practices, on the periphery of formal churches. Seeking out those that were less connected to churches would have perhaps rendered a higher rate of active practitioners seeking spiritual help from forms of popular religion. Among the more active church goers that I interviewed, these types of activities served as a symbolic boundary marker. Those who participated in this were outside acceptable church doctrine and practice.

Overlapping Spirit Worlds

Chapter 3 of this volume largely emphasizes how the spiritual experiences of Catholic and evangelical informants differed, especially as relates to altar encounters. While this present chapter also highlights several differences in the experiences of Catholics and evangelicals, here I find that Catholics and evangelicals held important commonalities. Generally, through forms of spiritual dialogue and expectations about the spirit world, both groups generated a sense of affirmation in the choices and commitments they made to particular faith communities amid the plethora of options before them. Catholic and evangelical theologies may differ on important points and adherents may emphasize how rituals and practices diverge, yet the sense of ongoing connection to the divine, a certain direct line of grace, seemed to remain vibrant in the lives of both groups of affiliates. Moreover, religious identities remained strong as affiliates were able to signal these ongoing points of divine contact. Identities were also shaped by the ways that Catholics and evangelicals distanced themselves from particular practices that were outside denominational orthodoxy. Practices of folk spirituality outside both Catholic and evangelical traditions in this case often served as recognizable boundaries to both sets of informants. The practices of divine dialogue and the recognition of unorthodoxy served to demarcate the boundaries of belonging within Catholic and evangelical affiliations.

Speaking particularly to lived religion, the spirit worlds engaged by Catholics and evangelicals overlapped in intricate ways. Moreover, there is more work to be done to theorize how these particular understandings about spiritual realities intersect and inform each other. Nelson (2005) synthesizes several helpful observations on the notion of how religion structures distinct experiential worlds for religious adherents:

> While we can agree with Eliade that, in a very general sense, those who are religious live in a different experiential world from those who are not, we must recognize that the religious do not all live in the same alternate reality. "Religions do not all inhabit the same world, but actually posit, structure, and dwell within a universe that is their own," William Paden (1994:51) rightly observed, and he might have added that within each of the major religious traditions there are what we may call "sub-worlds," and these can actually differ from one another as much as (or even more than) the major faiths differ from one another.

The "sub-worlds" of Catholics and evangelicals certainly exhibited differences, but in this case, it is inaccurate to say that they lived in completely separate worlds. Rather, there were significant overlaps in the sub-worlds of Catholics and evangelicals. This overlap was not coincidental, as the fact of the matter is that most evangelical informants were once Catholics. The expectations of divine dialogue were in part tied to Catholic religiosity. In my estimation, the Mexican Catholic imagination, as proposed by Castañeda-Liles (2018), permeated the sub-worlds—the spirit worlds—of Catholic and evangelical Santaneros. Their awareness of both human-centered relationships, and divine-centered interactions colored "how they enter[ed] into relationship with the sacred" (Castañeda-Liles 2018:210). Likewise, the rise and influence of Pentecostal and Charismatic brands of Christianity infused communities like Santa Ana with a "pneumatic" flavor of

Christianity (Chesnut 2003). So, while the altar encounters served as discursive centerpieces, and orienting experiences, that often distinguished Catholics and evangelicals, the ongoing worlds that Catholics and evangelicals inhabited tended to acknowledge the power of spirit beings, even if in distinct ways.

These experiences of a thin veil between the spirit world and the material world, helped to sustain the ethnic character of the city. As individuals recognized which places they were to avoid, and which places spoke to their spirits, they navigated the city in deeply personal ways. That is, these understandings of spiritual cartographies kept people tied to the ethnic spaces of Santa Ana. In as much as people contended to encounter the divine in consistent, life-giving ways, within the boundaries of the city, the city remained a spiritual haven for these Santaneros. Likewise, as people identified spaces to be avoided, as insiders, these too were spaces which provided ethnic meaning. After all, to be aware of the spiritual cartographies of a city, both the good and the bad, required direct experience. Only those who navigated the city directly would be experts of the city's spiritual wells and spiritual foundations.

6
Notions of Neighborhood

"If you really want to see what our religion is like, you have to come around here to *la comunidad* [the community]. This is where the true religion takes place." Edgar Olvera, a lay Catholic leader of stout build and gruff voice, looked me in the eye as he spoke these words of advice regarding my research in the community. Accentuating the term *la comunidad*, Edgar spread his arms in grandiose manner as if to embrace the row of bungalow homes surrounding us. *La comunidad*, for Edgar and many of his co-parishioners, encompassed both place and people. The Catholic ministry Edgar coordinated sponsored a procession that involved praying at homes within designated Santa Ana neighborhoods. This was part of a tradition called El Rosario de la Aurora, a morning gathering centered on praying the rosary at particular locations. As the group ambulated through the neighborhood, four participants at a time took turns shouldering a small platform mounted on poles carrying an image of the Virgen de Guadalupe, the focus of the gathering. Edgar transitioned his enthralled audience as the image of Guadalupe was brought to rest on the front lawn of a home, her final stop. "We think we are carrying her, but it is she who is carrying us!" Edgar pronounced. He was right. Guadalupe had mobilized the community in numerous ways, on various levels. The synergy she spurred sustained participants beyond the span of this event.

I soon learned that the draw of the Rosario de la Aurora was less contingent on Edgar's front-facing leadership than on the backstage efforts of Mercedes Uribe, a woman whose role was second only to Guadalupe at this event. Mercedes, the host at the final stop, saw it as her duty to welcome anyone in sight. A sixty-year-old immigrant from the Mexican state of Guanajuato, Mercedes would later gush about how she "loves the opportunity to host events at her home!" For the time being, motioning her hands downward, she invited all to sit at the tables set up on her front lawn to partake of a meal. The procession

The Saints of Santa Ana. Jonathan E. Calvillo, Oxford University Press (2020). © Oxford University Press.
DOI: 10.1093/oso/9780190097790.001.0001.

of a couple dozen participants swelled to nearly a hundred revelers, largely due to Mercedes' hospitality. The numbers ebbed and flowed as neighbors took freedom to exit and return through a chain-link gate. Beside the gate, on the edge of Mercedes's lawn, a Mexican flag perched atop a twenty-foot pole billowed overhead, welcoming visitors. The devotion embodied in the steamy bowls of stew, seasoned with fragrant spices, and accompanied by boisterous laughter, filled the community space. With precise auditory focus, Mercedes heard the inquiry of a teenage girl standing beyond the front yard fence. "Pasale mija!" (come in my dear) Mercedes exclaimed repeatedly. The young woman was searching for her mother, whose presence was being requested elsewhere. Mercedes continued to insist that the young woman enter. Surely Edgar's understanding of "true religion" in *la comunidad* was as present in Mercedes's hospitality as it was in the prayers and procession.

Faith in Community

This chapter explores the religiously informed dispositions with which faith adherents like Mercedes and Edgar relate to Santa Ana's barrios. Religious affiliation tended to inform particular neighborhood frames which were shaped and in turn shaped residents' patterns of engagement in the barrio (Small 2002). Catholics, I argue, demonstrated a stronger sense of the neighborhood as a place inhabited by a trust network. Furthermore, through devotional practices, Catholics worked to locally recreate an experience of the homeland spurred by an experience of nostalgia (see DuCross 2017). Catholic neighborhood nostalgia encouraged reproduction of homeland practices and symbols in public spaces, and imbued the ethnic enclave with value as a space where collective retrospection was possible. Consequently, Catholics were more likely than their evangelical neighbors to highlight positive aspects of the *barrio*.

Evangelicals, on the other hand, exhibited a "barrio reformation" perspective, a view that framed the neighborhood as a place to be reformed. The primary discourse that evangelicals deployed in relation to the neighborhood was one of transformation. Evangelicals invested in local neighborhoods intent on supplementing neighborhood deficits. I argue that as the barrio is an important generator of social resources, or social capital, these diverging relationships to the barrio correlate with differential modes of resource access for members of each religious group.

Building a Space of Resource Exchange

The sharing of resources is an important aspect of *la comunidad* that was on display at El Rosario de la Aurora. Most obvious, food was accessible to whosoever would set foot on Mercedes's front lawn. Some participants, though not most, came primarily to have a meal. Many volunteers, especially women, contributed to preparing and serving the food. More subtle exchanges of resources were also at play. Cultural, emotional, and cognitive resources were being transmitted. Physical exertion was being asked of people for setup and cleanup of the event. The event was organized, and various people had pre-designated roles, but impromptu opportunities abounded for visitors to become volunteers. Volunteers interacted as they worked side by side. People experienced a sense of camaraderie as they laughed and reminisced. Neighbors with busy schedules, some working multiple jobs, were able to deepen familiarity with others in the neighborhood. In getting to know each other better, people found opportunities for continued interaction beyond the event. Some of these exchanges were directly related to Guadalupan devotion, other exchanges were byproducts of face-to-face interaction, and sometimes one type of interaction led to the other. In all cases, the sense of religious community and ethnic community were further anchored in the neighborhood.

The concept of social capital captures well the harnessing of potential resources taking place through this gathering. According to Pierre Bourdieu, social capital is "the aggregate of the actual or potential resources which are linked to possession of a durable network of more or less institutionalized relationships of mutual acquaintance or recognition" (1986:248). Social capital provides people access to a set of assets predicated on membership within a trust-infused network (Bourdieu 1986; Coleman 1988; Putnam 1995). Neither "membership" nor networks need to be formal for social capital to be activated. What matters is that trust and ties are present, even if still in nascent form. The multiplexity of ties being made and strengthened through El Rosario de la Aurora, for example, broadened the neighborhood's social capital capacity. When a religious network of this type overlays an ethnic community, faith identities and ethnic identities function in mutually reinforcing ways.

Observing Social Capital

As *El Rosario de la Aurora* was thinning out, a woman in her late twenties, with a toddler-laden baby stroller, spoke to a group of women at a table. "She doesn't know how to pray the rosary and she wants to learn how," a woman furtively noted to a handful of people at an adjacent table. A male lay leader from the ministry sponsoring the event promptly stood up in response. I listened as the young woman engaged this man in conversation and inquired about the rosary. As she spoke, her intonation revealed an accent associated with people in Southern Mexico primarily of indigenous heritage. Her long, shiny black hair was pulled back tightly, as she held the baby stroller handles with both hands. She explained that she was never taught to pray the rosary where she came from. The mustached man that spoke to her wore a buttoned shirt tucked in at his waist. He hunched over to converse with this woman of shorter stature than he. Both the man and the woman were locked into serious conversation.

In magician-like fashion, the man drew a pamphlet from his shirt pocket which explained how to pray the rosary. He began to share with this woman, speaking in a deep, pedantic tone, the proper way to pray. The man was sharing a type of expertise with this woman. He then connected her to some of the women who were part of the sponsoring ministry. Several women took down her contact information. The woman wanting to learn the rosary thanked them. The ties being formed between these individuals gave way to another form of social capital: the first woman was being more fully connected to the local parish, an institution. Other conversations like these were taking place. The questions were different, but new ties were being made and existing ones were being strengthened around religious commonality. Official parish activities were being promoted from time to time, reinforcing institutional connections between those with strong parish connections and those with weak ones. People were becoming more embedded within *la comunidad*.

Attitudes toward the Barrio

Juanita Vargas in both word and deed was a champion for the parish model of church, wherein churches are anchored in and serve their surrounding neighborhoods. She demonstrated enthusiasm for having the church close by even as she expressed positive opinions about her working-class community. Juanita declared that she was "thankful to God for living close to the church." She says that when she first arrived in the United States "[I] began to go, little by little, [to church], and what I am most thankful for is that God brought me to *this* neighborhood that is so close to the church and the church is what has brought me so close to my kids." Before coming to the United States, family members had warned her that "kids go bad over there," meaning in the United States. When she moved to her neighborhood of Townsend St, she observed that some young people did struggle to establish healthy life patterns. But she also saw opportunities in her community. For her, though many judged her neighborhood negatively, it was rife with opportunity. The link between the neighborhood and the church was one of several important resources that Juanita gushed about. Juanita essentially embraced an asset-awareness outlook of the barrio. She recognized positive resources and potentialities present in her neighborhood.

Juanita described how she communicated the importance of the parish model to her son. Her son, Jose Luis, was preparing to go to college the following fall, but had not yet decided what college to attend.[1] Jose Luis asked his mother what she thought about him attending college far away, which in this case simply meant having to move away

[1] Jose Luis would later be admitted to and would graduate from a prestigious university in California.

from home. She responded in the following manner: "I tell him, wherever you go, pay attention to where the closest church is. Even if it's an hour, if that's the closest that's where you have to go. God is everywhere and our [Catholic] churches are everywhere. Find the one that is closest to you." Juanita assumed that if Jose Luis was going to look for a church, the closest Catholic church would be the natural choice.

The church added value to Juanita's experience in her neighborhood, even though the block she lived on was in one of the toughest neighborhoods in the city. During the span of field work, the neighborhood was placed under a gang injunction by the Santa Ana Police Department. Despite being fully aware of the manner in which her neighborhood was judged, Juanita made it a point to reveal how she had confronted negative assumptions about her neighborhood. One particular exchange that she recalled involved one of her children's school teachers:

> I am very happy where I live. I know that it's a lower neighborhood, but I am happy because I know my community. We don't complain about where we live. A teacher once told us, a lady said to us, "I don't know why people from Townsend St. don't buy homes but they buy jewelry and cars." I said that's true, but a lot of people have to bring in other people to afford a house. But I do love the neighborhood where I live. We live by ourselves [as a family not having to rent to other tenants]. We are independent. We have two bathrooms. The only thing we lack is room to run. I learned if you can't afford a house, work for your community.

Essentially, Juanita had defended her neighborhood. Juanita was committed to working with her neighbors to ensure her neighborhood was a great place to live. Much of this came through her participation in neighborhood-based church activities, as well as participation in a local community center. Countering the teacher's perspective, Juanita believed that moving to a higher-income neighborhood would actually bring more risks to her family, as it would force the family to live above their means. For her, staying in her current neighborhood was less risky because her family could live at a sustainable socioeconomic level and continue to benefit from the resources of her ethnic community. Juanita's children were all involved with the local parish, and Juanita believed that the church had contributed to the success of her children. A married mother of three children, two teens and one young adult, all of Juanita's children were enrolled in honors courses.

Hearing Juanita describe her love of the neighborhood did not conjure up images of a place plagued by gang violence, police raids, and drug dealers. Instead, her talk painted the picture of a neighborhood that was stable and safe. Juanita would seem like an ideal candidate for seeking social mobility via neighborhood mobility. She studied to be a nurse in Mexico, and served in that role for nearly a decade. She arrived in the United States more educated than many of her co-ethnic neighbors. Still, Juanita felt very much at ease living in her working-class neighborhood, given the resources she learned to access there. Her family was of mixed legal status so that also highly influenced where her family felt safe. Juanita drew a sense of safety through her involvement in the church and in community-based organizations.

Neighborhood unity through religion was a benefit that various subjects described when talking about life in their barrio. In one conversation with Francisca and Ricardo Delgado, Francisca observed that faith was a unifying factor in their neighborhood, primarily "for those of us that are Catholic." Her husband, Ricardo, expressed that Ash Wednesday was an example of how religion unified the neighborhood. He said it strengthened the relationships "with those we [already] have a connection with." Ricardo explained that the last time Ash Wednesday came around, he did not go to church as he had done in the past. Instead,

> A group from the church came and administered the customary ashes for Ash Wednesday in the neighborhood. A deacon was present, as a representative of the Inmaculado Corazón, and placed the ash markings on people's foreheads in the form of a cross as is typically done for Ash Wednesday. It was nice to have it in the neighborhood.

These types of experiences forged institutional ties and also strengthened ethnoreligious networks in the community.

Delia Carrillo, her husband, and her son, were a household that chose to stay in the barrio, despite having had the resources to move out. Her college-educated daughter and son-in-law actually did move out to a suburb in a neighboring city. Delia introduced me to her brother, Beto Flores, who lived across the street from her. I interviewed both Delia and Beto, and had several follow up conversations with them in their neighborhood. Delia and Beto's life experiences were more akin to that of second-generation Chicanos, because they came to the United States as young children in the 1950s. They both had little recollection of Mexico. Both being of lighter olive skin tone, Beto recalled, "Sometimes people at work would ask me if I'm Italian. I'd have to tell them, no, I'm Mexican." Delia had worked for a number of years in the local school district as an instructional assistant. She was accustomed to moving about through the systems of the city. Still, they grew up in the Artesia-Pilar neighborhood of Santa Ana, one of the oldest barrios in the city. They had a sense of ethnic space tied to their early memories in their childhood neighborhood.

For Delia and Beto, Catholicism was an important aspect of life in the barrio, but it was an aspect that was primarily staged in the home. Beto explained, "at home, we always had faith symbols." According to Delia's description, "We only had La Virgen or San Martin de Porras. All those other Saints or Virgins, that's from Mexico. We didn't have that here." Delia added that families like hers were strict about "baptizing your children through the church, and staying at the same church. It wasn't like today where people don't always stay at the same church." Beto attributed the lack of public religion in the barrio to the fact that "the church was basically white back then. We only had one mass in Spanish. We mainly kept our traditions at home." Delia explained that "we only used to do candle lighting at church. Now they do a lot of the traditions in the streets. That's more recent."

The barrios experienced by Delia and Beto were setting the stage for the barrios of today. Beto conjured up a memory of "the *jamaicas* that we had." *Jamaicas* were festivals organized by the Catholic church to raise funds but also for the enjoyment of the community. These were essentially carnivals with games and rides. Beto elaborated, "they would usually have them at a corner lot, there at the park and everyone would come out. We come from a time when we didn't have so many religions, like we do now. Almost everyone was Catholic, so everyone would come out to the *jamaicas*." So while public displays of faith were more subtle in the barrios of yesteryear, Delia and Beto memorialized the traditions that they had, sustained them in practice, and spoke of them with nostalgia.

Taking a longitudinal view of local barrios, Beto was opinionated about what barrios in the United States represented for Mexican immigrants in recent years. Having lived for five decades in the barrio, Beto had interacted extensively with his more recently arrived neighbors. In addition, Beto's work as a real estate agent consistently brought him into contact with more recently arrived Latinx immigrant clients. Based on his experiences as a realtor, Beto opined, "Mexicans really like to live in neighborhoods where they're the majority." He recalled that having shown a great number of homes to Mexican clients, many of them ended up eschewing neighborhoods where they were in the minority, even if they could afford them.

I prodded further for Beto to explain to me why he thought that it was the case that Mexicans highly valued living in the barrio. His response: "Mexican people look at a crowded neighborhood and say I want to live here. I can throw my parties, *quinceañeras*." His sister Delia, who was part of this particular conversation, interjected: "That comes from Mexico," meaning that those types of celebrations originated in Mexico, and that the desire to maintain those customs was also Mexican. Their observation was that the barrio affirmed practices which would not be permitted in other neighborhoods. "They know they can't do that in the other neighborhoods," Beto asserted. His argument was further fleshed out by his proposition that "[Mexicans] will throw a *quinceañera* [party] before they buy a car." In other words, Beto believed that these types of celebrations were of utmost importance to Mexicans and that Mexicans would attempt to secure an environment that would facilitate these types of celebrations.

Beto's statements, though intended to be an opinion about others, also reflected his, and to some extent his sister's, perception of their neighborhood. They themselves had hosted parties in the neighborhood where they invited neighbors and played loud music. They, as a number of my other informants had, invited me to several of their home celebrations. The family customarily brought out a commercial quality grill the length of a full table, had a full DJ set-up, and held all-out dance parties in their backyard until the late hours of the night. The freedoms of the barrio were certainly something that they had taken advantage of. Thus, the generalization that he had made about most Mexican households was exemplified by his own family's lifestyle. In this sense, Beto's assertion was partially a projection of his own customs. Beto and Delia suggested that for some Mexicans the desire for residential upward mobility was attenuated by a desire to maintain ethnic traditions which would be less palatable in non-Latinx neighborhoods. This view finds support in Alba and Logan's (1993) suggestion that the higher likelihood of Mexicans to reside in co-ethnic barrios may be influenced by preference. While structural barriers are most dominant, personal preference does have a role to play in neighborhood choice.

Neighborhood Nostalgia

"It's a very heavy nostalgia that one feels." As he uttered the phrase, Jesus Ibarra took a deep breath and paused, drawing a solemn hand toward his heart. It was as if the very nostalgia he had described began to set in. In a very reflective tone, Jesus proceeded to describe the type of festivities that he would frequently participate in in his hometown in Mexico:

> On the fourteenth day of December they had a fiesta at the Capilla Señor de los Milagros [the Chapel of the Lord of Miracles] where most of the town would attend. Then, they had a pilgrimage from the "rancherias" [the rural ranch areas], where people from the outskirt villages would come into town. When those pilgrimages were completed, the barrios from within the town would participate in their own pilgrimages. This was all to honor la Virgen de Guadalupe. On the 12th of December they would gather to sing Las Mañanitas. The whole pueblo would participate in pilgrimages. Then the posadas would start, at the barrios until Christmas. I really miss those days.

Jesus further elaborated, "It was difficult for me to move away from those celebrations, but it was even harder for my wife." Jesus, who had already been in the United States for a decade prior to his wife coming here, recalls his wife's experience once in the United States. Their families were from the same hometown in Mexico and they met during a season of festivities while Jesus and his family were visiting their hometown from the United States. Eventually, their paths would cross again at a pueblo festival, when Jesus and his family were in town. After a brief courtship, Jimena and Jesus married in Mexico and she returned with him to the United States. Jimena also elaborated on the events related by Jesus:

> With the neighbors, we the young people would make piñatas, fruit punch. There were a lot of people. We would get together as youth, right there in the middle of the piñata breaking. We would all share in these moments together.

Both Jesus and Jimena were emphatic about the communal aspects of their holiday celebrations in Mexico. These experiences were shared "with the neighbors." Devotional capital, a type of social capital which requires a performative investment in the religious sphere according to Peña (2011), was shared in this experience. That is, as people participate in public, collective religious activity, they are viewed with more respect, and ties are strengthened. Unlike the consumer traditions of American holidays, there were few material spoils to be acquired from the holidays that they reminisced about in Mexico. The experience for the Ibarra family was most memorable because of the communal aspect of these traditions, not necessarily because of material goods exchanged.

Several other respondents echoed similar sentiments related to missing the same level of localized community that was facilitated by the traditions in Mexico. In conversing with Ricardo and Francisca Delgado, the couple stressed that they missed the protracted aspect of the religious festivals. What mattered to the Delgados was that the community came together for an extended period of time.

RICARDO: Here they don't do what one does in Mexico. I came [here] with that illusion.

JONATHAN: What's missing here? What do you miss most?

RICARDO: The processions that they do over there. They're different. Maybe it's that over there they are done in the open field. We would walk from station to station far away. We would leave at 10[a.m.] and would return at 10[p.m.]. It was an all-day activity.

I interviewed Ricardo and his wife Francisca several months before the winter holiday season. When I participated in some of the neighborhood festivities during that winter, Ricardo and Francisca were at the forefront. The experience was different from what it was in Mexico, but it was still an opportunity to approximate the homeland context. Ricardo expressed that he was not able to make mass on many occasions, because his job as a construction worker left him very tired. His wife, a homemaker who doubled as a caretaker for friends' children, often attended mass without him. Yet, when neighborhood-based festivities came around, I observed that they participated together, consistently.

There were two dimensions of nostalgia specified by many Catholic subjects: remembrance and reenactment. On the one hand, there was an intentional effort made to recall the past and to describe it. Catholics described a yearning for what they had in their Mexican hometowns. There was a remembered experience, and an imagined community that was not physically present with them in the United States. This dimension of nostalgia reflected a retrospective aspect of Catholic spatial spirituality. In many ways, this aspect of Catholic spirituality paralleled the spatial-temporal ties discussed in Chapter 4 of this volume (see also Tweed 1997).

In addition, there was a strong motivation to reenact that which was lost. While subjects could not bring Mexico to Santa Ana, and many respondents could not readily return back because of their legal status, participants could expend energies to replicate what they had in Mexico. Reenactment required not only an emotional investment, but also material and physical investments. While most Santaneros recognized that they could not perfectly replicate what was back in the homeland, many shared a sense of satisfaction in working toward the goal of reenactment.

Mercedes Uribe was a shining example of someone for whom communal religious expression was a way to bridge temporal and geographical boundaries. In the surrounding homes and apartments, there were residents that considered Mercedes to be very devout. Among the people I interviewed, at least four subjects from the same parish referred me to her as someone that was a clear example of a faithful Catholic. After meeting her at an event she hosted at her home, I made arrangements to follow up with her. We sat and spoke on the front steps of her home. In her sixties, Mercedes's brown complexion was spry, her voluminous hair drawn back and shiny. She wore casual, comfortable sandals as she was often up and about; rarely standing still, her hands were typically busy producing something. Her nieces and nephews ran in and out of the house as we sat on the steps at the front of her home on a Saturday afternoon.

Mercedes was known for the frequency with which she volunteered her home for church festivals and celebrations. For example, leading up to Christmas time, Mercedes would open up her home for the tradition of *posadas* to take place.[2] However, when I asked Mercedes about her church attendance, she had very little to say. She casually acknowledged that she tried to attend mass weekly but was not always able to. Noticing that many of the community prayer events were hosted by specific prayer groups tied to the local parish, I asked if she was part of one of those. "No. I'm not part of those prayer groups or any of those teams," Mercedes responded in a disinterested tone. At neighborhood festivals, she was surrounded by people who exhibited some of the highest levels of church commitment that I met, yet she herself was indifferent to these opportunities. Her interest was in neighborhood-based spirituality.

Mercedes spoke elaborately of the neighborhood events she enjoyed organizing and of all the people that attended her events. She made sure I understood that people came from other cities in the county to her events. For Mercedes, the primary locus of faith expression was the barrio. According to her, "this is what I know that the people want

[2] Posadas reenact the Christian tradition of the Holy Family traveling to the city of Bethlehem while Mary was pregnant with Jesus; in Bethlehem they sought shelter for the night, but kept meeting rejection (Matovina 2011).

to participate in." Mercedes's practices and explanations helped to elucidate why neighborhood nostalgia was so important to people. Mercedes believed that neighborhood festivities met an emotional need by experientially reminding immigrants of what life was like in Mexico.

Mercedes jubilantly clasped her hands as she recounted how a new guest at one of her celebrations opined, "It's exactly like over there [in Mexico]!" This guest was surprised that the decorations and the activities involved were so similar to what he recalled from Mexico, according to Mercedes. The guest did not live in Santa Ana, and he told Mercedes, "I thought I would not see these types of celebrations in the United States again." Mercedes believed that "many people are surprised that way when they first come to see." Her efforts are partially an attempt to offset the gloom that overcomes some immigrants having to let go of ritual and celebration.

While these types of celebrations certainly would take place in other parts of Orange County, the magnitude, frequency, and spatial freedom exhibited by these events in Santa Ana were unparalleled. On some occasions, multiple celebrations would take place in close proximity to each other. People could hop across to different sites to experience different iterations of the same holiday. The support of local parishes, neighborhood associations, and other local institutions translated to ongoing support for communal celebrations throughout the year. Furthermore, the manner in which these celebrations occupied space in Santa Ana is of import. Amplified sound systems for music, in some cases loud bands, and the traversing across neighborhood sites in procession, amplified a sense of spatial belonging. This spatial spirituality ensured that nostalgia was not merely private and silent, but rather inscribed upon a communal space that extended across neighborhoods and conveyed a sense of ownership.

Local Miracles and Material Objects of Devotion

In visiting numerous community-based celebrations, it became clear that neighborhood nostalgia could not be understood without accompanying physical markers. The statues, altars, stickers, and images in general that were prevalent throughout the barrio were not merely accessories to faith and ritual, they themselves were often the focus of ritual. Saintly images were more than mere images, they were treated as guests of honor at celebrations of faith. These were also transportable and replicable representatives of culture.

As I attended a procession making its way through a central Santa Ana neighborhood, the story of one young couple captivated those in attendance. The Ayon family lived in a weathered but well-manicured home with a chain link fence around it and a wide front lawn. They were invited by the lay leader in charge to share a *testimonio* of a special occurrence they had witnessed. I pushed in on the edge of the small crowd to listen to the story that the couple related.

The husband, Giovani Ayon, walked forward, stepping out from his front porch with fidgety movements. He seemed reluctant to speak but his body language reflected a sense of excitement. He began by pointing to the altar on their front porch and stating how important it was to them. The altar contained a statue, about a foot and a half tall, of the Virgen de Guadalupe. Giovani said that the family was worried during a recent spell of the Santa Ana winds when the altar fell over. Before describing more, he choked up. Estefania, Giovani's wife, stepped in to continue the story. Estefania explained that she found out about the initial happenings when her husband called her on her cell phone. She rushed home to inspect the altar. She communicated a sense of urgency to the crowd, over the concern that possibly their statue of *La Virgen* had not survived the extended gust of wind. This would be a terrible tragedy. To the surprise of Estefania and Giovani, the statue was perfectly fine. Giovani and Estefania recognized this as a miracle.

The sharing of these testimonies publicly, coupled with the continued placement of these images in public spaces, helped to fortify the connection between physical sites in the neighborhood and memorialized accounts of divine intervention. Numerous scholars highlight the presence of objects of devotion in migrants' spiritual practices before, through, and after journeying from Mexico to the United States (Hagan 2008; Durand and Massey 2020), as already explored in Chapter 4. In similar fashion, objects of devotion enabled residents to sustain publicly recognized moments of divine intervention, of promises made to God, or of pressing needs brought before God, associated with themselves or with neighbors. The neighborhood, and the memorialized sites throughout, thus functioned as living, ongoing accounts of spiritual renewal or spiritual promise. The transnational nature of these images and objects fused the living accounts with the neighborhood sites and with memories of the homeland.

Objects of devotion in some cases strengthened transnational ties communally in that an object of devotion was itself brought over from Mexico and displayed in public and semi-public ways. The case of La Virgen de Juquila provided one such example, as brought to my attention by Miguel Luna, and as introduced in Chapter 4 of this volume. Miguel Luna explained that a particular statue of La Virgen de Juquila was brought from his region in Mexico. La Virgen de Juquila represented a specific iteration of the Virgin Mary in a location in Oaxaca. As powerful as the presence of Our Lady of Guadalupe was to many Santaneros, different iterations of the Holy Mother represented a more personalized point of connection to Mary for some Marian devotees. Nabhan-Warren (2005) notes, for example, that a keeper of a shrine to La Virgen de Las Americas intentionally distinguished herself from devotees of La Virgen de Guadalupe.

Miguel explained that a particular statue of La Virgen de Juquila had been brought from Mexico and would be on display at a local home. On a designated day, *La Virgen*'s clothing and altar decorations would be changed and this would be an occasion for gathering and honoring her. After being introduced to *La Virgen de Juquila* by Miguel, I began to spot her around town. At one local restaurant, I spotted her picture on the wall. I asked the cashier if that was *La Virgen de Juquila*. The woman's eyes widened in disbelief as she asked, "Do you know her?" Other patron saints have been known to visit the area. A nearby visit of the image of Santo Toribio from the Mexican state of Jalisco, for example, was brought to public attention via an article in the *Los Angeles Times* (Bermudez 2014).

Veronica Ochoa's public interaction with material representations of La Virgen de Guadalupe stand out as one of the most devout cases among interviewed subjects. Some neighbors that had referred me to Veronica stated that her devotion to La Virgen de Guadalupe and her involvement at the local parish increased because she needed God's help to deal with her young adult son's delinquent tendencies. When I visited Veronica at her home, I immediately noticed that she had numerous religious objects on display that were from Mexico, several indicating the town or state where they were made. "Recuerdo de Michoacan" (souvenir from Michoacan), one image of la Virgen de Guadalupe read. Most of these were Marian icons but several of them were also representations of Christ. "Those were brought to me by different family members when they returned from Mexico," Veronica explained. This was a fusion of transnational location and religious symbolism orienting the faithful toward the homeland.

Alongside these transnational items rested some US-origin items. In particular, I noticed a drawing of La Virgen de Guadalupe displayed on the wall that had obviously been completed by hand. The intricate shading and attention to detail given to the Holy Mother's face suggested a strong devotion from the artist. "I received that from [one of the young men] that's in prison," Veronica explained. The young man who crafted the image, a friend of her son, was affiliated with the local neighborhood gang and was serving time in prison. This young man recognized Veronica for her Marian devotion and thus sent her the gift of the drawing. Perhaps the experience of this young artist paralleled the various testimonies I encountered through the years of inmates having religious conversions. Some of these conversion experiences were toward evangelical and Pentecostal faiths, but some were affirmations of Catholic faith. In the case of this young artist, Veronica's faith had encouraged him in his personal devotion. In Veronica, transnational faith expression converged upon neighborhood-rooted devotion.

In caring for a shrine at the corner of her apartment courtyard, Veronica's devotion was made public. The residents of this courtyard were given permission to build a shrine a decade ago in the corner of their apartment complex's open-air courtyard. The shrine started small, and initially had a rustic look, but it was now a precisely fashioned house-like structure, measuring about four feet by five feet at its base area and about eight feet tall. It had entryway pillars covered in a lightly stuccoed texture. In terms of its general design, the shrine was not necessarily different from most shrines I saw in the area. Yet, while some shrines were household or family based, given its placement, this was a communal shrine shared by the entire neighborhood. What further distinguished this shrine was that at various times in the year, it housed three statues of Guadalupe, almost identical in dimensions and design.

The three images of the Holy Mother that Veronica cared for were of geographical significance. Two of the three statues periodically traveled to other parts of the county. One image traveled about 20 miles away to Aliso Viejo, a city in South Orange County. Another statue traveled to another home in Santa Ana. Veronica's son, Rodolfo, explained the journeys of Guadalupe as I conversed with him next to the altar. Months after a procession commemorating the day of the Virgen de Guadalupe, which Veronica invited me to, several attendees alluded to this practice of transporting the statues elsewhere. Once these statues were received at another altar, they were then venerated there.

The practice of transporting objects of devotion illustrated how particular ethnic enclaves could serve as hubs of spirituality within ethnic space. Veronica lived in an economically depressed community. She made her living from taking care of children, selling items at swap meets, and occasionally by selling food around the neighborhood. Her adult children helped her pay the rent. Veronica rarely ventured far beyond her neighborhood. Yet, through her devotion to La Virgen in general, and her caring for the local altar in particular, she was able to play a role that had effects beyond the neighborhood she was anchored to. In her devotion, by adding value to an image and space valued by others, she gained significance, and devotional capital, beyond her immediate circle. As Peña and Frehill (1998) argue, some Latinas working at the periphery of the institutional Catholic church find spaces of empowerment on these edges.

Reforming the Barrio

Evangelical respondents tended to reflect a very different view of the barrio from Catholic respondents. Evangelicals did not exhibit the neighborhood nostalgia exhibited by Catholic co-ethnics. Warm narratives of a past way of life, let alone efforts to recapture a past neighborhood experience, were absent from evangelical discourse. Instead, evangelicals tended to frame their discussions of the barrio in what I call the barrio-reformation perspective. This framing emphasized that the barrio is in need of transformation through the evangelical gospel message (Orsi 1999). Phrases such as "being a light to my neighbors," "sharing the gospel," and "giving testimony" permeated the discourse that evangelicals used to describe their self-designated role in the community.[3]

The barrio-reformation outlook appeared to have some links to subjects' own personal reformation narratives, or *testimonios* (Flores 2014). Evangelicals communicated a desire for their neighbors to experience what evangelicals themselves testified to having experienced. Evangelicals were highly invested in barrio-reformation efforts as these efforts reified their own faith narratives. To see others change and embrace evangelical faith brought affirmation and confirmation to evangelical practice.

There were three dominant patterns of neighborhood engagement[4] which bolstered the barrio-reformation perspective: (1) A transformational presence outlook, (2) an apathetic engagement outlook, and (3) a retreat from hostility outlook. These engagement patterns characterized the primary framing that particular subjects used in order to make sense of and explain their relationship to the ethnic enclave. McRoberts (2004) documents very similar patterns of neighborhood engagement among the Protestant churches that he studied in the Four Corners neighborhood of Boston. The congregations in his research viewed themselves as foreigners to the world around them and constructed frames of community engagement that allowed them to distance themselves from "the street."

A small minority of evangelical subjects did express a more positive outlook about the barrio and had few negative observations to share. This small minority demonstrated a consciousness about being different due to their faith, but they were able to highlight the positive

[3] Orsi (1999) elucidates the history of Protestants in the United States viewing the city as lost places; he also points out that cities were viewed as Catholic spaces. See also Mulder (2015) on white evangelicals grappling with how to engage the city.

[4] These patterns of engagement can also be viewed as types of neighborhood narrative frames as presented by Small (2004).

relationships that they had established in their neighborhood, primarily with non-co-religionists. Those within this group verbalized some desire to see transformation in their neighborhoods, but were less driven by an outlook that problematized their neighborhoods. Essentially, they espoused a *barrio-asset-awareness* outlook similar to that of many Catholic Santaneros. The following section examines the varying approaches to the barrio-reformation perspective. I will then briefly discuss the barrio-asset-awareness outlook and will highlight some of the distinctions of those holding this outlook. Finally, I will discuss how the prevailing barrio-reformation outlook is lived out collectively by evangelicals.

A Transformational Presence

Many evangelicals expressed seeing themselves as potential catalysts for the transformation of their surrounding co-ethnic community. They expressed a sense of duty in having to provide a positive example to their neighbors. Patricia Martinez, a devout member of a Pentecostal church, embodied the transformational-presence outlook. My interview with Patricia took place at her home in a patio area facing the front yard. From that vantage point, most of her cul-de-sac neighborhood could be seen, a street lined with stucco-covered homes, long altered from their original facade and structure. As she described her experience in her neighborhood, she would often point to the places where particular interactions took place.

In order to illustrate her experience of interacting with her neighbors, Patricia recalled an incident with a group of young men that she identified as gang members. The neighborhood where Patricia and her family lived was a known gang territory. Patricia had lived in the neighborhood long enough to know that particular neighbors were gang affiliates. She also had teenaged children who knew many of their neighborhood peers. These young men would loiter close to the Martinez home, particularly along a fence at the front of the property. At one point in our conversation, she pointed to a specific space between two fence posts on her front yard, and offered the following description:

> Before, a group of cholos [people that exhibit Chicano gang styles and mannerisms] would come and drug themselves there. They would smoke marijuana and pass the time there. We had to pray about that! Now they don't hang out there anymore. Thank God that all of that is going away. If God has placed us in this place, we need to pray to be the light.

For Patricia, her household's presence made a difference in their community. "Being the light," as Patricia expressed, involved simply being present, even without having direct interaction with those holding to different views of spirituality. Prayer was a way that Patricia believed her family contributed to the well-being of their neighborhood. Her prayers helped to do away with the negative activity that the young men were engaging in on her front fence, Patricia believed.

Patricia asserted that it was critical for her household members to live lives in a manner different from her neighbors. The home-based celebrations that Patricia's neighbors hosted provided a type of opportunity that Patricia and her husband used to assert a moral boundary. Patricia explained it as follows:

> When they have parties, those neighbors over there [pointing to a home across the street], they see that we don't participate ever. We don't participate in the parties that any of these neighbors have. And when we have parties, they see the difference. We've had some problems with those neighbors across the street there. They have wanted to do bad things to us. But they haven't been able to. God has protected us. And we can continue to be a light in this neighborhood.

Some of the elements that Patricia disapproved of from her neighbors' parties involved certain music, and drinking. Patricia and her husband did not listen to the music that her neighbors listened to and abstained from drinking. The types of parties that Patricia and her husband hosted were typically smaller family parties. Patricia believed that through her example, her neighbors would change, which would in turn bring transformation to the neighborhood.

Patricia recognized that the door was open for her family to visit the celebrations that their neighbors hosted. Her statement, "they see that we don't participate," was in reference to the fact that they themselves did not attend any of the local parties hosted by neighbors. In these working-class communities, it was customary for neighborhood parties to be attended by neighbors and local friends. As mentioned previously, I was frequently invited to neighborhood parties by informants and had the opportunity to attend several festive occasions. When a relationship had been established with a neighbor, it was typical for an open invitation to stand in Patricia's community. Patricia and her husband chose to stay away from these events because they believed their faith precluded them from participating in certain elements of the party.

Sixto Nuñez also embodied the transformational-presence outlook. Like Patricia, one of the most salient interactions that Sixto shared had to do with living close to "cholos." Sixto explained that there was a group of cholos that lived close to his apartment home. He passed them on a regular basis, and often acknowledged them by nodding at them and saying "hello." As a single, young adult, Sixto was a prime target for getting interrogated by local gang members. Sixto's appearance looked far from that of a gang member. He often wore tight-fitting polos and fitted jeans. He sported a crew cut approximating a faux hawk. Nevertheless, Sixto attributed the respect that he had gained from these young men to one particular thing: "They see me with my Bible often." Sixto lived in close proximity to the church that he attended. He rented a room from other church members, all of whom were Central American. He believed that his carrying of the Bible both signaled to the gang members that he was different, and provided them with an example that they should attempt to follow.

Yolanda Herrera, a preschool teacher who worked at a school located in a tough, inner-city neighborhood, was well acquainted with the surrounding community. She lived in a neighborhood not far from her work, but also spent a significant amount of time in the neighborhood around her work. She often served as an informal counselor for many of the mothers and parents that she worked with. Her work in the community embodied observations made by Small (2004) about how local professionals in working-class communities often perform duties beyond their job description which is instrumental in the transmission of social capital.

Yolanda had spent time visiting the homes of many local families, and saw this as a duty tied closely to her faith commitment. She made it clear that her motivation was to see reformation take place in the neighborhood. She stated,

> It has been of great impact to be in this neighborhood where they don't know Christ. I see that they come to me and they ask for prayer. There is a conviction that when one prays, something is going to happen. Mara [a local mother] on several occasions has asked me for prayer. She asked me for something. She tells me, "guess what? My mom this. Guess what? My mom that." She says, "Oh you who pray. You can help me." So I don't miss the opportunity.

Having higher levels of social capital compared to most of her working-class co-ethnics might have been a significant factor in Yolanda's experience. Her position at work provided her with higher levels of social capital, and it likewise placed her in a position where she was accessible to others who had less social capital. This is likely a factor in why some of her neighbors came to her for help. It was clear, however, that Yolanda's personal migration narrative provided a sense of common ground with these neighbors. Yolanda was an immigrant who had lived in some of the lowest-income areas in her city. In fact, she still lived in a lower-income neighborhood close to her work. Having spent much time as a single mother, she identified with many of the struggles of the working mothers that she encountered via her job. Yet, her connection with these neighbors was not simply an outgrowth of the common ground she had with them. She was not merely there to commiserate. She communicated that it was imperative for her to reach out to them. They "don't know Christ," as she said, and she wanted to do what she could so that they would know him.

For some evangelical respondents, their transformational-presence outlook was expressed via formal and programmatic outreach activities. Rosario Galindo arguably provided the best typology for someone involved in neighborhood transformation work in a very systematic way. Rosario was involved in a ministry that went out into the streets to reach out to gang members. This ministry, called Lives Worth Saving, was active in some of the roughest neighborhoods of Santa Ana and interacted with gang members at the times that they were most likely to be hanging out on the street. The ministry was started by a retired police-officer-turned-minister who worked on the Santa Ana Police Department for over two decades. Because of the high levels of gang involvement that this officer witnessed in Santa Ana, he decided to start a gang-intervention ministry.

Rosario's involvement with the gang-intervention ministry expanded beyond the particular program itself. She explained that she initially used to participate in the program once a month by going out into the streets with a team of people trained within her ministry and reaching out to gang members. The outreach involved several components. Team members offered to pray with gang members, they offered words of encouragement and informal counseling to gang members, and they would inform gang members of social services and resources that were available to them locally. Then, Rosario began to participate in a human trafficking–outreach component of the program. The human trafficking component involved making contact with victims of human trafficking and attempting to rescue them from their work.

Through her work in Lives Worth Saving, Rosario became involved in a group called Reaching Our Community, or R.O.C. Based on her description of this collective, "this is a group that helps to educate local organizations about serving youth that are at-risk of joining gangs or are currently involved in gang activity." In other words, she was involved not only in outreach efforts to gang members but also in training others to do this work more effectively. This was all in addition to her regular church attendance.

Some subjects were subtle in their espousing of the transformational-presence outlook while others took it upon themselves to function as neighborhood clergy of sorts. Obed Herrera was perhaps the most fervent of the subjects interviewed in terms of how far he was willing to go to interact with his neighbors. During an interview conducted at his home, he relayed in detail a recent encounter he had with a Catholic neighbor, a woman who then introduced him to some of her friends and family members:

The neighbor over there was talking to me about how she listens to Guadalupe Radio [a Catholic radio station]. She had a lot of questions about how prayer works. She said that Father Juan Rivas on Guadalupe Radio said that he admired how evangelicals pray because they pray with fervor. She asked if I could do one of those prayers with fervor. She was having a number of problems at home and she invited me to pray at her home. One of her prayer requests had to do with some neighbors that they were having problems with. These neighbors had been fighting with them and were threatening them. She was starting to be concerned about her family living there next to these neighbors and she hoped that the neighbors would move out soon.

I prayed that the neighbor would leave, as she had asked. A couple of weeks later I ran into her again and she said, "they were evicted! They were very conflictive people. The prayer worked!"

She said, "now I want you to pray for some friends' kids. They smoke and we don't want them to smoke." These were teenagers that had no business smoking. Most of them only had the guidance of a mother. They were acting out however they wanted to. I said, "Okay."

I went the next Wednesday to her home as she had asked me to do, and I could see that the room was full of women with their grown kids. As I was walking in, I felt the Lord tell me, "Take your belt off." God told me this as I was at the entrance of the house. I said, "Really, God?" But I felt like that's what he was telling me to do. So I did it. I took my belt off as I was walking in, and said, "Orale, who's first? [As he related this phrase, he motioned as if he was hitting a belt on his hand.] You guys are doing this because you didn't have a father to discipline you. Because you don't let go of your addiction and your mothers are crying and asking me to pray for you to leave this addiction." And they started to put their heads down one by one. As I talked to them more, they began to throw away their cigarettes. They started to walk up to where I was standing and started to throw away the junk that they had with them. Now there needs to be follow up.

Obed had essentially conducted a Pentecostal altar call in the home of a neighbor. He lived for this type of encounter yet talked about it in a very nonchalant manner. He emphasized that through his neighborhood interactions, he believed, “when people pray, and they are faithful to obey what God is asking them to do, things begin to change.” As Obed walked me to my car after our interview, I noticed him greeting some of his neighbors. They smiled at him and he waved back, engaging in small talk with them along the way. That brief instance suggested that he had a positive relationship with at least some neighbors.

Apathy towards the Neighborhood

Several respondents spoke of the neighborhood in a manner that was not explicitly negative per se, but which reflected an underlying apathy towards the neighborhood. For these respondents, the neighborhood was simply a place to reside in and not necessarily a place for forging connections with others. In some cases, the factor that socially distanced people from their neighbors seemed to be their heavy involvement in church activities. While church activities provided an escape from a world that some adherents perceived to be hostile, high-frequency church participation also reified symbolic boundaries by limiting the amount of time that evangelicals could spend in their neighborhood.

Eduardo and Clarisa Aceves, a young married couple, had very little to say about their neighborhood. They both had extremely busy work schedules. Their jobs allowed them to spend time together as they waited tables for the same diner. Eduardo chuckled when he described how, “many can’t believe how me and my wife can work together. ‘How do you do it?’ they ask us.” Eduardo and Clarisa took pride in this. They saw this as part of the way in which they give a “good testimony.” Beyond their busy work schedules, Eduardo and Clarisa were heavily active at church. Their work schedules regularly held them back from being able to attend Sunday church services. Their response was to attend as many other church activities as they could throughout the week. A major part of their attendance involved taking their children to church activities for children, such as music and drama classes.

Eduardo and Clarisa had such busy schedules when it came to work and church participation that they had very little time to interact with neighbors. Consequently, they did not express particular concern for their neighborhood. Their reformative outlook was expressed as something that needed to take place among individuals, particularly among members of their extended family, but not in a manner that demonstrated investment in their neighborhood. Their notions of neighborhood and community were almost non-exist in their discussions of where they lived. Their emphasis on the nuclear family was highly salient, however. It would seem, then, that their notion of "giving a good testimony" was tied to the way in which they were able to manage and present their family life to others. For two individuals that came to the United States with very little material wealth, and limited social ties, all the while dealing with unauthorized statuses, the ability to maintain a strong nuclear family provided an important marker of success. The maintaining of the nuclear family became emblematic of not only "making it" in the United States but also of being spiritually "blessed."

Federico and Gloria Reyes spoke about their neighborhood along the same lines as Eduardo and Clarisa had. Their stories similarly stressed their opportune encounter with one another and their harmonious relationship. They too stressed that they were very busy with church and had little time to connect with people in their community. Federico described their neighborhood with the phrase "Nobody bothers nobody." Federico and Gloria did express a desire to see individuals change. People were viewed as individuals and not necessarily as members of a community. Perhaps this hinted at an individualization effect taking place within an evangelical framework.[5]

Negative Experiences of Neighborhood

For some, a reformative outlook was fueled by negative personal experiences in the barrio. According to Maite Barrera, her family moved out of Santa Ana to get away from the crime and violence that was there.

[5] While further research is needed to examine this correlation, a longstanding body of research since Durkheim (1897) and Weber (1930) has examined the individualistic tendencies of Protestants as compared to Catholics.

Maite is an office administrator in her early thirties and an evangelical. She recalled an incident that happened in the '90s, close to her home, which appeared to be a turning point in how she and her family related to the neighborhood. The incident in question involved Maite's uncle, Jacinto, her "primary male role model and father figure." On this occasion, Maite, her uncle, and another family member, needed to make a stop at a gas station close to their home to refuel their vehicle. After her uncle stepped out to purchase gas, he was assaulted. A man approached him from behind and told him to get on the floor, all the while holding a gun to his back. He was asked to give up his money. After Jacinto gave the assailant the money in his wallet, the man ran off.

The assault that Maite's uncle Jacinto experienced was the straw that broke the camel's back for her household in terms of their residence in Santa Ana. Soon after that, her family moved to the neighboring city of Anaheim. Maite experienced much of her schooling in Anaheim, and describes school as being better resourced there. Eventually, Maite and her family would move back to Santa Ana. She explained her reaction in the following manner: "When we moved back to Santa Ana from Anaheim, it was huge [it was a significant change]. I still had that mentality like Santa Ana is bad, it has gangs, they're going to hurt you. We only stuck to the perimeters." Maite's return to Santa Ana took place nearly two decades after initially living there. She eventually married a man with deep roots in Santa Ana.

It is important to stress that in spite of these negative experiences in the barrio, Maite still espoused a strong desire for the residents of central Santa Ana to have positive experiences in their neighborhoods, and more than anything for them to experience neighborhood transformation. She indicated that she enjoyed "going out into the community and doing evangelistic work." What is evident is that in her perception of Santa Ana, Maite strongly centered deleterious aspects and experiences of the city.

Barrio Asset Awareness

Some evangelical respondents expressed more positive views of the neighborhood and focused less on aspects that they perceived as negative. Those who were more positive in expressing their opinions still tended to lean towards less descriptive views of the neighborhood than their Catholic co-ethnics did. Simply stated, evangelicals had far less to talk about when it came to discussing their neighborhoods. Certainly, I could press questions further to obtain more information, but a clear trend that emerged was that for Catholics, it was far more natural to discuss positive aspects of their local neighborhood compared to evangelicals. Nonetheless, some evangelicals still referenced positive relationships that they had with neighbors along with other positive aspects of their neighborhood experience.

Arturo and Julieta Esparza verbalized the most positive opinion of the neighborhood among their co-religionists. Arturo and Julieta, both factory workers, had been married for more than thirty years and were faithful to their evangelical church. When asked about how they got along with their neighbors, Arturo recounted a moving story about how he helped to launch and coordinate a neighborhood soccer league. During this time, his children were in elementary school, and he had a desire to create a positive recreational activity for them to participate in. Arturo was a soccer aficionado. He himself was a committed soccer player in his teen years and into young adulthood. His idea was to create a soccer league for children in the neighborhood.

After planning out what a soccer league would look like, Arturo described the steps that he took to make the league a reality: "I went and knocked on doors and asked people if their kids wanted to be part of a soccer team. We got a bunch of kids to come out and play. We made teams in our neighborhood. Kids from all over the neighborhood were happy to participate and we had enough kids for half a dozen teams." For a summer season, Arturo coordinated this league, and his own children, along with the neighborhood children, participated. Friendships were forged between the Esparza family and their neighbors, and neighbors were very appreciative of what Arturo had done. Julieta added that neighbors, particularly other women in the neighborhood, developed a strong sense of trust with her. A woman next door said to Julieta, "I feel comfortable confiding a lot in you." Julieta was pleased that she could develop friendships of trust with her neighbors. This was partly an outgrowth of Arturo's connections in the neighborhood, and largely an outgrowth of Julieta's own capacity for building friendships with her neighbors.

Aside from the Esparzas, a few other evangelical respondents mentioned having positive relationships with their neighbors. Most of these references were brief. What stood out among evangelicals in this regard was that those who had more positive views of their neighborhood tended to be more established in the United States. Julieta and Arturo had worked in their respective factory jobs for more than two decades. They had a stable home life and lived on the edge of Santa Ana's inner corridor. Moreover, their neighborhood was more tranquil and suburban in its semblance. Their neighborhood was on the southern edge of central Santa Ana. Evangelicals who were more socioeconomically stable had less dependency on the barrio. They lived in neighborhoods with neighbors less reliant on each other when compared to under-resourced inner-corridor neighborhoods. Evangelicals appeared to be socially taxed when they broke with neighborhood expectations of interdependence. Yet, interdependence was more common in lower-income communities. Perhaps this led lower-income evangelicals to experience more tension in their neighborhoods. The evangelicals that were less dependent on the barrio were among those that had more positive things to say about it. It is possible that these evangelicals were less invested in distancing themselves from the neighborhood because they already were less reliant on, and had less expectations of, their co-ethnic peers in the barrio.

Conclusion

In discussing ethnic neighborhoods, numerous scholars provide insightful distinction between ethnic ghettos and ethnic enclaves (Lin and Zhou 2005; Marcuse 1997, 2005; Peach 2005; Romo 1983). Scholars acknowledge various similarities between these two types of neighborhoods. Both ghettos and enclaves are spaces that are composed primarily of one ethnic group experiencing high levels of segregation and minimal exposure to whites. Residents in said neighborhoods experience sub-standard housing conditions, and above average levels of criminal activity. Children growing up in both types of communities are likely to attend public schools that are overwhelmingly populated by co-ethnics of lower socioeconomic status. In both contexts, the majority of working adults tend to be in "low-skill" jobs with few prospects for promotion.

Differences emerge when considering the opportunities that both types of spaces present. Enclaves are populated by first-generation immigrants with a strong sense of ethnic identity. Enclaves embody an entrepreneurial spirit both structurally and culturally: co-ethnic neighbors assist each other with employment, and residents perceive that social mobility is possible. The enclave becomes a place that people return to in order to access cultural and economic resources. Ghettos, on the other hand, are plagued by social immobility. Immobility is manifested in that residents are native born ethnics rather than immigrants. Ghetto residents are conscious of structural barriers limiting their success and as such are disheartened by their condition. Identities emanating from the ghetto are stigmatized, and those who are able to leave the ghetto are likely to avoid returning.

Catholics tend to perceive central Santa Ana as an ethnic enclave; evangelicals' perceptions more closely approximate the ethnic ghetto description. As demonstrated through the words and actions of each tradition's respective adherents, opinions cluster around notions of barrio as concentration of ethnic resource, and barrio as a space needing improvement. In regard to ethnic identity, the Catholic perspective tends to strengthen the relationship between ethnic identity and the spatial enclave. Conversely, the evangelical perspective ties ethnic expression to church spaces in the barrio, but less so to the barrio as a broader community. For evangelicals, ethnicity is less clearly articulated as being tied to a local neighborhood, when compared to Catholic construction of ethnicity.

Given the differences in how the barrio is understood, Catholics and evangelicals contribute to the common good of their ethnic communities in distinct ways. Catholics contributed to a diffuse, general sense of trust that was particularly vital to vulnerable immigrants residing in ethnic enclaves. This phenomenon mirrors the migration trust networks that Flores-Yeffal (2013) conceptualizes, wherein immigrants "pay-it-forward" by contributing resources into the broader community. Evangelicals, on the other hand, excelled at providing a specialized safety net for very particular cases of need in the barrio. Evangelicals were attuned to the outliers, the most vulnerable, either in the community or in their own social networks. Evangelicals found ways to assist these individuals, both through their own resources, and through church resources. In this sense, both groups complemented each other. Indeed, the work of evangelicals in the barrio would typically not have been possible without the foundation that was laid by their Catholic co-ethnics. On the other hand, Catholics in general, displayed a weaker sense of normativized urgency to intervene in particular situations of need. Evangelicals were efficient at zeroing in on specific cases needing intervention: The victim of abuse, the drug addict, the gang member desiring to be reformed were prime cases of need that evangelicals would intervene in. Catholics were effective at generating a sense of trust that connected people in the community.

To conclude, while both Catholics and evangelicals expressed ethnic affinities, Catholics were more likely to express these within a localized ethnic community, and with more explicit ties to the homeland. Evangelicals, on the other hand, were more likely to express their ethnic affinities in their alternative church spaces. The localized ethnic neighborhood was less a place of resources for evangelicals, and more a place that needed to be resourced. Catholics, primarily, ensured that the barrio remained a space where ethnicity was performed and transmitted. Catholics helped to ensure that the keepers of ethnicity in the barrio were the poor, the immigrant, and the undocumented. These were the cultural brokers of the barrio and remained the localized bearers of ethnic authenticity, for Catholics. For evangelicals, these were individuals to be helped, and evangelicals were seeking opportunities to help them. For Catholics, ethnic identity was predicated on building collective community; for evangelicals, it was predicated on a mission of transformation in the barrio.

Sites Unseen

I walked past the couple of parked vendor trucks that provided residents with grocery options steps from their homes. Upon initial perusal, I noticed that save for a few coats of paint, the familiar row of apartment buildings on Myrtle St. had not changed much since I had visited the block the previous year. My family and I had moved away, but I was in town for a few days and made it a point to stop by. A fundraiser assisting a local resident in the neighborhood to pay medical bills offered a perfect opportunity to reconnect with a number of residents. A group of women in the community had gotten together to support their friend in need by selling food and many from the community were present for the event.

The *kermes*, as the fundraiser was called, would be held in an apartment courtyard at the center of the block. Before reaching the space where the *kermes* was being held, I passed a courtyard where I had previously participated in several festive occasions, including feast days to *La Virgen de Guadalupe*. This courtyard was home to one of the altars to *La Guadalupana* mentioned in previous chapters. I glanced over to the corner of the courtyard expecting to be met by the gaze of *Guadalupe*, and was bewildered by the barren sight that I beheld. The altar had been removed!

At the *kermes*, as I sat at a table enjoying a plate of enchiladas, amid thirty or so people coming and going, I noticed Doña Katia, a woman whose family frequently attended the celebrations in the neighborhood. Doña Katia greeted me warmly, and asked how I was doing. The conversation soon turned to the altar one courtyard over. I recalled that Doña Katia's husband had built the altar. "He had done such a good job in building it," I mentioned. "Yes, he had," she uttered, nodding her head sternly. "The owner of the building didn't want it there anymore," she explained. "The place doesn't look right like that—pelón

The Saints of Santa Ana. Jonathan E. Calvillo, Oxford University Press (2020). © Oxford University Press.
DOI: 10.1093/oso/9780190097790.001.0001.

[bald/bare]," she added. Her previously happy expression turned troubled as she recounted the state of the beloved altar.

Walking back to my car after my time at the *kermes*, I again passed the now-altar-less courtyard and ran into another neighbor that I knew, Doña Aide. "Hola Jonathan!" she called out to me. I walked over and inquired about her family. As the sun bore down on us, she said, "Come, stand here in the shade." We conversed under the shade of an iron and concrete staircase leading to the second level of apartments. Residents often sat or stood there and caught up with each other when the sun loomed over the open courtyard. After giving me a brief recap on the state of her three sons, our attention also turned to the site of the altar. With a raspy tone, and assertive pace, Doña Aide waxed on:

> No, well, it's just not the same anymore! We tried talking to the owner—the Chinese lady—but she wouldn't listen. She said she didn't want it there anymore. People walk by here, and they were so used to genuflecting. Now they just walk by and keep going, but a lot of them look over out of habit. People were so used to it. We were just so used to looking over to the little corner there.

It struck me how the space still held meaning for many of the residents, even in the absence of the altar. The altar was located adjacent to a walkway that residents walked through to get from the back alley and carports to the apartment courtyard. The back alley contrasted with the courtyard: It was the site of garbage dumpsters and gang graffiti, a place children were typically advised to avoid. To transition from the more familial environment of the courtyard to the alley, one would traverse the gaze of Guadalupe. Many returning back from work, before being greeted by anyone else, would be greeted by her. And thus, their bodies had been conditioned by the material image of Guadalupe with her particular placement and her close proximity to their residence.

It is of little surprise that the day-to-day acts of devotion toward Guadalupe and her altar had formed part of the habitus of many of these Santaneros. I was surprised, however, by the fact that my own bodily response, my habitus, had been shaped to some extent as well; my own line of sight immediately tracked over to the corner as

I initially walked down the street. I, too, had grown accustomed to the altar. I felt disoriented when I noticed that the space was now empty.

A short cement platform hinted that something had been in the corner of the courtyard before. The floor and the wall surrounding the area bore a new coat of paint. The space had been whitewashed, almost as if to erase the memory of the altar. The residents certainly had not forgotten. As I returned to my car, I contemplated how precarious and contingent the religious practices of many Santaneros could be. Their faith had not necessarily wavered, but the ability to sustain their traditions could be endangered by people in power. In this case, their lack of influence in the establishment of housing policies came to hurt their practices.

Before I left, Doña Aide pointed out that in an opposite corner of the courtyard, a group of residents had asked the tenant of one apartment to keep an image right outside of their apartment unit, as a small fenced off courtyard in that area provided some shelter for an image. The tenant in that unit agreed to the request, and now kept an image in the corner as a way to maintain Guadalupe's presence in the semi-public space. The image was not nearly as visible as the previous altar, but the tenants knew that she was there. Doña Aide insisted that they took some consolation in this. The loss of the altar demonstrated the contingent nature of popular Catholic devotional practices within the public spaces of Santa Ana. The raised awareness of residents about the altar also indicated the social nature of *lo cotidiano*, the everyday practices that Santaneros engaged in (Espín 2006). There was no indication that neighborhood demographics had shifted, or that gentrification in this part of town was a threat. It appeared that the opinion of the owner had shifted, and the devotional practices of a neighborhood had been affected.

In many ways, popular Catholic practices were particularly vulnerable to this type of constraint. Traditional practices anchored within local Catholic parishes seemed to have achieved relatively strong levels of legitimacy in the local diocese, from what I observed. Even translocalized practices that had been transplanted into Santa Ana were supported by the diocese, an approach which Matovina (2011) indicates is often helpful toward maintaining parish engagement among Latinxs. The practices of popular Catholicism when conducted independently, out in the community, however, necessitated spaces where these practices could take root. As vibrant as the practices were in the community, they were subject to the structural opportunities that practitioners had before them, and in some cases practitioners had little recourse to formally push against limitations. Even still, residents found ways to adapt and to reclaim spaces where they encountered resistance.

Along the same lines, I would find during that brief trip to Santa Ana that evangelical communities and their practices were also not immune to structural constraints. Some of the evangelical churches I had visited in Santa Ana had moved or were in the process of moving, I came to discover, because they encountered constraints in the spaces they operated within. La Gran Cosecha Sobrenatural, for example, was being challenged in that the church they rented space from was to be demolished and turned into the site of an affordable housing development. Some Latinx churches had also ceased to operate in the last few years. The entrepreneurial nature of evangelical churches and of evangelical devotion also meant that these churches were often subject to the needs and constraints of the market. Yet, evangelicals, too, found ways to adapt in order to sustain their faith communities. Furthermore, even as some evangelicals and their congregations left Santa Ana, others came in, with distinct visions for how to engage the city.

Retrospective Ethnic Spaces

Religion served as one of the primary containers for ethnicity to thrive within the working-class, immigrant communities of central Santa Ana. Ethnic space was especially cultivated by the partnerships that were sustained between local parishes and practitioners of lived religion in Santa Ana. The operation of popular Catholicism in the very spaces of Santa Ana that were most racialized, is precisely what made for a potent symbiotic relationship between religion and ethnicity among Catholic Santaneros. The histories of exclusion that many working-class Mexicans endured throughout the previous century were felt by the newer immigrants that now resided in central Santa

Ana. In these incubators, ethnic space was given life through practices of devotion. Religion gave many Santaneros a voice and a reason to celebrate, even as it provided the means of lament and the means of jubilation. At any given moment, religion could operate as the language of ethnicity, the language of culture, the language of belonging.

Widespread understandings in the community of how Catholicism and ethnicity intersected legitimized the notion for many Catholics that their faith and ethnicity were intricately intertwined. Catholics could speak with confidence that to be Mexican and to be Guadalupan were mutually reinforcing. Participation in local events was not merely an act of religious devotion but also an investment in cultural reproduction. Catholics could generally move about through the Catholic-majority spaces of Santa Ana affirmed that their expressions of ethnicity were authentic.

Some Catholics did experience altar encounters, points that in theory could have brought about drastic changes of identity, but for Catholics these tended to reinforce their existing belief system. The altar encounters that Catholics experienced served to safeguard them against overly enthusiastic narratives of transformation expounded by evangelicals. That is, these altar encounters provided Catholics with discursive tools with which to withstand the competitive efforts of evangelical outreach. The ties to the past that Catholics were able to maintain, then, sustained a sense of having a religious lineage. This religious lineage could be understood as closely overlapping with ethnic heritage, as it provided a sense of intergenerational transmission. Many Catholics even drew on indigeneity as a legitimating factor in their religious expression (Elizondo 2006). Likewise, moving about through ethnic spaces with perceptions of a spirit world reinforced Catholic belief systems. It was difficult for Catholics to turn away from the spiritual entities that they held dear. Ethnic spaces, for Catholics, were spaces of continuity.

Overall, Catholics had a stronger sense of place in their religious devotion. Their sense of ethnicity was largely rooted in their understandings of ethnic neighborhoods as community. Neighborhoods were not merely places to reside in, but they were places within which communal devotion structured the rhythms of life (DuCros 2017). Certainly, Catholics yearned for elements of their ethnic past, but they did their best to recreate these elements communally (Tweed 1997). The barrio was a redemptive place, as it was a place where the past could be recreated and renewed.

Reformed Ethnic Spaces

Evangelicals demonstrated a different relationship to the ethnic spaces of Santa Ana compared to their Catholic co-ethnics. Historically, Protestant affiliation would have given Latinxs more legitimacy within the white-dominant social institutions of the time. However, with the rise of immigrant-dominant evangelical churches, many with high levels of independence from white institutions, Latinx evangelical churches took on a life of their own. Still, many evangelicals, it turned out, struggled for ethnic legitimacy among co-ethnics in their neighborhoods. In part, some evangelicals were looked upon with suspicion because of their efforts to proselytize neighbors. In some cases, such efforts were the work of non-evangelical groups such as Jehovah's Witnesses, but often evangelicals themselves were engaged in evangelistic efforts. The intra-ethnic boundary that emerged within the ethnic space of Santa Ana along religious lines was given power by Santaneros. Evangelicals often removed themselves from ethnic spaces or envisioned themselves as changing the ethnic space. The process of living out ethnicity, for evangelicals, was largely relegated to life within the home and the church.

The centrality of altar encounters shaped the boundaries of evangelical religious identities as they were markers of membership for evangelicals. Altar encounters also shaped evangelical constructions of ethnicity as they most typically meant rupturing with the past. Ethnicity as an identity signaled by the commemoration of ancestral lineages and the transmission of particular cultural elements was less prevalent among evangelicals. This is not to say that none of the evangelicals I engaged with had Protestant ancestors. Neither is it to say that evangelicals had no traditions to transmit. The critical point is that evangelical identity was largely predicated on starting anew, on being born again. Ethnic space as a space that sustained ethnic memory was less tenable to evangelicals who were more focused on being renewed and on encountering an eternal future.

Still, the promise of new life and the particular mode of divine dialogue espoused by evangelicals was a powerful draw for many Santaneros. Whereas Catholicism was inculturated in its symbols and practices, the testimonios of evangelicals, increasingly polished and rehearsed with time, were inculturated epistles unto themselves, narrating encounters with God in geographies familiar to Santaneros. The familiarity with which evangelicals talked about God, the direct, unmediated access, functioned as a potent discursive strategy that evangelicals had at their disposal when among Santaneros.

The experiences of change and of direct dialogue with God expressed by evangelicals in many ways spurred evangelicals to view the barrio as a mission field, a place to be transformed. The barrio was not primarily a place to feast and celebrate in, but a place to evangelize. Church provided a space for celebration. Certainly, evangelicals could enjoy cultural establishments around town, but they were less invested in producing celebratory spaces for the broader public to enjoy. When they did produce such spaces, they typically included an element of evangelism.

Evangelicals were, nonetheless, committed to ethnic space as a place in which they wanted to help people. They were committed to ethnic networks as an extension of their mission to help others. Evangelicals largely saw themselves as helpers within their communities, or within their family networks. Ethnic space for evangelicals was a space to be transformed.

Divergent Ethnic Projects

In the end, Catholics produced an ethnic space that was imbued with memory. Evangelicals engaged ethnic space as a project of envisioned reformation. Catholics built trust by inviting the broader community in. Evangelicals built trust by reaching out to those in need. Catholics recognized their traditions as majority culture, and took for granted that their practices were ethnic. Evangelicals saw themselves as ethnic, but carried the burden of religious difference while forging alternative ethnic expressions. Catholicism generally seemed stronger at sustaining an intentional and fervent community of memory in the neighborhood. Evangelicalism generally seemed better at motivating affiliates to fervently pursue the needs of individuals in their community.

These distinct visions of ethnic community in central Santa Ana did not merely operate side by side in isolation, but rather interacted one with the other, as evangelicals and Catholics engaged with each other and embodied these approaches within shared neighborhood spaces. The negotiations and contestations taking place around the role of religion in defining ethnic identity might themselves serve to maintain the salience of ethnic difference. That is, the existence of distinct visions of ethnicity need not mean that ethnic boundaries were waning. These intra-ethnic processes may, in fact, have energized the salience of ethnic boundaries from within. When investment in these processes wanes, perhaps then ethnicity will wane in significance. As co-ethnics continue to internally negotiate the meanings, markers, and membership of ethnicity, they are signaling commitment to upholding some level of broader ethnic distinction. Investment in ethnic distinction and a commitment to some form of ethnic authenticity, however that might be expressed, sustain an ethnic boundary from within, contributing to a sense of persistent ethnic identity. Apathy and disinterest, when co-ethnics are no longer interested in negotiating the meanings of authentic ethnicity, potentially contribute to the decline of ethnic identity.

Shifting Affiliations

A relevant question remains as to whether religious traditions themselves will survive into the future as ethnically distinct religious expressions in Santa Ana and beyond. My arguments in this book will likely be mediated by the type of future that one or the other affiliation has in the Latinx communities of Santa Ana. David Lopez's (2009) contention that the Catholic church has contributed little toward the future mobility of Mexican Americans is suggestive in regards to weakening Catholic affiliation among ethnic Mexicans. Nevertheless, the Mexican majority Catholic parishes of Santa Ana are far from withering and many of the parishioners that are most integrated into parish life also reflect high degrees of social mobility. Though this does not prove causality, it suggests that Catholic affiliation does not preclude socioeconomic success among ethnic Mexican households and may in fact contribute to success. There is room, nevertheless, to theorize about the extent of loss and the type of loss that is taking place in the Catholic church. After all, the conversion narratives of so many evangelicals indicate that some Catholics are indeed converting to evangelicalism. Who might these Catholics be who are converting to evangelicalism? Furthermore, who are the Catholics that remain steadfast in their Catholic faith? I begin with the latter group and then work my way back to the question of those who are switching their religious affiliation from Catholicism to evangelicalism.

Among the Catholic informants highlighted throughout this volume, three sub-groups of Catholics emerged: (1) Home Catholics, who primarily practiced their faith within private and semi-private spaces, usually at home, and possibly with family members;[1] (2) Neighborhood Catholics, who primarily practiced their faith communally with neighbors and friends from a particular neighborhood; and (3) Parish Catholics, who had a strong commitment to their local parish and regularly attended mass. Such groups were not completely isolated from each other and could have crossed over into each other's lives quite frequently. The core distinction here is in regard to where their primary site of religious engagement rested. For the first group, faith commitment was invested in the home and with immediate family; for the second group, it was invested among family, friends, and neighbors in the neighborhood; and for the third group, the greatest commitment was enacted within the formal life of the parish.

An excellent example of Home Catholicism was Rodrigo Alonzo, introduced in Chapter 1 of this volume.[2] Rodrigo mentioned visiting the local parish, and also mentioned having an affinity towards

[1] This would be similar to the "family traditioning" proposed by Chen and Jeung (2012).

[2] Bane notes that "US parishes report lower proportions of Latino parishioners" than "there are in the overall population and in the self-reported Catholic population" (2019:158). These might well be Home and Neighborhood Catholics.

another parish in town, where apparently he had lived close to in the past. However, he admitted that he hardly attended mass these days, except for special occasions such as weddings. Most of his outward faith expression, per his own accounts, revolved around his devotion to *La Virgen de Guadalupe*. He did mention a high level of respect toward the Holy See and also a deep love of the Pope, signaling that he was not opposed to the formal structure of the Catholic church.

Neighborhood Catholics were strongly represented by Mercedes Uribe, whose involvement in the community is detailed in Chapter 6 of this volume. Mercedes did claim to attend mass with far more frequency than someone like Rodrigo. However, her greatest relational investments and social network ties in terms of religious community were primarily anchored in her neighborhood, and cultivated through her offering up of her home for collective devotional practices. Mercedes admitted to most taking pride in the activities she was able to organize in the neighborhood.

Parish Catholics were well represented by Jimena and Jesus Ibarra, who were greatly invested in parish life. I strategically use the term "Parish" Catholics to draw from the fullest sense of the word parish, as these Catholics tended to be invested in the communities surrounding the local church as well as in the activities taking place within the church facilities (Adler, Bruce, and Starks 2019). What distinguished Parish Catholics from Neighborhood Catholics was that they were much more committed to the formal programming of parish life. Jimena and Jesus, for example, had formal duties and responsibilities within the parish. They bore identifiable roles and were expected to show up and lead particular activities. Jimena and Jesus had close ties to people in the parish, as I observed, and as they shared in our conversations. Many of the Parish Catholics I interacted with blended in well with Neighborhood Catholics because of their high levels of involvement in the local community. There were some Parish Catholics that had little involvement in the neighborhood, but only one or two Parish Catholics that I interviewed reflected this latter participation pattern.

My observations suggest that the Catholics most vulnerable to religious switching would have been Home Catholics. Home Catholics exhibited weaker social ties to other Catholics. They were perhaps more vulnerable to teachings deemed unorthodox by the church given that they had less interaction with formalized teaching, at least on a consistent basis. Some Home Catholics were especially isolated from Catholic community.

On the other hand, I do not minimize the faith commitment of Home Catholics. For some Home Catholics, such as Rodrigo, their faith was of utmost importance. Rodrigo was fiery, downright evangelistic, when talking about his faith. Still, in lacking strong Catholic ties, and in not consistently attending mass and/or not partaking of Catholic teaching in a collective context, such members might be open to visiting other types of religious gatherings, when social ties are developed with religious others. Also, some Home Catholics were more open to forms of popular religion not squarely within Catholicism. Such practices provided a gateway of sorts to seeking out other types of religious experiences, particularly those of Pentecostal inclination.

It is far more difficult to envision Neighborhood Catholics and Parish Catholics switching to another religious tradition. Because these Catholics had strong ties in their surrounding community and/or within their local parishes, they would have faced high levels of social sanctions if they were to distance themselves from the Catholic church. Likewise, on a personal level, it would have been more difficult to walk away from a faith that they had highly invested in, within a social context.

Examining evangelicals who were former Catholics provides additional clues about the religious shifts happening in the Mexican community. Most evangelicals who were former Catholics did not describe a life of participating in a vibrant Catholic faith. Their descriptions of Catholic practice were inconsistent. Some of them, such as Vicente Garza, shared about negative experiences that he had with Catholic clergy. Evangelicals who were former Catholics also often emphasized tensions with family members even while they were Catholic. The types of tensions typically centered on parental shortcomings, and/or acts of domestic violence. Finally, the role of religious experience seemed prominent in the accounts of former Catholics, wherein they contrasted their current evangelical lives of worship with former Catholic practices which they found less fulfilling (Mulder, Ramos, and Martí 2017). On the other hand, it is important to note that some former Catholics did have memories of Catholic participation in their childhood that were generally positive, or at least neutral. Some recalled doing their first communion or attending mass with parents and/or grandparents. Most of these individuals, those that had some positive memories of Catholicism, were not completely estranged from the Catholic church when they ventured into evangelicalism.

The Catholic faith reflected in the accounts of former Catholics lacked deep roots in consistent social networks of faith and strong institutional connections, bolstered by consistent religious teaching, and fortified through sequential and consistent participation in the sacraments. This type of profile seemed to fit many converts whether they converted in the United States or in Mexico. Those most likely to convert, then, appeared to be those with weak ties of Catholic community and weak Catholic socialization. Moments of crisis, but in particular a tumultuous home life, either during their upbringing or in their current adult household, also provided a sense of urgency for pre-converts. These moments likely contributed to an instability which encouraged people to seek help beyond their usual network or to accept help when it arrived, even if it came from a source outside of their religious community. Often, evangelicals were the ones ready to provide the help needed by these individuals, and help often involved visiting some type of evangelical gathering. Of relevance, Matovina posits that some immigrants who visit evangelical and Protestant churches "fail to recognize they have begun to participate in a Protestant congregation" (2011:103). For the Santaneros I spoke to, this was not the case, however. All respondents I spoke with, Catholic and evangelical, were quite aware of the differences in their respective denominational traditions, particularly when they visited gatherings of distinct denominations.[3]

In the larger scheme of things, Catholics who were rooted in their faith were far less likely to explore the possibility of becoming evangelical. Most Catholics articulated being highly satisfied within their faith communities and were not looking for any other spiritual

[3] One informant, Jesús Ibarra, featured in Chapter 1, did articulate a concern similar to Matovina's observation, but primarily in reference to other Catholics and not necessarily in reference to his own experience.

options. Among immigrants, the faith seemed to be strong for a core group of Santa Ana residents. One challenge for the Catholic churches was that parishes worked with such an extensive population that most parishioners had limited access to clergy. Lay leaders could supplement that need, but many parishioners would need to shift in their cultural expectations of legitimate religious leadership to fully accept the contributions of lay leaders.

The ongoing partnerships with neighborhood-based Catholic networks of devotion and local parishes appeared from my observation to be a critical component for further sustaining the faith communities of Catholics in Santa Ana. Catholic parishes such as *Inmaculado Corazon* seemed to be succeeding in this regard. Experiences outside the church that pointed people to the sacraments seemed a powerful mechanism of retention for many informants. Perhaps further opportunities were available as church leaders continued to cultivate ties outside the walls of the church.

Informants' aspirations of intergenerational success also proved a significant motivator toward Catholic retention. To a select group of Catholic informants, access to a broader array of Catholic institutions beyond the parish proved especially beneficial to their household (Smith et al. 2014). Several informants had children that attended local Catholic schools, for example. Jimena and Jesus Ibarra were one such case, as their daughter attended high school at the famed Mater Dei High School. Jose Luis Vargas attended various camps and youth gatherings through his involvement in a parish youth group. These resources shaped these young people in notable ways. The young people that had accessed these educational and extra-curricular resources available through the Catholic church were poised to succeed in life, several of them already on track to complete college degrees at the time of my interviews. In similar fashion, several informants who raised children to consistently participate in parish life, and to partake of church sacraments, boasted of having adult children who were now highly educated and held white-collar jobs. Saúl, for example, shared that all of his adult children were college graduates, some with graduate degrees, and were leading successful professional lives. Miguel Luna also indicated that his adult children were employed in prestigious professional sectors. Catholic affiliation, for some informants, seemed to correlate with a Latinx culture of professionalism and success that was cultivated within the next generation. Since my data focused on the first generation, these observations are primarily suggestive, nevertheless they are worthy of future exploration.

Focusing on the themes prevalent in existing literature on Catholic decline and evangelical growth among Latinxs, few scholars address the possibility of evangelical decline. Some scholars, such as Matovina, point out that with the increased religious pluralism in the United States, as well as a reigning attitude of religious voluntarism, people have options and a will to try these options out. Matovina (2011) further suggests that adherence to evangelicalism tapers off across generations, an observation that only partially matches up with recent findings. As more current data reveals (Cooperman et al. 2014), 16% of Latinx immigrants are evangelical, compared to 15% of second- generation Latinxs, a figure that appears to match Matovina's projection. However, at the third generation, the evangelical share jumps to 18% of the Latinx population, ultimately an increase. Nevertheless, Matovina may still be correct in that the 18% figure may be indicative of a cohort effect, influenced by an older generation of Latinx Protestants present throughout the southwestern United States. It is quite possible that among younger cohorts of the third generation, this trend of Protestant growth is not holding. Conversely, other scholars, such as Mulder, Ramos, and Marti (2017), predict that this growth will continue.

Some scholars also consider the possibility of Latinx evangelicals leaving their co-ethnic congregations for predominantly white congregations (Rodriguez 2011) or multiethnic congregations (Mulder, Ramos, and Marti 2017). This exemplifies a pattern similar to Min's research on the Korean second generation in which he argues that Korean Protestant immigrants are successful at transmitting their faith to their children but are not successful at transmitting their ethnic identity. That is, some ethnic evangelicals select churches where they are in the ethnic minority, as they still find commonality in a shared faith tradition with non-co-ethnics. Rodriguez (2011) offers Latinx church leaders solutions such as the creation of second-generation, English-dominant Latinx congregations. In either scenarios of religious decline, or of ethnic waning, the concern is that some form of interconnectedness to the previous generation is lost.

The challenge that looms ahead, for both Catholics and evangelicals, is found in the second generation and beyond, particularly as represented by younger cohorts. Questions of faith as a vehicle for maintaining ethnic identity presuppose that faith will be sustained, but what if faith is not transmitted to the next generation? National survey data indicates that many later generation Latinxs disaffiliate from formal religion altogether, contributing to a 9% increase in non-affiliation from the first generation (15%) to the second (24%; see Cooperman et al. 2014). Among unaffiliated Latinxs, 19% were raised Protestant and 61% were raised Catholic (Cooperman et al. 2014).

If Catholic or evangelical affiliation tapers off among younger generations, then both faith traditions will falter as mechanisms of ethnic maintenance (Min 2010; Warner 2007). Younger generations may lose a sense of ethnic continuity, or they may emphasize other practices that connect them to aspects of an ethnic past. Indeed, the practices of some younger-generation Santaneros suggest that this is precisely what is happening. Yes, there are young people who are faithful to either Catholic or evangelical parishes as indicated by several young adults that participated in this study. However, there is also a growing number that is finding not just ethnic community but also spiritual community through alternative means. In the final vignette, I point to these emerging expressions of spirituality among young Santaneros.

Altars Re-Imagined

The streets of Santa Ana were alive with the sounds of hip-hop music booming through the speakers set atop an expansive portable stage. The words of the hip-hop group Salvajes performing live on the platform echoed beneath the silhouette of the Ronald Reagan Federal Building, an act of celebration and an act of resistance (Hughes et al. 2015). "This is indigenous land! Let 'em know!" the voice of Mic Hempstead reverberated through the crowd of thousands. The energy from Salvajes ricocheted from one member to the other as each commandeered the microphone. In unison they uttered the hook of one of their songs:

Salvajes en la cultura desde criatura.
Aqui no cabe duda, cultura cura
[Savages in the culture since childhood.
Here there is no doubt, culture cures]

La Cuatro, or 4th St., in the downtown area of Santa Ana, had been closed off to vehicles for an event attracting one of the largest crowds among the various public events hosted in the city. The event, Noche de Altares, has been an event which honors El Dia de Los Muertos, or Day of the Dead, a celebration also known in Mexico as Dia de Muertos. The event opened at sunset with a blessing spoken in the Nahuatl language by some artists and performers of Mexica dance. The Uto-Aztecan linguistic family at the root of Nahuatl derives from the same linguistic root as the Acjachemen language, spoken by the natives of the land.[4]

El Dia de Muertos, as it is more commonly known in Mexico, has come to coincide with All Saints Day, though much of the tradition associated with the celebration predates European contact and is tied to Mesoamerican practices. An occasion to commemorate the lives of deceased loved ones, the event does more than embody a solemn tone of mourning. Rather, the event presents an opportunity to celebrate the lives of those that have passed on. Some believe those who have passed, come into the present at that time. Many also take the opportunity to promote social justice issues particularly when these issues involve the deaths of individuals identified with marginalized communities; violence against transgender individuals and a commemoration against students murdered in Iguala, Mexico, were among issues featured in the last event I attended.

Noche de Altares is an event planned largely by young community leaders, organizers, and activists affiliated with El Centro Cultural de Mexico, a community organization "where the community can find cultural, educational, and artistic activities that strengthen their identities, develop their talents and develop a

[4] This is not to say that Nahuatl and Acjachemen are necessarily intelligible to speakers of each respective language, but merely that they shared common linguistic roots.

sense of leadership in their community" (Anon. n.d.). The organization is a hotbed of activity where members of the community are empowered to do everything from organizing classes for ethnic musical genres, to mounting campaigns around political issues in the city. As the event has grown, an increasing number of community members have been drawn into the organization of the event. Second generation Santaneros are involved alongside first generation Santaneros.

While the Dia de Muertos might be considered an ancient celebration in its origins, many of the lead organizers are actually younger Santaneros. Even as the event draws people of all ages, and resonates with older Santaneros, younger Santaneros play key roles in designing the event. Noche de Altares represents a cultural resurgence of sorts, where second-generation and 1.5-generation Mexicans and Latinxs invest in the preservation of culture. Dozens, perhaps hundreds, of performers invest in the showings of culture that are displayed throughout the event. Not all performances hearken back to ancient times, in wooden, literal fashion. Some performers, such as the hip-hop group, are clearly adaptations of more modern artforms. Still, nearly all performers find ways to signal explicitly or implicitly a sense of ethnic rootedness, of collective origins. This event is an opportunity for Santaneros of the "next" generation to create their own spaces of ethnic cultural reproduction.

As I walked through the display of altars, one particular question sparked my curiosity: Is there any sign of formal religious affiliation among participants at this event? Certainly, there was a pervasive sense of spirituality present that night. Altares can function as spiritual symbols, pointing to how the ancestors live on, and for some people acknowledging the continued influence of ancestors in the present. The opening ceremony, the Mexica invocation accompanied by the burning of incense could be understood as having spiritual implications. As people walked around and took in the altars dedicated to deceased loved ones, I observed moments of solemn bonding. Indeed, I had instances where I could not help but inquire of altar keepers regarding their particular loved ones. I was surprised by the honesty and sincerity with which people shared. It was as if church, in its most essential sense of spiritual community, had been brought out to the streets, and had taken over the cityscape, as people took moments to contemplate and commune with deep reverence among the altars.

Clearly, this was not a church in the formal, institutional sense. For some, it may very well have been the antithesis of church. There was no expectation that participants needed to have a worldview that allowed for an afterlife, for spirit beings, or for God. There were no signs of any formal church involvement, neither Catholic nor Protestant. Here and there I spotted *La Virgen de Guadalupe*, but *la Catrina*, the elegantly dressed skull lady, was far more visible at this event. At one altar, I noticed a Bible verse, Jeremiah 29:1, displayed alongside the images of a young man who had died in a car accident. I asked family members what that reference signified. "It was a tattoo that he had gotten," they mentioned. They were happy to share a bit more about his life as well. Aside from these symbols, there were very little tie-ins to more formalized religious expression.

Ethnic culture was here being harnessed in a deeply spiritual way, but aside from formal religion. This was a spirituality untethered to any religious institutions. Was this the future of ethnoreligiosity? For thousands of participants, La Noche de Altares was an opportunity to experience community and deep reflection. It was an opportunity to belong to something beyond themselves, to reconnect ties to the ancestors and to reignite a sense of collective memory. These young leaders in the city had found a way to harness the sense of ethnicity often tied to religion, but to do so aside from religion. The saints lived on in the churches, temples, and shrines of Santa Ana, but they were also found in these temporary altars, these impromptu spaces of contemplation that would be gone before the next sunrise.

Young Santaneros were not replicating exactly what their parents had demonstrated to them, but were rather adapting aspects of tradition. In some cases, they were digging farther back to a past that some believed was forgotten. These Santaneros were embracing Santa Ana as an ethnic space by reconstructing and performing a sense of collective memory upon it. Regardless of whether or not the traditions were authentic and historical, as theologian Orlando Espín (218:142) proposes, "continuity in Tradition exists if and when the people believe that continuity exists."[5] As I contemplated the participants at the Noche de Altares, I observed many who believed. And as the blood, sweat, and tears of the past mingled with the hopes of the future, it would be up to the next generation to decide whether *la comunidad* would be *sagrada*.

[5] Espín is here referencing Catholic Tradition, but his general point is applicable in a broader sense as well.

APPENDIX A

Methodological Considerations

To understand how religious affiliation influences the ethnic identity formation of Mexican immigrants, I juxtaposed the experiences of the two largest religious groups among ethnic Mexicans: Catholics and evangelicals (Cooperman et al. 2014). The bulk of data for this project was collected through two primary methods: interviews and participant observation. I conducted in-depth, semi-structured interviews with fifty parishioners from Santa Ana, and spent time within their spiritual communities to gain understanding of their social networks and lived religious practices. The project in its totality took over five years to complete. In the sections to follow I outline the steps undertaken to develop this investigation.

First Steps

More than wanting to know about religion and ethnic identity, I entered the field with a commitment to understanding Santa Ana's religious ecology, the constellation of churches and organizations serving the city's Latinx-majority neighborhoods. Having spent most of my life in Orange County, I was aware of the complex system of religious institutions that operated within the region, yet I also recognized that Santa Ana was distinct given its ethnoreligious history. I began by spending time among leaders and within organizational networks throughout Santa Ana, making myself available for events and gatherings that allowed me to observe the interconnectedness and diversity of Santa Ana churches. My work several years prior within faith-based non-profit and educational sectors allowed me to interact with a variety of leaders in Santa Ana's religious ecology. Availing myself of the knowledge I had of Santa Ana's religious communities via my experience in local neighborhoods, I retraced some of the ties I had previously made within Santa Ana's Catholic and evangelical communities, among formal leaders, lay leaders, and participants. For about a year, I visited community meetings and church events throughout the city. I reached out to leaders that I was not previously familiar with along with some that I already knew. I gained knowledge of the organizational networks facilitating collaboration within local Latinx religious communities. I also noted that some churches worked in isolation.

Sampling Methods

In my second year of fieldwork, I identified churches that were especially active in serving Mexican-majority communities within central Santa Ana. I decided to focus on six primary churches as sites from which to sample interviewees. Four of these churches were evangelical, and two were Catholic. I selected churches based on the demographics of their constituency and based on church commitments to the local community. I selected churches that were located in Santa Ana and served a substantial number of Santa Ana residents. The churches I selected all offered services or masses in Spanish. Some churches offered activities in both Spanish and English. During this year, I spent time visiting activities sponsored by some of these churches. I also worked to gain familiarity with leaders from these churches and informed them of my study. This strategy paid off as I gained leader-endorsed entree into particular circles within these religious communities.

In selecting churches to sample from, I was mindful of any pronounced socioeconomic disparities among members and across congregations. In visiting these churches, I confirmed that these churches primarily served working-class parishioners. There was some variation related to socioeconomic status in my sample, but generally, the churches I selected served similar communities across Catholic and evangelical traditions.

One point of difference that was evident across churches was that some churches had a broader geographic base of membership than others. Evangelical churches tended to have a broader geographic reach than Catholic ones, for example, at least in proportion to the size of their congregation. It should be noted that Catholic parishes in Santa Ana counted on much higher memberships than the vast majority of evangelical churches in the city, which was part of the reason why I only sampled from two Catholic churches in contrast to the four evangelical ones I drew from. There was one Latinx evangelical mega-church which approximated the membership count of local Catholic parishes and was part of the study.

In thinking through the types of churches to sample interviewees from, I noted which classifications mattered to Santa Ana residents. I retain the term evangelical to describe the Protestant churches in the sample because this is the primary term used by the congregants themselves as well as by a substantial portion of the local community. Similar to the nomenclature used in Latin America, many Protestants self-identify as evangelicals, or more typically using its Spanish cognate, *evangelicos*. In Santa Ana, the category of those that identify as evangelicals is made up in large part by congregants of Pentecostal persuasion. In this study I did not sample directly from congregants of Mainline congregations, though some evangelicals proved to have ties with local Mainline churches.

Next, I set out to conduct a total of fifty in-depth interviews of parishioners from both Catholic and evangelical churches. Completion of interviews was roughly a year-long process. The sample was divided between twenty-five Catholic parishioners, and twenty-five evangelical parishioners. Interviewees were all adult residents of Santa Ana, immigrants from Mexico, and members of the six selected parishes. While a sub-sample of interviewees[1] had recently moved out of Santa Ana, they all retained a connection to the city at least through their church participation, and many through relational ties to the city, and/or through employment in the city. Those that moved out of the city resided less than a mile outside of the city. Moreover, all of the interviewees maintained strong social connections to the city of Santa Ana through a variety of channels. The majority of interviewees were of working-class status. Most worked in the service sector, in construction, or in light industry. A subsample of interviewees were of higher socioeconomic status. These nine interviewees mostly worked in the fields of education and/or human services. Still, even these upwardly mobile informants retained ties to working class neighborhoods of central Santa Ana through their place of residence, their employment, and their church participation. By extension, their social networks were concentrated within central Santa Ana. Interviewees ranged in age from nineteen years of age to sixty-five years of age. The sample included twenty six women and twenty four men. Interviewees had been in the United States in the range of ten years to sixty years. Moreover, there were no significant differences between the Catholic and evangelical samples of interviewees in terms of socioeconomic status or immigration status. Both groups represented a similar sampling of residents from central Santa Ana's working-class-majority, Mexican-majority neighborhoods.

I connected with an initial wave of interviewees through referrals from leaders I built rapport with from the churches I had identified. In some cases, church leaders put me in contact with parishioners that met the requirements I set forth, as detailed previously. In other cases, church leaders encouraged me to attend certain church events and gatherings where I could readily build rapport with parishioners. In these latter cases, I was often given names of people that I could consider reaching out to who participated in these specific ministries. The spaces I was most typically led to were prayer groups and neighborhood focused ministry groups. These proved to be spaces where people were open to talking and typically trusted me given the endorsements I had received from pastors and leaders. Having interviewed an initial cluster of slightly over a dozen informants, I then sought referrals from these informants for other potential interviewees. Along the way, as I continued to visit the contexts of spiritual community that my interviewees were a part of, I established additional connections there, and conducted more interviews.

[1] Three interviewees had moved out of the city.

In order to grasp the contexts in which interviewees experienced spiritual community, when appropriate, I shadowed interviewees within their faith communities and conducted participant observation there. The types of activities I conducted participant observation within varied widely. In some cases, interviewees' spiritual communities were primarily rooted in neighborhood-based activities. In this case, I took part in neighborhood prayer gatherings, processions, and family celebrations. This was especially the case for Catholics interviewees. I also made it a point to visit activities taking place at the parishes that parishioners belonged to. I had the opportunity to visit different types of masses, services, and community events hosted by interviewees' churches. Some of these visits were of traditional Sunday morning worship gatherings, such as masses and services, while others were of special activities, such as outreach events or community forums, organized at churches. Through these visits, I had the opportunity to conduct dozens of informal interviews with other community members. In all, I was able to gain a multifaceted perspective of how the Latinx-dominant churches of my interviewees were intertwined with the life of local neighborhoods in central Santa Ana. Being available to impromptu invitations, though not always possible, was of paramount importance to this study. Living in the city was of significant help in this regard. While the bulk of the data collection took place in the span of three years (2013–2016), I had made forays into the field prior to this time frame, and periodically, after.

Data Documentation and Analysis

Documentation throughout this study primarily involved the transcription of recorded interviews and the maintenance of fieldnotes. I conducted all interviews in face-to-face settings, either in home contexts, in church facilities, or in semi-public neighborhood-based spaces. Interviewees were read a prompt explaining that their participation in the study was voluntary, to which all invited interviewees gave verbal consent. Likewise, all interviewees agreed to have their interviews recorded. Interviews generally followed the interview guide included in this volume, but I also took a more flexible approach, allowing interviewees to elaborate on particular themes that were meaningful to them. Interviews typically lasted about an hour and in many cases I had follow up interactions with informants. I transcribed interviews into a Word document myself. The overwhelming majority of interviews and field interactions took place in Spanish.

Along with my interviews, I kept a journal of my engagement in the field. Fieldnotes were typically typed up within twenty four hours of my field engagements. In some cases I wrote memos reflecting on particular themes and patterns that I was observing in the field and that emerged from my fieldnotes. Both transcribed interviews and fieldnotes were then coded to highlight key themes and patterns, which were then further grouped into broadly encompassing thematic clusters. The themes that ultimately compose the structure of this volume largely emerged from my interactions in the field as documented in my fieldnotes and interview notes.

In regards to language, it is important to reiterate that the overwhelming majority of my interviews and interactions were conducted in Spanish. Those that had come to the U.S. as children typically preferred to interact in English, but roughly 80% of my informants communicated with me in Spanish. As a person of Mexican American heritage, who grew up speaking Spanish, language posed no challenge, other than informants' occasional use of regional colloquialisms that I was unfamiliar with. My ability to code switch into regional terminology at strategic moments, both in English and Spanish, typically served to build trust with informants. Linguistic familiarity also proved helpful as I translated into written form the social interactions that I had and that I observed in the field. I attempted to capture in this volume some of the colloquial terminology prevalent among Santaneros, even as I worked to make the phraseology intelligible in English.

Limitations and Future Directions

One critical distinction to make between this study and others that similarly sample from church populations, is that much of my conceptual focus centered on how congregants engaged with each other and with religious others in their neighborhoods. This was a focus that I chose to make clearer while in the field. Rather than focusing on the experiences of socialization within the congregations, I turned my attention to the patterns of intergroup engagement and to the social maps that congregants generated in relation to coreligionists and non-coreligionists. My research questions were centered on how intergroup interactions contributed to processes of ethnic identity formation. Moreover, in not framing this as a parish or congregational study, I limited the analysis of institutional factors in the identify formation of informants. As of the completion of this project, I have turned additional attention to how parishes and congregations contribute, as institutions, to the distinct modes of ethnic identity formation of Latinxs. There is much comparative work to be done to understand how notions of not just ethnicity, but also of race, are made real through church-based experiences within predominantly Latinx churches.

APPENDIX B

Interview Schedule (English) Affiliation and Acculturation Questionnaire

Background Information

1. Sex
2. Age
3. Please list the people that you consider to be part of your current household including name and relationship
4. Marital status
5. Length of residence (years) in the United States
6. Education
7. Occupation

Ethnic and Religious Self Identification

1. What label would you use to describe your ethnic background?
   a. Latino b. Hispanic c. Mexican d. Mexican-American e. American f. Other:________
2. What labels best describe your faith beliefs? (For example, Catholic, Christian, Baptist, Pentecostal.) Which is the most important?
3. What do you think is more important, that people identify you because of your faith, or that people identify you because of your ethnicity?
4. What brought you to the United States?
5. Can you tell me about how you came to the faith and beliefs that you now have?
6. Please describe to me what a typical week of church participation looked like for you last year. Were there any other special events that came up throughout the year? Any events with other churches?
7. When you were in Mexico, was your church participation similar to or different from what it is today? Please explain.
8. How long have you been at your current church?

Religious Boundaries and the Policing of Ethnicity

1. Who do you feel more connected to?
   a. people of the same faith as you,
   b. other Mexican people,
   c. both about the same?
2. How does your faith influence your relationships with your immediate and extended family? (Think about both positive and negative responses you get from others.)
3. How does your faith influence your experience of living in your neighborhood?
4. Are there places or events you will not go to because you feel that people of your faith should not be there? Please describe.
5. Have you ever felt discriminated against because of your faith? By who? Was it ever by other Mexican people?

Social Network

1. In a crisis situation, who are the first three people you would call for help?
   What is your relation to them? Friend or family member?
   What is their age and occupation?
   Are any of them members of the same church as you?
   If not, are they of the same faith as you?
2. Have you ever obtained work through someone from your church?
   If so, who are they and what was the job you obtained?
3. When you think about your close friends, what are different characteristics that describe them?
   a. Mexican
   b. Latino, but not Mexican
   c. Not Latino
   d. Same faith as you / comparten la misma fe
   e. Not of the same faith as you / no comparten la misma fe
4. Do you contribute time or money to any other organizations related to being Mexican or Latino?

Cultural Transmission

1. Do you share the same beliefs as your immediate family? How do you express faith as a family?
   If yes, how so at home and at church? Is there any resistance?
2. What is the preferred future that you desire for your children's lives as adults?
3. What elements of Mexican culture do you think should be passed on to the next generation and which elements would you not want to pass on?
4. What language do you speak at home with your family members?

APPENDIX C

Interview Schedule (Spanish)

Affiliation and Acculturation Questionnaire

Este es un estudio sobre cómo las creencias espirituales, fe personal, y participación en una iglesia tienen influencia en la vida de personas inmigrantes. Estaré haciendo preguntas sobre su identidad, su cultura, y los recursos sociales que ha recibido por tomar parte en una iglesia.

Información Personal—Background Information

1. ¿Cuántos años ha vivido en los Estados Unidos?
2. ¿Ocupación?
3. ¿Educación?
4. ¿Estatus matrimonial?
5. ¿Edad?
6. ¿Género?

Identificación Propia—Self Identification

1. ¿Que terminó usaría usted para describir su trasfondo étnico?
   a. Latino b. Hispano c. Mexicano/a d. Mexico-Americano e. Americano f. Otro:
2. ¿Qué término describe mejor sus creencias y su fe? Por ejemplo: Cristiano, Católico, Católico Romano, Bautista, Pentecostal.
3. ¿Qué piensa usted que es más importante? ¿Que las personas le identifiquen por su fe, o que las personas le identifiquen por ser Mexicano/a?
4. ¿Me pudiera dar un corto relato de lo que lo trajo a los estados unidos?
5. ¿Me pudiera dar una descripción de lo que lo trajo a la fe y creencia que usted tiene hoy?
6. Pensando en el año pasado, ¿Cómo describiría usted una semana típica para usted en su participación en la iglesia? Hubieron eventos especiales que se llevaron a cabo a través del año? Hubo algún evento que incluyó la participación de otras iglesias?
7. ¿Cuando usted vivió en México, fue diferente su participación de iglesia?
8. ¿Que tanto tiempo ha estado en su iglesia?

Demarcaciones Religiosas y Supervisión de Etnicidad—Religious Boundaries and the Policing of Ethnicity

1. ¿Con qué tipo de persona siente usted más coneccion?
   a. Personas que comparten la misma fe que usted
   b. Personas que comparten la misma cultura que usted
   c. Los dos aspectos más o menos igual
2. ¿De qué manera influye su fe la forma en la que usted y su familia se relacionan unos con los otros? (tanto lo positivo como lo negativo)
3. ¿De qué manera es influenciada por su fe la experiencia que tiene viviendo en su vecindario?
4. ¿Hay lugares o eventos a los cuales usted no va porque cree que personas de su fe no deben ir allí?
5. ¿Alguna vez ha sentido discriminación a raíz de su fe? De parte de quien? (eran Mexicanos o Latinos?)

Red Social—Social Network

1. ¿Cuales son las personas que usted considera como parte de su hogar? Incluya nombre y relación a usted.
2. ¿En una crisis personal, quienes serían las tres primeras personas que llamaría?
   ¿Cual es tu relación hacia ellos?
   ¿Que edad y ocupación tienen?
   ¿Algunos de ellos son miembros de la misma iglesia que usted?
   Si no, ¿Son de la misma fe que usted?
3. ¿En alguna ocasión ha obtenido trabajo con la ayuda de alguien de su iglesia?
   Si la respuesta es "si," ¿Quienes son, y cuál fue el trabajo?
4. ¿Cuando piensas en tus amigos más cercanos, cuales son diferentes características que los describen? (Amistades en las que tienes confianza)
   a. Mexicanos
   b. Latinos, pero no Mexicanos
   c. No Latinos
   d. Comparten la misma fe
   e. No comparten la misma fe
5. ¿Contribuye usted tiempo o dinero a cualquier otra organización relacionada con ser de trasfondo Mexicano o Latino?

Transmisión de Cultura—Cultural Transmission

1. Comparten las mismas creencias usted y su familia? ¿Cómo expresan su fe como familia?
   ¿De qué forma en la casa, y de qué forma enla iglesia? ¿Hay resistencia de alguien?
2. ¿Cual es el futuro que usted desea para sus hijos cuando sean adultos?
3. ¿Que elementos de la cultura Mexicana piensa usted que deben ser adoptados por la próxima generación y que elementos piensa usted que deben ser eliminados?
4. Que idioma habla usted en casa con sus miembros de familia?

Bibliography

Adler, Gary J., Tricia C. Bruce, and Brian Starks. 2019. *American Parishes: Remaking Local Catholicism*. New York: Fordham University Press.

Agius Vallejo, Jody. 2012. *Barrios to Burbs the Making of the Mexican-American Middle Class*. Stanford, CA: Stanford University Press.

Alba, Richard D., and John R. Logan. 1993. "Minority Proximity to Whites in Suburbs: An Individual-Level Analysis of Segregation." *American Journal of Sociology* 98(6):1388–427.

Alba, Richard. 2005. "Bright vs. Blurred Boundaries: Second-Generation Assimilation and Exclusion in France, Germany, and the United States." *Ethnic and Racial Studies* 28(1):20–49.

Alcoff, Linda, Michael Hames-García, Satya Mohanty, Michael Hames-García, and Paula M. L. Moya. 2006. *Identity Politics Reconsidered*. New York: Palgrave Macmillan.

Almaguer, Tomas. 1994. *Racial Fault Lines: The Historical Origins of White Supremacy in California*. Berkeley: University of California Press.

Alvarez, Daniel. 2015. "No More Violence! Renewal Theological Reflections on Violence in the Context of Honduras and Its Immigrants to the United States." Pp. 81–95 in *Pentecostals and Charismatics in Latin America and Latino Communities*, edited by N. Medina and S. Alfaro. New York: Palgrave Macmillan.

Ammerman, Nancy Tatom. 1997. *Congregation & Community*. New Brunswick: Rutgers University Press.

Ammerman, Nancy Tatom. 2007. *Everyday Religion: Observing Modern Religious Lives*. Oxford University Press.

Anon. n.d. "Mission." *El Centro Cultural de México*. Accessed August 26, 2019. http://elcentroculturaldemexico.org/mission-and-vission.

Anzaldúa, Gloria. 1999. *Borderlands*. San Francisco: Aunt Lute Books.

Arellano, Gustavo. 2008. *Orange County: A Personal History*. New York: Simon and Schuster.

Arellano, Gustavo. 2013. "Santanero: A Zine to Be Seen." *OC Weekly*, April 4.

Armor, Samuel. 1921. *History of Orange County, California: With Biographical Sketches of the Leading Men and Women of the County Who Have Been Identified with Its Earliest Growth and Development from the Early Days to the Present*. Los Angeles: Historic Record Company.

Arriola, Christopher. 1995. "Knocking on the Schoolhouse Door: Mendez v. Westminster, Equal Protection, Public Education, and Mexican Americans in the 1940's." *La Raza Law Journal* 8:166–207.

Badillo, David A. 2004. "Mexicanos and Suburban Parish Communities: Religion, Space, and Identity in Contemporary Chicago." *Journal of Urban History* 31(1):23–46.

Badillo, David A. 2008. *Latinos and the New Immigrant Church*. Baltimore, MD: Johns Hopkins University Press.

Bailey, Stanley R. 2008. "Unmixing for Race Making in Brazil." *American Journal of Sociology* 114(3):577–614.

Bane, Mary Jo. 2019. "A House Divided." Pp. 153–70 in *American Parishes, Remaking Local Catholicism*, edited by G. J. Adler, T. C. Bruce, and B. Starks. New York: Fordham University Press.

Barth, Fredrik. 1969. *Ethnic Groups and Boundaries: The Social Organization of Culture Difference*. Boston: Little, Brown and Company.

Berger, Peter L. 1967. *The Sacred Canopy: Elements of a Sociological Theory of Religion*. Garden City, NY: Doubleday.

Bermudez, Esmeralda. 2014. "Faithful Flock to See Statue of Santo Toribio, the Immigrants' Saint." *Los Angeles Times*, July 12.

Blum, Edward J. 2012. "Gods of the Golden Coast: Sacred Topographies." *Boom: A Journal of California* 2(2):82–85.

Bourdieu, Pierre. 1984. *Distinction: A Social Critique of the Judgement of Taste*. Cambridge, MA: Harvard University Press.

Bourdieu, Pierre. 1986. "The Forms of Capital." Pp. 241–58 in *Handbook of Theory and Research for the Sociology of Education*, edited by J. G. Richardson. New York: Greenwood.

Bowen, Kurt. 1996. *Evangelism and Apostasy: The Evolution and Impact of Evangelicals in Modern Mexico*. Vol. 23. Montreal: McGill-Queen's Press-MQUP.

Brazil, Ben. 2019. "Juaneño Spiritual Leader Seeks to Preserve the Old Ways." *Daily Pilot*, May 16.

Brenneman, Robert. 2011. *Homies and Hermanos: God and Gangs in Central America*. New York: Oxford University Press.

Bricken, Gordon. 2011. *Legacy of Faith : The First 124 Years of Saint Joseph Catholic Church*. Santa Ana, CA: The Bricken Press.

Brubaker, Rogers. 2002. "Ethnicity without Groups." *European Journal of Sociology/Archives Européennes de Sociologie* 43(2):163–89.

Brubaker, Rogers. 2004. *Ethnicity without Groups*. Cambridge, MA: Harvard University Press.

Brunner, Edmund de S., and Mary V. Brunner. 1922. *Irrigation and Religion: A Study of Religious and Social Conditions in Two California Counties*. New York: G.H. Doran.

Brusco, Elizabeth E. 2011. *The Reformation of Machismo: Evangelical Conversion and Gender in Colombia*. Austin: University of Texas Press.

Cal-Pac UMC. 2014. *Historical Section*. California-Pacific Conference United Methodist Church.

Calvillo, Jonathan E., and Stanley R. Bailey. 2015. "Latino Religious Affiliation and Ethnic Identity." *Journal for the Scientific Study of Religion* 54(1):57–78.

Carcamo, Cindy. 2011. "Immigrants' Return to Mexico Alters Santa Ana." *Orange County Register*, November 14.

Carter, Prudence L. 2003. "Black Cultural Capital, Status Positioning, and Schooling Conflicts for Low-Income African American Youth." *Social Problems* 50(1):136–55.

Case, Alden. 1902. *The Pacific*. Thursday, February 27, edited by W. W. Ferrier. Publishing Company of the Pacific.

Cassaniti, Julia L., and Tanya Marie Luhrmann. 2014. "The Cultural Kindling of Spiritual Experiences." *Current Anthropology* 55(10):333–43.

Castañeda, Ernesto. 2018. *A Place to Call Home: Immigrant Exclusion and Urban Belonging in New York, Paris, and Barcelona*. Redwood City, CA: Stanford University Press.

Castañeda-Liles, María Del Socorro. 2018. *Our Lady of Everyday Life: La Virgen de Guadalupe and the Catholic Imagination of Mexican Women in America*. New York: Oxford University Press.

Chavez, Leo. 2013. *The Latino Threat: Constructing Immigrants, Citizens, and the Nation*. Stanford, CA: Stanford University Press.

Chen, Carolyn, and Russell Jeung. 2012. *Sustaining Faith Traditions: Race, Ethnicity, and Religion among the Latino and Asian American Second Generation*. New York: New York University Press.

Chesnut, R. Andrew. 1997. *Born Again in Brazil: The Pentecostal Boom and the Pathogens of Poverty*. New Brunswick: Rutgers University Press.

Chesnut, R. Andrew. 2003. "A Preferential Option for the Spirit: The Catholic Charismatic Renewal in Latin America's New Religious Economy." *Latin American Politics and Society* 45(1):55–85.

Christie, Les. 2011. "America's Most Overvalued and Undervalued Housing Markets—Jan. 11, 2011." *CNN Money*. Accessed September 23, 2019. https://money.cnn.com/2011/01/10/real_estate/overvalued_housing_markets/index.htm.

Coleman, James S. 1988. "Social Capital in the Creation of Human Capital." *American Journal of Sociology* 94:S95–S120.

Cooperman, Alan, Mark Hugo Lopez, Cary Funk, Jessica Hamar Martínez, and Katherine Ritchey. 2014. *The Shifting Religious Identity of Latinos in the United States*. Washington, DC: Pew Research Center.

Coutin, Susan Bibler. 2013. "In the Breach: Citizenship and Its Approximations." *Indiana Journal of Global Legal Studies* 20:109.

De Genova, Nicholas. 2004. "The Legal Production of Mexican/Migrant 'Illegality.'" *Latino Studies* 2(2):160–85.

De Genova, Nicholas, and Ana Y. Ramos-Zayas. 2003. "Latino Racial Formations in the United States: An Introduction." *Journal of Latin American Anthropology* 8(2):2–16.

De la Torre, Miguel A. 2009. *Hispanic American Religious Cultures*. Santa Barbara, CA: ABC-CLIO.

Deck, Allan Figueroa. 2015. "Latino Migration and the Transformation of USA Catholicism: Framing the Question." *Perspectiva Teológica* 46:89–112.

Dias, Elizabeth. 2013. "The Latino Reformation." *Time Magazine*. April 15. Accessed May 15, 2013. http://www.time.com/time/magazine/article/0,9171,2140207,00.html

Dillon, Michele. 2003. *Handbook of the Sociology of Religion*. New York: Cambridge University Press.

Do, Anh. 2016. "Crystal Cathedral Enters a New Era as It Transforms into Christ Cathedral." *LA Times*, September 17. Accessed January 3, 2019. https://www.latimes.com/local/lanow/la-me-ln-orange-county-catholics-adv-snap-story.html

Dochuk, Darren. 2010. *From Bible Belt to Sunbelt: Plain-Folk Religion, Grassroots Politics, and the Rise of Evangelical Conservatism*. New York: W. W. Norton & Company.

Dowling, Julie A. 2005. "'I'm Not Mexican. . . Pero Soy Mexicano': Linguistic Context of Labeling among Mexican Americans in Texas." *Southwest Journal of Linguistics* 24(1–2):53–64.

Dowling, Julie A. 2014. *Mexican Americans and the Question of Race*. Austin: University of Texas Press.

Doyle, Dennis M. 2012. "The Concept of Inculturation in Roman Catholicism: A Theological Consideration." *U.S. Catholic Historian* 30(1):1–13.

DuCros, Faustina M. 2017. "Creating Transregional Collective Nostalgia: The Organising Role of Catholic Parishes among Louisiana Migrants in Great Migration-Era Los Angeles." *Journal of Ethnic & Migration Studies* 43(5):830–48.

Durand, Jorge, and Douglas S. Massey. 2020. *Miracles on the Border: Retablos of Mexican Migrants to the United States*. Tucson: University of Arizona Press.

Durkheim, Émile. 1897. *Suicide: A study in sociology*. Paris: F. Alcan.

Durkheim, Émile. 1912. Elementary Forms of Religious Life. New York: Oxford University Press.

Eiesland, Nancy L. 2000. *A Particular Place: Urban Restructuring and Religious Ecology in a Southern Exurb*. New Brunswick: Rutgers University Press.

Eliade, Mircea. 1959. *The Sacred and the Profane: The Nature of Religion*. Boston: Houghton Mifflin Harcourt.

Elizondo, Virgilio P. 1997. *Guadalupe, Mother of the New Creation*. New York: Orbis Books.

Elizondo, Virgilio P. 2006. "Converted by Beauty." Pp. 73–78 in *The Treasure of Guadalupe*, edited by V. P. Elizondo, A. F. Deck, and T. Matovina. Lanham, MD: Rowman & Littlefield.

Emeka, Amon, and Jody Agius Vallejo. 2011. "Non-Hispanics with Latin American Ancestry: Assimilation, Race, and Identity among Latin American Descendants in the US." *Social Science Research* 40(6):1547–63.

Epting, Charles. 2014. *Orange County Pioneers: Oral Histories from the Works Progress Administration*. Mount Pleasant, SC: Arcadia Publishing.

Espín, Orlando O. 2002. "Mexican Religious Practices, Popular Catholicism, and the Development of Doctrine." Pp. 139–52 in *Horizons of the Sacred: Mexican Traditions in U.S. Catholicism*, edited by T. Matovina and G. Riebe-Estrella. Cornell University Press.

Espín, Orlando O. 2006. "Tradition: Culture, Daily Life and Popular Religion, and Their Impact on Christian Tradition." Pp. 12–24 in *Futuring Our Past: Explorations in the Theology of Tradition, Studies in Latino/a Catholicism*, edited by O. O. Espín and G. Macy. Maryknoll, NY: Orbis Books.

Espinosa, Gastón. 2014. *Latino Pentecostals in America: Faith and Politics in Action*. Cambridge, MA: Harvard University Press.

Espinosa, Gastón. 2017. "'Let the Spirit Fly': Marilynn Kramar and the History of the Latino Catholic Charismatic Movement in the U.S.-Mexico Borderlands." Pp. 30–52 in *California Dreaming: Society and Culture in the Golden State*, edited by R. A. Wells. Eugene, OR: Wipf and Stock.

Fishman, Joshua A. 1968. "Nationality-Nationalism and Nation-Nationism." Pp. 39–51 in *Language problems of developing nations*, edited by J. A. Fishman, C. A. Ferguson, and J. D. Gupta. New York: John Wiley & Sons.

Flores, Edward. 2014. *God's Gangs: Barrio Ministry, Masculinity, and Gang Recovery*. New York: New York University Press.

Flores-Yeffal, Nadia Yamel. 2013. *Migration-Trust Networks: Social Cohesion in Mexican US-Bound Emigration*. College Station, TX: Texas A&M University Press.

Fortuny Loret de Mola, Patricia. 1994. "El Pentecostalismo. Su Capacidad de Transformación En Jalisco y Yucatán." *Nueva Antropología* 13(45):49–63.

Fortuny Loret de Mola, Patricia. 2002. "The Santa Cena of La Luz Del Mundo Church: A Case of Contemporary Transnationalism." Pp. 15–50 in *Religion Across Borders: Transnational Religious Networks*, edited by H. R. Ebaugh and J. S. Chafetz. Walnut Creek, CA: Altamira Press.

Foster, George M. 1966. "Euphemisms and Cultural Sensitivity in Tzintzuntzan." *Anthropological Quarterly* 39(2):53–59.

Freier, Luisa Feline. 2008. "Religion, Ethnicity and Immigrant Integration: 'Latino' Lutherans versus 'Mexican' Catholics in a Midwestern City." *Studies in Ethnicity and Nationalism* 8(2):267–89.

Freier, Luisa Feline. 2009. "How Our Lady of Guadalupe Became Lutheran: Latin American Migration and Religious Change." *Migraciones Internacionales* 5(2):152–90.

Garces-Foley, Kathleen. 2008. "Comparing Catholic and Evangelical Integration Efforts." *Journal for the Scientific Study of Religion* 47(1):17–22.

García, Mario T. 1994. *Memories of Chicano History: The Life and Narrative of Bert Corona*. Berkeley: University of California Press.

Garcia, Mary. 2007. *Santa Ana's Logan Barrio: Its History, Stories, and Families*. Santa Ana, CA: Santa Ana Historical Preservation Society.

Gittelsohn, John. 2008. "WaMu Loaned Millions to O.C. Home Flippers with Fraud History." *Orange County Register*, September 19.

Gonzalez, Gilbert G. 1994. *Labor and Community: Mexican Citrus Worker Villages in a Southern California County, 1900–1950*. Urbana: University of Illinois Press.

Gonzalez, Erualdo R. 2017. *Latino City: Urban Planning, Politics, and the Grassroots*. New York: Routledge.

Grammich, Clifford, Kirk Hadaway, Rich Houseal, Dale E. Jones, Alexei Krindatch, Richie Stanley, and Richard H. Taylor. 2012. *US Religion Census (2010). Religious Congregations & Membership Study*. Kansas City, MO: Association of Statisticians of American Religious Bodies.

Greeley, Andrew. 2000. *The Catholic Imagination*. Berkeley: University of California Press.

Green, Mary. 1987. *St. Joseph Church 1887–1987: The Celebration of a People, a Place, a Presence*. Santa Ana, CA: St. Joseph Parish.

Guinn, James Miller. 1902. *Historical and Biographical Record of Southern California: Containing a History of Southern California from Its Earliest Settlement to the Opening Year of the Twentieth Century*. Chicago: Chapman.

Guinn, James Miller. 1911. "History of the Cahuenga Valley and the Rancho La Brea." Pp. 82–94 in *Annual Publication of the Historical Society of Southern California*. Los Angeles: Historical Society of Southern California.

Gurza, Agustin. 2000. "Mexico's Holy War Is Part of Many Family Histories." *Los Angeles Times*, October 17.

Haas, Lisbeth. 1995. *Conquests and Historical Identities in California, 1769–1936*. 1st pbk. printing. Berkeley: University of California Press.

Haas, Lisbeth. 2013. *Saints and Citizens: Indigenous Histories of Colonial Missions and Mexican California*. Berkeley: University of California Press.

Hagan, Jacqueline, and Helen Rose Ebaugh. 2003. "Calling upon the Sacred: Migrants' Use of Religion in the Migration Process." *International Migration Review* 37(4):1145–62.

Hagan, Jacqueline Maria. 2008. *Migration Miracle: Faith, Hope, and Meaning on the Undocumented Journey*. Cambridge, MA: Harvard University Press.

Hagerty, Barbara Bradley. 2011. "US Hispanics Choose Churches Outside Catholicism." *National Public Radio, October 19*. Accessed March 2, 2014. https://www.npr.org/2011/10/19/141275979/u-s-hispanics-choose-churches-outside-catholicism

Hagerty, James R. 2009. "Bidding Wars Are Emerging on Foreclosures." *Wall Street Journal*, April 23. Accessed September 22, 2019. https://www.wsj.com/articles/SB124044612611045827

Hall, Matthew, Emily Greenman, and George Farkas. 2010. "Legal Status and Wage Disparities for Mexican Immigrants." *Social Forces* 89(2):491–513.

Harwood, Stacy, and Dowell Myers. 2002. "The Dynamics of Immigration and Local Governance in Santa Ana." *Policy Studies Journal* 30(1):70–91.

Harwood, Thomas. 1910. *History of New Mexico Spanish and English Missions of the Methodist Episcopal Church from 1850 to 1910, in Decades.* Albuquerque: Abogado Press.

Higgins, Michael J. 1990. "Martíres y Virgenes: La Religión Popular En México y En Nicaragua." *Nueva Antropología* 11(37):85–106.

Hirschman, Charles. 2004. "The Role of Religion in the Origins and Adaptation of Immigrant Groups in the United States." *International Migration Review* 38(3):1206–33.

Hoiles, Raymond Cyrus, ed. 1939. "Churches of Santa Ana: Mexican Methodist Episcopal Church." *The Santa Ana Register* (March 18):13.

Holland, Clifton L. 1974. *The Religious Dimension in Hispanic Los Angeles: A Protestant Case Study.* Pasadena, CA: William Carey Library.

Hoover, Brett. 2017. "The 'Ownership' of Churches: Ethnic, Racial, and Language Groups in US Catholicism." *Eurostudia* 12(1):105–24.

Hoover, Brett C. 2014. *The Shared Parish: Latinos, Anglos, and the Future of U.S. Catholicism.* New York: NYU Press.

Hughes, Jennifer Scheper, James Kyung-Jin Lee, Amanda Lucia, and S. Romi Mukherjee. 2015. "Take It Outside: Practicing Religion in Public." *Boom: A Journal of California* 5(4):54–63.

Huntington, Samuel P. 2004. *Who Are We?: The Challenges to America's National Identity.* New York: Simon and Schuster.

Hurtig, Janise D. 2000. "Hispanic Immigrant Churches and the Construction of Ethnicity." Pp. 29–55 in *Public Religion and Urban Transformation: Faith in the City*, edited by Lowell Livezey. New York: New York University Press.

Hutchinson, Mark. 2009. "'Second Founder': A C Valdez Sr and Australian Pentecostalism." *Australasian Pentecostal Studies* 11.

INEGI. 2015. *Encuesta Intercensal 2015: Principales Resultados.* Mexico: Instituto Nacional de Estadística y Geografía.

Iribarren, Roman. 1974. *Our Lady of the Pillar, Our Lady of Guadalupe Parish: Fifty Years 1922–1972.* North Hollywood, CA: Churchill.

Itzigsohn, José. 2004. "The Formation of Latino and Latina Panethnic Identities." Pp. 197–218 in *Not Just Black and White*, edited by N. Foner and G. M. Fredrickson. New York: Russell Sage Foundation.

Jimenez, Tomas. 2010. *Replenished Ethnicity: Mexican Americans, Immigration, and Identity.* Berkeley: University of California Press.

Jimenez, Tomas R. 2008. "Mexican Immigrant Replenishment and the Continuing Significance of Ethnicity and Race." *American Journal of Sociology* 113(6):1527–67.

Jiménez, Tomás R., Corey D. Fields, and Ariela Schachter. 2015. "How Ethnoraciality Matters: Looking inside Ethnoracial 'Groups.'" *Social Currents* 2(2):107–15.

Jones, Robert P., Daniel Cox, and Juhem Navarro-Rivera. 2013. "How Shifting Religious Identities and Experiences Are Influencing Hispanic Approaches to Politics." *Public Religion Research Institute*, Washington, DC 48.

Kandil, Caitlin Yoshiko. 2017. "Want to See the Catholic Church's Future? Go to Mass in the Fast-Growing Diocese of Orange." *Latimes.com*, October 5.

Knott, Kim, Volkhard Krech, and Birgit Meyer. 2016. "Iconic Religion in Urban Space." *Material Religion* 12(2):123–36.

Koerper, Henry Carl, and Nicholas M. Magalousis. 1988. *The Natural and Social Sciences of Orange County*. Newport Beach, CA: Natural History Foundation of Orange County.

Kopetman, Roxana. 2012. "Crystal Cathedral Renamed Christ Cathedral." *Orange County Register*, June 10.

Kosmin, Barry Alexander, and Ariela Keysar. 2009. *American Religious Identification Survey (ARIS 2008): Summary Report*. Hartford, CT: Trinity College.

Krekelberg, William F. 2016. *Call To Mission: The Diocese of Orange Forty Years and Counting*. Eckbolsheim: Éditions du Signe.

Kresge, Lisa. 2007. "Indigenous Oaxacan Communities in California: An Overview." Davis: California Institute for Rural Studies.

Lacayo, Celia. 2016. "Latinos Need to Stay in Their Place: Differential Segregation in a Multi-Ethnic Suburb." *Societies* 6(3):25.

Lawrence, Anthony L. 2012. *The First Catholic Church in Huntington Beach, California: A Chronological Illustrated History of Sts. Simon and Jude Parish*. Huntington Beach, CA: Saints Simon and Jude Catholic Church.

Lee, Ellen K. 1969. "Helena Modjeska and the Francisco Torres Affair, Summer 1892." *Southern California Quarterly* 51(1):35–56.

Lee, Jennifer, and Frank D. Bean. 2007. "Reinventing the Color Line Immigration and America's New Racial/Ethnic Divide." *Social Forces* 86(2):561–86.

Lefebvre, Henri. 1991. *The Production of Space*. Cambridge, MA: Blackwell.

Lin, Mingang, and Min Zhou. 2005. "Community Transformation and the Formation of Ethnic Capital: Immigrant Chinese Communities in the United States." *Journal of Chinese Overseas* 1(2):260–84.

Lint Sagarena, Roberto. 2009. "Migration and Mexican American Religious Life, 1848–2000." Pp. 56–70 in *Immigration and Religion in America: Comparative and Historical Perspectives*, edited by R. D. Alba, A. J. Raboteau, and J. DeWind. New York: New York University Press.

Lopez, David. 2009. "Whither the Flock? The Catholic Church and the Success of Mexicans in America." Pp. 71–98 in *Immigration and Religion in America: Comparative and Historical Perspectives*, edited by R. D. Alba, A. J. Raboteau, and J. DeWind. New York: New York University Press.

Lopez, Mark Hugo. 2013. "Hispanic or Latino? Many Don't Care, except in Texas." Washington, DC: Pew Research Center.

Lopez, Mark Hugo, Ana Gonzalez-Barrera, and Gustavo López. 2017. *Latino Identity Declines Across Generations as Immigrant Ties Weaken*. Washington, DC: Pew Research Center.

López-Sanders, Laura. 2012. "Bible Belt Immigrants: Latino Religious Incorporation in New Immigrant Destinations." *Latino Studies* 10(1–2):128–54.

Loveman, Mara. 1999. "Is 'Race' Essential?" *American Sociological Review* 64(6):891–98.

Lovett, Ian. 2018. "Lasting Tributes Meet Early End in Bankruptcy." *The New York Times*, October 19.

Lugo, Luis, and Allison Pond. 2007. *¡Here Come 'Los Evangélicos'!* Washington, DC: Pew Research Center.

Luhrmann, T. M. 2012. *When God Talks Back: Understanding the American Evangelical Relationship with God*. New York: Knopf Doubleday.

Mahlberg, Jean Dolores. 1968. "The History of St. Peter Evangelical Lutheran Church of Santa Ana, California." Fullerton, CA: California State University Fullerton.

Manglos, Nicolette D. 2010. "Born Again in Balaka: Pentecostal versus Catholic Narratives of Religious Transformation in Rural Malawi." *Sociology of Religion* 71(4):409–31.

Manglos-Weber, Nicolette D. 2018. *Joining the Choir: Religious Memberships and Social Trust among Transnational Ghanaians*. New York: Oxford University Press.

Marcelli, Enrico A., Manuel Pastor, and Steven P. Wallace. 2015. *Toward a Healthy California*. Los Angeles: University of Southern California, Center for the Study of Immigrant Integration.

Marcuse, Peter. 1997. "The Enclave, the Citadel, and the Ghetto: What Has Changed in the Post-Fordist U.S. City." *Urban Affairs Review* 33(2):228–64.

Marcuse, Peter. 2005. "Enclaves Yes, Ghettos No." Pp. 15–30 in *Desegregating the City: Ghettos, Enclaves, and Inequality*, edited by D. P. Varady. Albany, NY: State University of New York Press.

Marquardt, Marie Friedmann. 2005a. "From Shame to Confidence: Gender, Religious Conversion, and Civic Engagement of Mexicans in the U.S. South." *Latin American Perspectives* 32(1):27–56.

Marquardt, Marie Friedmann. 2005b. "Structural and Cultural Hybrids: Religious Congregational Life and Public Participation of Mexicans in the New South." Pp. 189–218 in *Immigrant Faiths: Transforming Religious Life in America*, edited by K. I. Leonard, A. Stepick, M. A. Vasquez, and J. Holdaway. Lanham, MD: Rowman Altamira.

Martí, Gerardo. 2018. "Maranatha (O Lord, Come): The Power–Surrender Dynamic of Pentecostal Worship." *Liturgy* 33(3):20–28.

Martinez, Juan F. 2013. "Remittances and Mission." Pp. 204–23 in *Spirit and Power: The Growth and Global Impact of Pentecostalism*, edited by D. E. Miller, K. H. Sargeant, and R. Flory. New York: Oxford University Press.

Martinez, Juan Francisco. 2011. *Los Protestantes: An Introduction to Latino Protestantism in the United States*. Santa Barbara, CA: ABC-CLIO.

Massey, Douglas S., Jorge Durand, and Nolan J. Malone. 2003. *Beyond Smoke and Mirrors: Mexican Immigration in an Era of Economic Integration*. New York: Russell Sage Foundation.

Matovina, Timothy. 2009. "Theologies of Guadalupe: From the Spanish Colonial Era to Pope John Paul II." *Theological Studies* 70(1):61–91.

Matovina, Timothy. 2011. *Latino Catholicism: Transformation in America's Largest Church*. Princeton, NJ: Princeton University Press.

Matovina, Timothy M. 2017. "Hispanic Lay Movements in the Postconciliar Church." Pp. 136–50 in *What We Have Seen and Heard: Fostering Baptismal Witness in the World*, edited by M. E. Connors. Eugene, OR: Wipf and Stock.

Mayrargue, Cédric. 2001. "The Expansion of Pentecostalism in Benin: Individual Rationales and Transnational Dynamics." Pp. 274–92 in *Between Babel and Pentecost: Transnational Pentecostalism in Africa and Latin America*, edited by A. Corten and R. Marshall-Fratani. Bloomington: Indiana University Press.

McArthur, Helen M. 1948. *A History of First Methodist Church Santa Ana: November 29, 1873–November 29, 1943*. Santa Ana, CA: Quality Printers.

McGirr, Lisa. 2015. *Suburban Warriors: The Origins of the New American Right: The Origins of the New American Right*. Princeton, NJ: Princeton University Press.

McLellan, Dennis. 2005. "Msgr. John V. Coffield, 91; Southland Cleric and Social Activist." *Los Angeles Times*, February 6.

McNerney, Eileen. 2005. *A Story of Suffering and Hope: Lessons from Latino Youth*. New York: Paulist Press.

McRoberts, Omar M. 2003. *Streets of Glory: Church and Community in a Black Urban Neighborhood*. Chicago: University of Chicago Press.

McWilliams, Carey. 1946. *Southern California Country: An Island on the Land*. New York: Duell, Sloan & Pearce.

Menjívar, Cecilia. 1999. "Religious Institutions and Transnationalism: A Case Study of Catholic and Evangelical Salvadoran Immigrants." *International Journal of Politics, Culture, and Society* 12(4):589–612.

Menjívar, Cecilia. 2003. "Religion and Immigration in Comparative Perspective: Catholic and Evangelical Salvadorans in San Francisco, Washington, D.C., and Phoenix." *Sociology of Religion* 64(1):21–45.

Meyer, Birgit. 1998. "'Make a Complete Break with the Past.' Memory and Post-Colonial Modernity in Ghanaian Pentecostalist Discourse." *Journal of Religion in Africa* 28(3):316–49.

Miller, Courtney, and Veronica Ramirez. 2016. "'Wealthiest' Cities: How Income, Home Values and Credit Limits Stack Up Around the US."

NerdWallet. Accessed June 26, 2019. https://www.nerdwallet.com/blog/finance/high-roller-cities-wealth-credit-highest/.

Miller, Donald E., Kimon H. Sargeant, and Richard Flory. 2013. *Spirit and Power: The Growth and Global Impact of Pentecostalism*. New York: Oxford University Press.

Min, Pyong Gap. 2010. *Preserving Ethnicity through Religion in America: Korean Protestants and Indian Hindus across Generations*. New York: New York University Press.

Mindiola, Tatcho, Jr., Yolanda Flores Niemann, and Nestor Rodriguez. 2009. *Black-Brown Relations and Stereotypes*. Austin: University of Texas Press.

Mitchell, Don. 2012. *They Saved the Crops: Labor, Landscape, and the Struggle over Industrial Farming in Bracero-Era California*. Athens: University of Georgia Press.

Montiel, Lisa M., Richard P. Nathan, and David J. Wright. 2004. *An Update on Urban Hardship*. Albany, NY: Nelson A. Rockefeller Institute of Government.

Montrose, Donald. 1961. *The Story of a Parish: Its Priests and Its People. Published on the Occasion of the Centennial of St. Boniface Church, Anaheim, California*. Anaheim, CA: St. Boniface Parish.

Mora-Torres, G. Cristina. 2006. "What's so Ethnic about Ethno-Religious Identity? Contemporary Evidence from Latino Immigrant 'Conversion' Narratives" Paper presented at the annual meeting of the American Sociological Association. August 11, Montreal Convention Center, Montreal, Quebec, Canada.

Mora, G. Cristina. 2014. *Making Hispanics: How Activists, Bureaucrats, and Media Constructed a New American*. Chicago: University of Chicago Press.

Morris-Young, Dan. 2018. "Fr. Figueroa Deck Says the Latino Catholic 'sleeping Giant' Is Awakening." *National Catholic Reporter*, March 8.

Mulder, Mark T. 2015. *Shades of White Flight: Evangelical Congregations and Urban Departure*. New Brunswick, NJ: Rutgers University Press.

Mulder, Mark T., Aida I. Ramos, and Gerardo Martí. 2017. *Latino Protestants in America: Growing and Diverse*. Lanham, MD: Rowman & Littlefield.

Mull, J. Dennis, and Dorothy S. Mull. 1983. "A Visit with a Curandero." *Western Journal of Medicine* 139(5):730–36.

Murray, Florence. 1947. *The Negro Handbook*. New York: Current Books Inc.

Nabhan-Warren, Kristy. 2005. *The Virgin of El Barrio: Marian Apparitions, Catholic Evangelizing, and Mexican American Activism*. New York: New York University Press.

Nabhan-Warren, Kristy. 2013. *The Cursillo Movement in America: Catholics, Protestants, and Fourth-Day Spirituality*. Chapel Hill, NC: University of North Carolina Press Books.

Nagourney, Adam, and Jennifer Medina. 2016. "This City is 78% Latino, and the Face of a New California." *The New York Times*, October 11.

Navarro, Carlos Garma. 1998. "The Socialization of the Gifts of Tongues and Healing in Mexican Pentecostalism." *Journal of Contemporary Religion* 13(3):353–61.

Ngai, Mae M. 1999. "The Architecture of Race in American Immigration Law: A Reexamination of the Immigration Act of 1924." *The Journal of American History* 86(1):67–92.

Ninh, Thien-Huong. 2014. "Colored Faith: Vietnamese American Catholics Struggle for Equality within Their Multicultural Church." *Amerasia Journal* 40(1):80–96.

Ocaña Perez, Damarys. 2011. "Medal of Freedom Recipient Sylvia Mendez Is Ready for Her Closeup." *LATINA*, February 8. Accessed July 3, 2018. http://www.latina.com/lifestyle/-news/medal-freedom-recipient-sylvia-mendez-ready-her-closeup

Odem, Mary E. 2004. "Our Lady of Guadalupe in the New South: Latino Immigrants and the Politics of Integration in the Catholic Church." *Journal of American Ethnic History* 24(1):26–57.

Omi, Michael, and Howard Winant. 2014. *Racial Formation in the United States*. New York: Routledge.

Orsi, Robert A. 1999. *Gods of the City: Religion and the American Urban Landscape*. Bloomington: Indiana University Press.

Ortiz, Vilma, and Edward Telles. 2012. "Racial Identity and Racial Treatment of Mexican Americans." *Race and Social Problems* 4(1):41–56.

Ospino, Hosffman. 2014. *Hispanic Ministry in Catholic Parishes: A Summary Report of Findings from the National Study of Catholic Parishes with Hispanic Ministry*. Boston, MA: Trustees of Boston College.

Paden, William E. 1994. *Religious Worlds: The Comparative Study of Religion*. Boston: Beacon Press.

Padilla, Felix M. 1985. *Latino Ethnic Consciousness: The Case of Mexican Americans and Puerto Ricans in Chicago*. Notre Dame, IN: University of Notre Dame Press.

Palmer-Boyes, Ashley. 2010. "The Latino Catholic Parish as a Specialist Organization: Distinguishing Characteristics." *Review of Religious Research* 51(3):302–23.

Peach, Ceri. 2005. "The Ghetto and the Ethnic Enclave." Pp. 31–48 in *Desegregating the City: Ghettos, Enclaves, and Inequality*, edited by D. P. Varady. Albany, NY: State University of New York Press.

Peña, Elaine. 2011. *Performing Piety: Making Space Sacred with the Virgin of Guadalupe*. Berkeley: University of California Press.

Peña, Milagros, and Lisa M. Frehill. 1998. "Latina Religious Practice: Analyzing Cultural Dimensions in Measures of Religiosity." *Journal for the Scientific Study of Religion* 37(4):620–35.

Ponce, Albert. 2014. "Racialization, Resistance, and the Migrant Rights Movement: A Historical Analysis." *Critical Sociology* 40(1):9–27.

Portes, Alejandro, and Rubén G. Rumbaut. 2014. *Immigrant America: A Portrait*. Berkeley: University of California Press.

Putnam, Robert D. 1995. "Tuning In, Tuning Out: The Strange Disappearance of Social Capital in America." *PS: Political Science & Politics* 28(4):664–83.

Ramirez, Daniel. 1999. "Borderlands Praxis: The Immigrant Experience in Latino Pentecostal Churches." *Journal of the American Academy of Religion* 67(3):573–96.

Ramírez, Daniel. 2015. *Migrating Faith: Pentecostalism in the United States and Mexico in the Twentieth Century*. Chapel Hill: University of North Carolina Press Books.

Ramos, Aida I., Robert D. Woodberry, and Christopher G. Ellison. 2017. "The Contexts of Conversion among U.S. Latinos." *Sociology of Religion* 78(2):119–45.

Reiff, David. 2006. "Nuevo Catholics." *New York Times Magazine*, December 24.

Reyes, David. 1995. "Bell Tolls for Church: Santa Ana's Church of the Brethren, a Victim of Changing Times and Demographics, Holds Its Last Service in the Building It Had Occupied since 1923." *Los Angeles Times*, May 29.

Ridgely, Susan B. 2019. "The Generational Ties That Bind American Roman Catholics: Attending to Age and Region in the Roman Catholic Imaginary." *Exchange* 48(3):251–67.

Robbins, Joel. 2004. "The Globalization of Pentecostal and Charismatic Christianity." *Annual Review of Anthropology* 33(1):117–43.

Robeck, Cecil M. 2006. *The Azusa Street Mission and Revival*. Nashville, TN: Thomas Nelson.

Rodríguez, Clara E. 2000. *Changing Race: Latinos, the Census, and the History of Ethnicity in the United States*. New York: New York University Press.

Rodriguez, Daniel A. 2011. *A Future for the Latino Church: Models for Multilingual, Multigenerational Hispanic Congregations*. Downers Grove, IL: InterVarsity Press.

Romo, Ricardo. 1983. *East Los Angeles: History of a Barrio*. Austin: University of Texas Press.

Rosenthal-Urey, Ina. 1984. "Church Records as a Source of Data on Mexican Migrant Networks: A Methodological Note." *The International Migration Review* 18(3):767–81.

Salguero, Gabriel. 2013. "Latino Evangelicals Trending. A Closer Look and What's Next." *The Huffington Post*, April 8. Accessed January 30, 2015. https://www.huffpost.com/entry/latino-evangelicals-trending-a-closer-look-and-whats-next_b_3037438

Sanchez-Walsh, Arlene. 2003. *Latino Pentecostal Identity: Evangelical Faith, Self, and Society*. New York: Columbia University Press.

Sanchez-Walsh, Arlene. 2018. *Pentecostals in America*. New York: Columbia University Press.

Sassen, Saskia. 2002. "The Repositioning of Citizenship: Emergent Subjects and Spaces for Politics." *CR: The New Centennial Review* 3(2):41–66.

Scauzillo, Steve. 2014. "L.A. Ranks 45th out of 60 U.S. Cities in Park Space; Long Beach Ranks 24th in Trust for Public Land Study." *San Gabriel Valley Tribune*, May 30.

Schermerhorn, Richard Alonzo. 1978. *Comparative Ethnic Relations: A Framework for Theory and Research*. Chicago: University of Chicago Press.

Schiller Nina Glick, Çaglar Ayşe, and Guldbrandsen, Thaddeus C. 2008. "Beyond the Ethnic Lens: Locality, Globality, and Born-again Incorporation." *American Ethnologist* 33(4):612–33.

Sears, David O., Mingying Fu, P. J. Henry, and Kerra Bui. 2003. "The Origins and Persistence of Ethnic Identity among the 'New Immigrant' Groups." *Social Psychology Quarterly* 66(4):419–37.

Selective Service System. 1917. "James Verdgo Cruz, 'United States World War I Draft Registration Cards, 1917–1918.'" FamilySearch.org. Accessed July 20, 2019 /ark:/61903/1:1:KZV5-SW5.

Small, Mario Luis. 2002. "Culture, Cohorts, and Social Organization Theory: Understanding Local Participation in a Latino Housing Project." *American Journal of Sociology* 108(1):1–54.

Small, Mario Luis. 2004. *Villa Victoria: The Transformation of Social Capital in a Boston Barrio*. Chicago: University of Chicago Press.

Spencer, Madeleine, and Victoria Carty. 2017. "Gentrification, Gang Injunctions, and the Impact on Latin@ Communities in Southern California." Pp. 33–47 in *Mobilizing Public Sociology: Scholars, Activists, and Latin@ Migrants Converse on Common Ground*. Leiden, NL: Brill.

Starkloff, Carl F. 1994. "Inculturation and Cultural Systems (Part 2)." *Theological Studies* 55(2):274–94.

State of California. 1941. "Affidavits for Correction of a Record, s.v. 'James R. Cruze.'" FamilySearch.org. Accessed July 20, 2019. https://www.familysearch.org/ark:/61903/1:1:QGLW-7NWV

State of California. 1949. "Delayed Certificate of Birth, s.v. 'Della Acedlia Molina.'" FamilySearch.org. Accessed July 20, 2019. https://www.familysearch.org/ark:/61903/1:1:HSPS-4N6Z

Suro, Roberto, Gabriel Escobar, Gretchen Livingston, Shirin Hakimzadeh, Luis Lugo, Sandra Stencel, John Green, Gregory A. Smith, Daniel Cox, and Sahar Chaudhry. 2007. *Changing Faiths: Latinos and the Transformation of American Religion*. Washington DC: Pew Research Center.

Taylor, J. Benjamin, Sarah Allen Gershon, and Adrian D. Pantoja. 2014. "Christian America? Understanding the Link between Churches, Attitudes, and 'Being American' among Latino Immigrants." *Politics and Religion* 7(2):339–65.

Taylor, Paul, Mark Hugo Lopez, Jessica Hamar Martínez, and Gabriel Velasco. 2012. *When Labels Don't Fit: Hispanics and Their Views of Identity*. Washington, DC: Pew Research Center.

Tienda, Marta, and Norma Fuentes. 2014. "Hispanics in Metropolitan America: New Realities and Old Debates." *Annual Review of Sociology* 40(1):499–520.

Traslosheros, Jorge E. 2002. "Señora de la historia, Madre mestiza, Reina de México. La coronación de la Virgen de Guadalupe y su actualización como mito fundacional de la patria, 1895." *Signos históricos* 7:105–47.

Treviño, Roberto R. 2006. *The Church in the Barrio: Mexican American Ethno-Catholicism in Houston*. Chapel Hill, NC: University of North Carolina Press.

Tweed, Thomas A. 1997. *Our Lady of the Exile: Diasporic Re*. New York: Oxford University Press.

Tweed, Thomas A. 2009. *Crossing and Dwelling: A Theory of Religion*. Cambridge, MA: Harvard University Press.

U.S. Census Bureau. 1900. "1900 U.S. Census. Long Beach, Los Angeles County, California. Population Schedule, Digital Image s.v. 'James Cruz.'" FamilySearch.org. Accessed July 20, 2019. https://www.familysearch.org/ark:/61903/1:1:M9P2-Q5D

U.S. Census Bureau. 1910a. "1910 U.S. Census. Santa Ana, Orange County, California. Population Schedule, s.v. 'Della Molina.'" FamilySearch.org. Accessed July 20, 2019. https://www.familysearch.org/ark:/61903/1:1:MVLV-L32

U.S. Census Bureau. 1910b. "1910 U.S. Census. U.S.S. Tennessee. Population Schedule, s.v. 'James V. Cruz.'" FamilySearch.org. Accessed July 20, 2019. https://www.familysearch.org/ark:/61903/1:1:MRSP-H9V

U.S. Census Bureau. 1920. "1920 U.S. Census, San Diego, San Diego County, California. Population Schedule, s.v. 'Della Cruz.'" FamilySearch.org. Acccessed July 20, 2019. https://www.familysearch.org/ark:/61903/1:1:MHW6-YT6

U.S. Census Bureau. 1930. "1930 U.S. Census. Santa Ana, Orange County, California. Population Schedule, s.v. 'Della Cruz.'" FamilySearch.org. Accessed July 20, 2019. https://www.familysearch.org/ark:/61903/1:1:XCDG-C66

U.S. Census Bureau. 1940. "1940 U.S. Census. Santa Ana, Orange County, California, Population Schedule, s.v. 'Della Cruz.'" FamilySearch.org. Accessed July 20, 2019. https://www.familysearch.org/ark:/61903/1:1:K948-DHB

US Census Bureau. 2010. *State and County Quick Facts*.

U.S. Census Bureau. 2017. "American FactFinder—Results." Accessed June 25, 2019. https://factfinder.census.gov/faces/tableservices/jsf/pages/productview.xhtml?src=CF.

U.S. Census Bureau. 2018. "U.S. Census Bureau QuickFacts: Santa Ana City, California." Accessed March 2, 2019. https://www.census.gov/quickfacts/fact/table/santaanacitycalifornia/POP010210.

Valdez, A. C., and James F. Scheer. 1980. *Fire on Azusa Street*. Los Angeles: Gift.

Vasquez, Manuel A. 1999. "Pentecostalism, Collective Identity, and Transnationalism among Salvadorans and Peruvians in the U.S." *Journal of the American Academy of Religion* 67(3):617–36.

Vega, Sujey. 2015. *Latino Heartland: Of Borders and Belonging in the Midwest*. New York: New York University Press.

Vélez, Karin. 2017. "Stones and Bones: Catholic Responses to the 1812 Collapse of the Mission Church of Capistrano." *Material Religion* 13(4):437–60.

Vila, Pablo. 2000. *Crossing Borders, Reinforcing Borders: Social Categories, Metaphors, and Narrative Identities on the US-Mexico Frontier*. Austin: University of Texas Press.

Vila, Pablo. 2003. "Processes of Identification on the U.S.-Mexico Border." *The Social Science Journal* 40(4):607–25.

Vila, Pablo. 2005. *Border Identifications: Narratives of Religion, Gender, and Class on the U.S.-Mexico Border*. Austin: University of Texas Press.

Walker, Helen. 1928. "The Conflict of Cultures in First Generation Mexicans in Santa Ana, California." Master's thesis, University of Southern California. Accessed March 12, 2018. http://digitallibrary.usc.edu/cdm/ref/collection/p15799coll40/id/217428

Warner, R. Stephen. 1993. "Work in Progress toward a New Paradigm for the Sociological Study of Religion in the United States." *American Journal of Sociology* 98(5):1044–93.

Warner, R. Stephen. 2007. "The Role of Religion in the Process of Segmented Assimilation." *The ANNALS of the American Academy of Political and Social Science* 612(1):100–115.

Waters, Mary C. 1990. *Ethnic Options: Choosing Identities in America*. Berkeley: University of California Press.

Weber, Max. 1930. *The Protestant Ethic and the Spirit of Capitalism*. New York: Routledge.

Weber, Max. 1968. *Economy and Society: An Outline of Interpretive Sociology*. New York: Bedminster Press.

Williams, Philip J., and Patricia Fortuny Loret de Mola. 2007. "Religion and Social Capital among Mexican Immigrants in Southwest Florida." *Latino Studies* 5(2):233–53.

Wilson, Catherine E. 2008. *The Politics of Latino Faith: Religion, Identity, and Urban Community*. New York: New York University Press.

Wiltz, John E. 1958. "APA-Ism in Kentucky and Elsewhere." *The Register of the Kentucky Historical Society* 56(2):143–55.

Wimmer, Andreas. 2009. "Herder's Heritage and the Boundary-Making Approach: Studying Ethnicity in Immigrant Societies." *Sociological Theory* 27(3):244–70.

Wimmer, Andreas. 2013. *Ethnic Boundary Making: Institutions, Power, Networks*. New York: Oxford University Press.

Winchester, Daniel. 2015. "Converting to Continuity: Temporality and Self in Eastern Orthodox Conversion Narratives." *Journal for the Scientific Study of Religion* 54(3):439–60.

Wuthnow, Robert J. 2011. "Taking Talk Seriously: Religious Discourse as Social Practice." *Journal for the Scientific Study of Religion* 50(1):1–21.

Yoshikawa, Hirokazu, and Ariel Kalil. 2011. "The Effects of Parental Undocumented Status on the Developmental Contexts of Young Children in Immigrant Families." *Child Development Perspectives* 5(4):291–97.

Young, Julia G. 2015. *Mexican Exodus: Emigrants, Exiles, and Refugees of the Cristero War*. New York: Oxford University Press.

Index

For the benefit of digital users, indexed terms that span two pages (e.g., 52–53) may, on occasion, appear on only one of those pages.

www.ingramcontent.com/pod-product-compliance
Ingram Content Group UK Ltd.
Pitfield, Milton Keynes, MK11 3LW, UK
UKHW021051270726
13967UKWH00012B/220